INTERNATIONAL MISSIONARY COUNCIL CENTENARY SERIES

T0279979

Creative Collaborations

INTERNATIONAL MISSIONARY COUNCIL CENTENARY SERIES

Creative Collaborations:
Case Studies of
North American Missional Practices

Edited by
Dana L. Robert, Allison Kach-Yawnghwe,
and Morgan Crago

Copyright © World Council of Churches 2023

First published 2023 by Regnum Books International
This edition is published under license from the World Council of Churches

Regnum is an imprint of the Oxford Centre for Mission Studies
St. Philip and St. James Church
Woodstock Road
Oxford, OX2 6HR, UK
www.regnumbooks.net

The rights of the World Council of Churches to be identified
as the editor of this work has been asserted by them
in accordance with the Copyright, Designs and Patents Act 1988.

*All rights reserved. No part of this publication may be reproduced, stored in a retrieval system, or
transmitted, in any form or by any means, electronic, mechanical, photocopying, recording or
otherwise, without the prior permission of the publisher or a license permitting restricted copying.
In the UK such licenses are issued by the Copyright Licensing Agency, 90 Tottenham Court Road,
London W1P 9HE.*

British Library Cataloguing in Publication Data
A catalogue record for this book is available from the British Library

ISBN: 979-8-8898-3325-3
eBook ISBN: 979-8-8898-3326-0

Typeset by Words by Design
www.wordsbydesign.co.uk

This series has been published with the financial support of EMW and CWME

Distributed by 1517 Media in the US, Canada, India, and Brazil

Series Preface

This series of books arises from a study process that marked the centenary of the International Missionary Council (IMC), founded in 1921 at Lake Mohonk, USA. It has its origin in the Commission on World Mission and Evangelism of the World Council of Churches, which wanted to celebrate the work of its historical predecessor IMC (1921-1961). In 2020, it therefore initiated a global and ecumenical study process, which was strongly supported by the Oxford Centre for Mission Studies (OCMS) in the UK and the Association of Protestant Churches and Missions in Germany (EMW) in Hamburg. The 18-month study process involved some 15 academic and ecumenical study centres or groups around the world, practically in all eight regions of the World Council of Churches, paying special attention to those sectors which were not represented at Lake Mohonk a hundred years earlier.

The International Missionary Council Centenary Series edited by the steering committee of the process in cooperation with the director of the CWME of the WCC presents the most interesting parts of the study process. The IMC was founded to foster mission cooperation and unity, and the study process wanted to identify important topics and challenges for mission and mission cooperation, not only in the past, even if the history of the IMC is to be celebrated, but also in the present and future. The steering committee of the study process was delighted to discover that some previously unheard voices have been heard through the process. Indeed, in order to honour the legacy of the IMC, the study process itself was implemented in an interactive and inclusive way that produced more mission cooperation and more unity among various actors in academy, church and mission bodies.

The volumes in the International Missionary Council Centenary Series present mainly, but not only, regional aspects and dimensions of world mission that has become polyphonic. The polyphonic character of mission opens and offers new common spaces for discussion and reflection on how all actors, churches, academy, mission bodies and transnational networks, can work together in creative and innovative ways, both in missiology and mission practice.

This Regnum Series builds on three foundational books that were generated by the study process and published by WCC Publications in 2022-23. A comprehensive Jubilee volume appeared as Risto Jukko ed., *Together in the Mission of God: Jubilee Reflections on the International Missionary Council*, Geneva: WCC Publications, 2022. Additionally, two mission studies anthologies gathered up the initial fruits of the study process: Risto Jukko ed., *A Hundred Years of Mission Cooperation: the Impact of the International Missionary Council 1921-2021*, Geneva: WCC Publications, 2022; and Risto Jukko ed., *The Future of Mission Cooperation: the Living Legacy of the International Missionary Council*, Geneva: WCC Publications, 2023. Now the Regnum Series offers a much more extensive harvest of the work completed by the study centres which collaborated in the IMC centenary study process.

The steering committee is delighted to be able to make the results of the study process accessible to a wider readership while recognising that opinions expressed in the book chapters are those of their authors and claim no wider authority.

Series Editors:

Marina Ngursangzeli Behera
Michael Biehl
Risto Jukko
Kenneth R. Ross
Tito Paredes
Peter Cruchley
Jingqin Gu

Contents

Introduction

Dana L. Robert, Allison Kach-Yawnghwe, and Morgan Crago

What does it mean to be in mission today? This book shows that for North American Christians, mission remains a touchstone for Christian identity and a core marker of faithfulness to Jesus Christ. The case studies herein show that rather than collapsing under the strain of massive challenges, many North American Christians are reaching across divisions and differences to connect with people and contexts unlike themselves. The research in this book highlights multiple ways in which North American Christians are collaborating with others to witness to their faith. Such collaborations are like the mustard seeds of the Kingdom (Mt. 13:31–32), often small and yet creative actions of believers who push beyond Christian divisions and paralyzing social problems.

It is no surprise that many are asking where is the good that comes from following Jesus Christ in mission? Today people who profess no religion are the fastest-growing "religious" population.[1] Instead of being an ambassador for justice, equality, and peace, the legacy of North American Christianity seems tied to colonialism and oppression. War and climate crisis hover over the world and threaten to destroy it. Millions of humans are migrating from their homes, and global pandemics are on the increase.

In such times as these, creative collaborations become testimonies of hope. In the midst of political crises and church splits, North American Christians persist in reaching across human differences. The authors of these case studies examine the intersection of three concepts – mission, North America, and collaboration – and apply them to a specific context. Authors represent Roman Catholicism, mainline Protestantism, evangelicalism, and pentecostalism. While each case study is fascinating on its own, together they suggest an exciting range of missional practices. The narratives are based on the particular interests and experiences of individual scholars and practitioners who have agreed to participate in this book project. No effort has been made to monitor the theological assumptions of the authors or to judge their analyses of the problems and the challenges that they found. Nor do the case studies have all the answers. Yet, they bring fresh imagination to shaping Christian witness in the world and – we trust – to reinvigorating North American Christianity. In compiling snapshots of diverse boundary crossings undertaken by North American Christians, this book shows that missional collaboration opens creative insights into the present and future of mission itself.

---

[1] Gregory A. Smith, "About Three-in-Ten U.S. Adults Are Now Religiously Unaffiliated," Pew Research Center, 14 December 2021, https://www.pewresearch.org/religion/2021/12/14/about-three-in-ten-u-s-adults-are-now-religiously-unaffiliated/

The meaning of mission, collaboration, and North America have been shaped by the participants and authors of this research. In the spirit of Paulo Freire, who noted that the road is made by walking,[2] this volume has privileged concrete, specific examples of mission. These allow tentative definitions of mission to emerge from praxis. Collaboration has similarly taken many forms, several of which we have identified as organizing principles for the essays. Although at the outset we loosely defined "North America" as Canada and the United States, we quickly realized that North America encompasses diverse and contested terrain. The Canadian case studies, for example, describe church organizations that are deeply committed to collaboration with First Nations peoples who were subject to colonization abetted by Christian mission. Today, these ecclesial bodies are invested in generous understandings of indigenized Christian faiths. The migration of people across continental boundaries – including those from the Caribbean, Central America, and Latin America – also shapes the meaning of a "North American" identity. Accordingly, the case study on Latinx mission, describing the physical and cultural mobility of different generations, is an important feature of the book. Urban centres are magnets for migration and home to diverse ethnicities, gender identities, and ecclesial groups. Several case studies thus address the complexities of "North America" in these urban spaces. Finally, some case studies explore outreach by North American Christians to persons and places outside North America. In these ostensibly classic forms of mission outreach, the very notion of being North American is sharpened and expanded in the crucible of relationships. The intersections of North America plus mission plus collaboration have provided us with rich insights to expand our understanding of all three.

The introduction first discusses the background and rationale for the book, including its anchorage in the global mission study process launched in 2021 by the Commission on World Mission and Evangelism of the World Council of Churches. Secondly, we introduce the case studies in missional collaboration and explore the patterns they reveal about how North American Christians engage in mission together. Finally, we discuss some of the implications of the case studies and what they might mean for North American mission today, especially in light of relational practices and the larger research project that frames the volume.

Background to the Volume

In 2010, mission leaders from around the world met in a series of meetings in Edinburgh, Cape Town, Aarhus, Boston, Tokyo, San José, and elsewhere to commemorate the centennial of the 1910 World Missionary Conference. A renaissance in mission theology flowed from these meetings: important statements were produced that represented significant theological convergence

---

[2] Myles Horton and Paulo Freire, *We Make the Road by Walking: Conversations on Education and Social Change*, ed. Brenda Bell, John Gaventa, and John Peters (Philadelphia, PA: Temple University Press, 1991).

among a wide spectrum of Christian communions.[3] A 35-volume book series from Regnum Press featured multiple topics and perspectives on mission contexts and themes.[4] Despite significant differences in ethnicity, ecclesiology, and politics, major Christian communions shared a basic commitment toward holistic mission theology – that mission is essential to Christian identity itself. Mission reflects the movement of the triune God. It includes both evangelism and charitable outreach, concern for individual salvation and social transformation, and care for all of God's creation, including the "least of these."[5]

A decade after the 2010 meetings, the 100th anniversary of the founding of the International Missionary Council (IMC) in 1921 provided a further opportunity to take stock of mission over the past century, and also its current trends and hopes for the future. Instead of organizing discussions according to ecclesial groupings, as in 2010, the Commission on World Mission and Evangelism (CWME) of the World Council of Churches (WCC) launched a study process in which 15 academic centres around the world took responsibility to research the history and current realities of mission in their own regions. The historical reflections and analyses of core mission issues were presented to the WCC at its Karlsruhe Assembly in August/September 2022 in order to help guide missional priorities for the next decade.[6]

During the 2021 study process, each regional study centre chose its own questions and contributed to the several phases of the project as each was able. As coordinator for North America, the Center for Global Christianity and Mission at the Boston University School of Theology selected the intersection of three concepts – North America, mission, and collaboration – as the framework for its investigations. The purpose of examining mission practices, in collaboration across multiple boundaries, had several purposes. We hoped to investigate new missional energy at the grassroots level and to move beyond the typical narrative of North American mission as polarized and dying. We wished to avoid theological and ecclesiological siloes that locked research into familiar patterns. We determined that research into missiological collaboration and

---

[3] "Edinburgh 2010 Common Call," in *Edinburgh 2010: Mission Today and Tomorrow*, eds. Kirsteen Kim and Andrew Anderson (Oxford: Regnum Books International, 2011), 1–2; Third Lausanne Congress on World Evangelization, *The Cape Town Commitment: A Confession of Faith and a Call to Action* (The Lausanne Movement, 2011); Pontifical Council for Interreligious Dialogue, "*Christian Witness in a Multi-Religious World: Recommendations for Conduct*," 25–28 January 2011, https://www.vatican.va/roman_curia/pontifical_councils/interelg/documents/rc_pc_inter elg_doc_20111110_testimonianza-cristiana_en.html. This third document is a joint statement of the Vatican, the World Council of Churches, and the World Evangelical Alliance.
[4] Regnum Books, "Edinburgh Centenary," Regnum Books, https://www.regnumbooks.net/collections/edinburgh-centenary.
[5] On holistic mission, see Al Tizon, *Whole and Reconciled: Gospel, Church, and Mission in a Fractured World* (Grand Rapids, MI: Baker Academic, 2018).
[6] Risto Jukko, ed., *Together in the Mission of God: Jubilee Reflections on the International Missionary Council* (Geneva: World Council of Churches, 2022); Risto Jukko, ed., *A Hundred Years of Mission Cooperation: The Impact of the International Missionary Council 1921–2021* (Geneva: WCC Publications, 2022).

convergences had not been undertaken in a serious way since the heyday of ecumenical partnership as a model in the 1960s and 1970s. In the intervening decades, entirely new ecclesial groupings had emerged that merited renewed scholarly attention. We ascertained that although tremendous research into converging mission theologies had taken place since the 2010 meetings, little research on converging mission practices had been undertaken.

Accordingly, a small team under the leadership of Professor Dana L. Robert designed an ambitious grassroots study process and advertised it on the website of the Center and at the 2021 meeting of the American Society of Missiology.[7] A group of leading North American missiologists were recruited to launch the study process and to evaluate the results that flowed from the initial research. A second group of researchers volunteered to write longer case studies that would result in this volume – one of a series representing approaches to mission in various world regions. Missiologists involved in the project fielded a panel for the centennial celebration of the IMC in November 2021. The preliminary report from North America was submitted to the WCC in January 2022;[8] and, in June 2022, another panel of researchers presented their results at the American Society of Missiology. This volume of case studies, therefore, flows from the larger global research process launched by the CWME in 2021. Some content overlaps with the North American report submitted in January 2022, but this case study book has proceeded separately from the preparation of the report.

Case Studies and Patterns of Missional Collaboration

The case studies in this volume demonstrate a variety of approaches and models for missional collaborations. They draw upon different ecclesial traditions of collaboration and expand those into multiple directions. Because each case study illuminates multiple angles of collaboration, it makes sense to organize the papers along a rough spectrum. We group them under four main descriptors, but this organizational scheme does not box them into mutually exclusive categories. The four descriptors are 1. Ecumenical Unity, 2. Mutual Partnerships, 3. Cooperative Projects, and 4. Decolonizing Frontiers. Each descriptor links to historical emphases that we selectively employ as a framework for the volume. The range of practices that each encompasses helps to frame the meaning of mission for the group engaged in them.

Ecumenical Unity

Often when people think about cooperation and collaboration among Christians, the image of mid-20th century "ecumenism" comes to mind. During the high

---

[7] School of Theology, Center for Global Christianity and Mission, "North American Missional Collaborations, 2021–2022", Boston University, https://www.bu.edu/cgcm/imc/.

[8] For the North American report, see Dana L. Robert, with contributions by D. Benac, B. Carlson and C. Cardoza-Orlandi, J. Laxton, W. Gregory, A. Kach, D. Scott, "Missional Collaborations 2021: A Report from North America," in Jukko, ed., *A Hundred Years of Mission Cooperation,* 369–412.

point of the 20th century ecumenical movement, churches worked together on matters of shared doctrine and outreach with the end goal of organic unity.[9] By the 1970s, despite the progress made by the Second Vatican Council and denominational church mergers, the official ecumenical movement was losing steam in North America. A case in point was the 1970 refusal of laity in mainline Protestant denominations to support the "Plan of Union" put forward by the Consultation on Church Union.[10] Secularization, theological discord, and the privatization of religious practices and beliefs washed over North America, and the public witness of united churches lost favour. Competing evangelical movements, push-back from traditional Catholics, and divisions and decline among mainline Christians weakened the official ecumenical movement among North Americans. Nevertheless, visions of church unity continued to inspire shared mission, and engagement in mission inspired visions of Christian unity.

Today, it can be said that the vision of Ecumenism with a capital "E" has in mission largely given way to ecumenism with a small "e." In other words, instead of unity being a matter of global organization or top-down pushing for denominational mergers, a range of regional and local movements model Christian unity through their intentional collaborations. More than one informant for the case studies noted that ecumenism today is local. The volume opens with three case studies that demonstrate a broad sweep of commitments to Christian unity, as well as unity based on common humanity, as intrinsic to their core missional identities.

In his research on contemporary Roman Catholic collaborations, William Gregory undertakes an ambitious survey of US Catholic ecumenism in relation to outreach. He opens his case study by affirming the central importance of Christian unity to Pope Francis and to the policy and doctrine of the largest church in North America, and he puts the idea of ecumenical unity into dialogue with major missional collaborations through examining "Catholic Charities, the Society of Saint Vincent De Paul, the pregnancy help movement, and the faith-based community organizations supported by the Catholic Campaign for Human Development."[11] Through interviews with leaders, Gregory uncovers a high degree of collaboration "on the ground" with other churches and community organizations on behalf of those dealing with poverty or addiction, those who have been incarcerated, refugees, and other groups of people in need. Justice and charity for the "least of these" take place across ecclesial boundaries in reference to the kingdom spirit of Matthew 25 – "I was hungry and you gave me food, I was thirsty and you gave me something to drink, I was a stranger and you welcomed me, I was naked and you gave me clothing, I was sick and you took

---

[9] Classic works on mission and ecumenical unity include W. Richey Hogg, *Ecumenical Foundations: A History of the International Missionary Council and Its Nineteenth Century Background* (New York: Harper, 1952); Ruth Rouse and Stephen Charles Neill, eds., *A History of the Ecumenical Movement: 1517–1948*, vol. 1 (Geneva: WCC, 2004).
[10] On COCU, see Keith Watkins, *The American Church that Might Have Been: A History of the Consultation on Church Union* (Eugene, OR: Pickwick Publications, 2014).
[11] William Gregory, "Contemporary US Catholic Collaborative Mission," p.21 in this volume.

care of me, I was in prison and you visited me." Gregory finds surprising intersections, such as both Mormons and evangelicals donating substantially to Catholic Charities for the sake of their common mission. Behind the impressive range of practical cooperation, however, Gregory asks the nagging question as to whether practical collaboration can lead ultimately to ecumenical unity in terms consistent with Roman Catholic theological commitments that stretch from the period of the Second Vatican Council (1962–65) to the present.

The case study by Dustin Benac and Christopher James, like that of William Gregory, engaged in comprehensive research through over 40 interviews, in this case with leaders and participants in citywide church networks. In their research, Benac and James identified up to 100 North American cities with active evangelical church networks devoted both to serving the city and to Christian unity. For the case study, Benac and James looked in depth at two groups – Transforming the Bay with Christ (TBC) in San Francisco and UniteBoston (UB). Commitment to locality, across a range of evangelical groups, is a new phase of Christian unity. Although evangelicalism and ecumenism were often seen as enemies in the past, the reality of a North America in which large percentages of people are now unchurched has inspired evangelicals to take seriously the classic Christian unity text of John 17, the "high priestly prayer" of Jesus that his followers may be one. Collaboration with other Christians "amplifies" the witness of city networks. The question of theological and geographic limits to unity remains a challenge for the city networks.

Another model for ecumenical unity is demonstrated in the work of Latin Americans from a variety of ethnic backgrounds networking together to improve Latinx theological education. In their chapter, Carlos Cardoza-Orlandi and Britta Meiers Carlson describe the history and mission of the *Asociación para la Educación Teológica Hispana* (*AETH*), a network which brings together Latinx scholars from across the theological spectrum – Catholic, mainline Protestant, evangelical, pentecostal, and neo-pentecostal. Established in 1991, this organization hosts conferences, publishes scholarly and accessible theological literature relevant to the Latinx community, and provides certification to various theological schools and Bible institutes in partnership with the Association of Theological Schools (ATS). Because of its commitment to facilitating the Latinx community's access to theological education and highlighting this community's specific concerns, *AETH* seeks to "challenge the boundary between accredited theological schools and non-accredited Bible institutes" and widen the boundaries even further to include "community organizing networks and producers of online content."[12] *AETH* brings scholars into community in order to theologize *en conjunto*, or "together." As *AETH* enters its fourth decade of existence, Cardoza-Orlandi and Carlson report that the network's constituency is increasingly pentecostal and non-denominational, with less participation from mainline Protestants and Catholics than previously. They also note that *AETH* must adapt to reflect the concerns of immigrants coming from different parts of

---

[12] Britta Meiers Carlson and Carlos Cardoza-Orlandi, "Mission and Theological Education Among Latinx Christians: Contributions of *La Asociación para la Educación Teológica Hispana*," p.53 in this volume.

Latin America as well as the issues relevant to second and third generation Latinx Christians.

Mutual Partnerships

In mission circles, the idea of partnership became a dominant motif during the late 1960s and the 1970s, as a reaction against colonial mission models in which Western churches and missionaries dominated the non-Western "recipients" of their outreach. As North American and European churches declined in number relative to the growing Christian movements of Africa, Asia, and Latin America, it was clear that cooperation among groups needed to be on equal bases, with recognition and appreciation for what each group could bring to the table. Various experiments in partnership emerged during the height of the ecumenical movement. The limitations of partnership as a 1970s model soon became apparent, as old colonial patterns of Westerners supplying money to "worthy" supplicants remained common practice. Even now, many churches in Latin America dislike the term partnership, as it reminds them of paternalistic arrogance and financial dependency in relation to North American "partners."[13] By the 1980s, especially with the deregulation of the airline industry and the rise of easier forms of global communication, the short-term mission trip arose as a chief way of establishing relationships with racial, ethnic, or national "others." The rise of the STM movement from the 1980s resulted in the reduction of long-term missionary infrastructure, as churches began diverting their mission money to support service trips by their own members.[14]

Over the past few decades, ideas of partnership have developed strongly in the direction of mutuality and reciprocity as their core values, where give and take between the partners is the norm.[15] Formal ecumenical dialogue continues

---

[13] For the classic study of partnership in mission, see Max Warren, *Partnership: The Study of an Idea* (London: SCM Press, 1956). On the history and struggles of partnership, see Wilbert van Saane, *From Paternalism to Partnership: Protestant Mission Partnerships in the History of the Netherlands Missionary Council (1900– 1999)*, Studies in the Intercultural History of Christianity 164 (Lausanne: Peter Lang, 2019); Knut E. Larsen and Knud Jørgensen, eds., *Power and Partnership* (Oxford: Regnum Books, 2014); Jonathan S. Barnes, *Power and Partnership: A History of the Protestant Mission Movement* (Eugene, OR: Pickwick Publications, 2013); Graham Duncan, *Partnership in Mission: A Critical Historical Evaluation of the Relationship between 'Older' and 'Younger' Churches, with Special Reference to the Church of Scotland* (Saarbrücken: VDM Verlag Dr Müller, 2008).

[14] Important evaluations of the short-term mission trip are found in Robert J. Priest, ed., *Effective Engagement in Short-Term Missions: Doing It Right* (Pasadena, CA: William Carey Library, 2008); Brian M. Howell, *Short-Term Mission: An Ethnography of Christian Travel Narrative and Experience* (Downers Grove, IL: IVP Academic, 2012).

[15] Partnership in mission is a subject that continues to produce helpful contemporary reflection. See, for example, Robert Heaney, John Kafwanka, and Hilda Kabia, *God's Church for God's World: A Practical Approach to Partnership in Mission* (New York: Church Publishing, 2020); Samuel Cueva, *Mission Partnership in Creative Tension: An Analysis of Relationships within the Evangelical Missions Movement with Special Reference to Peru and Britain from 1987–2006* (Carlisle: Langham Partnership, 2015);

among church leaders, and shared projects remained important for mission agencies of all types. But ordinary church members seek partnerships that flow through personal connections. They often but not always use their own denominational family as a framework for the partnerships across ethnic, racial, economic, or national lines. Or they partner with specialized agencies and non-governmental agencies that provide valuable expertise for their hands-on outreach. In the "old days," partnership needed to be managed by denominational executives who could handle currency exchanges, book travel, and tap into long-term missionary infrastructures. As building relationships across differences has become a chief personal goal for congregations and individuals invested in partnerships, the range of possibilities has expanded.

At the same time, truly mutual partnerships require hard work and the willingness to work through misunderstandings over time. The four examples of partnership as mutuality explored in this section exemplify long-term, multi-generational commitments to relationships, friendships, loving care, and social justice as ways of being in mission. Although the individual partners have changed over time, as have the details and programs of the partnership, long-term commitment is the signature feature of collaboration as mutuality.[16]

Through her case study focused on Dallas, Texas, Glory Dharmaraj presents the history of Bethlehem Centers – multi-racial neighbourhood centres in urban communities organized by southern Methodist women around the turn of the 20th century. By looking at the pronouncements of Methodist women's organizations from 1911 to the present, she identifies the concept of "sistering" as a key theological motivation and uncovers the theological shift of "mission to" women and children in need to "mission with" these partners.[17] Dharmaraj shows how the partnerships of the Dallas Bethlehem Center (DBC) evolve to meet the urgent needs of the people among whom it is located. She does this by charting the ups and downs experienced by the centre – from its origins under an interracial board in the 1940s, to the DBC's solidarity with the African American community in their geographic displacement after the construction of a new highway, to the DBC's recent collaborations with neighbourhood community services in the 21st century. Her case study highlights the importance of locality in mission partnerships, in connection with regional networks for transformational social change.

James R. Krabill describes over 50 years of partnership between North American Mennonites and African Independent Churches (AICs) in western and

---

David Wesley, *A Common Mission: Healthy Patterns in Congregational Mission Partnerships* (Eugene, OR: Resource Publications, 2014).

[16] On mutuality in mission, see Glory E. Dharmaraj and Jacob S. Dharmaraj, *A Theology of Mutuality: A Paradigm for Mission in the Twenty-first Century* (New York: United Methodist Women, 2014); Jonathan Barnes and Peter E. Makari, eds., *Restoring Dignity, Nourishing Hope: Developing Mutuality in Mission* (Cleveland, OH: Pilgrim Press, 2016); Christopher L. Heuertz and Christine D. Pohl, *Friendship at the Margins: Discovering Mutuality in Service and Mission* (Downers Grove, IL: IVP Books, 2010).

[17] Glory E. Dharmaraj, "Sisterhood and 'Sistering': Restating Relationships in the Cartography of Missional Collaborations: Dallas Bethlehem Center, A Case Study" in this volume.

southern Africa. This inspiring case study describes partnerships across ethnicities, nationalities, and ecclesial bodies, and persistent commitment to relationships over multiple generations. His case study emphasizes their African-initiated nature, beginning with the first call from Nigerian congregations to the Mennonite Board of Missions in 1958, made after the Nigerians heard of the Mennonites through a Mennonite international radio programme. He describes how historical and practical features of the Mennonite faith – such as their principled disassociation from the state, commitment to a "believers' church," and history of persecution by established Catholic and Protestant groups – facilitate friendly connections with the AICs, since many AICs share these characteristics. In shaping their partnerships, the North American Mennonites often worked in the area of biblical training or coordinating gatherings for AICs across the continent, and they steered away from one-sided colonial models such as bringing in large sums of money for church projects.

Another study that focuses on the struggle toward mutuality in mission is Christopher Ney's narrative of the 50-year partnership between the United Churches of Christ (UCC) in the USA and The Pentecostal Church of Chile (IPC). Beginning in 1980, when an IPC missionary to North America met UCC leaders in Brooklyn, NY, this relationship grew into a regular association between the two denominations, with representatives of each attending the other's annual meetings and the appointment of a full-time missionary to anchor the infrastructures. The partnership's Missionary-in-Residence programme – in which an IPC family would come to New England for a period – produced mixed results. The North American congregations appreciated the opportunity to learn about pentecostalism, but the Chilean family experienced many logistical difficulties as they returned home. A later manifestation of the partnership – the CONPAZ youth programme in which North Americans and Chileans undertook a retreat at a Chilean creation-care centre – promoted the values of cultural respect and friendship-building among the participants. With partnership as the framework, different practices emerged depending on the persons involved and the needs of the times.

Locating her study in the context of landmark papal and episcopal documents, Angelyn Dries presents another longstanding international partnership – a "parish twinning" relationship between Catholic parishes in Wisconsin, USA, and Nkokonjeru, Uganda. In this instance, the partnership was initiated by the North American parish, St Eugene's. Nevertheless, the parish's decision to look to Uganda for a "twin" emerged from a friendship between St Eugene's pastor and a Ugandan priest studying at a Catholic university in Wisconsin, in addition to some connections forged by the Little Sisters of St Francis, an English group working in Uganda. As in Ney's study, this twinning relationship proceeded by trial and error, as when the Wisconsin parish sent an enormous amount of requested goods to Nkokonjeru without considering the logistics of getting these gifts across the sprawling Uganda diocese. However, as with all of the studies in this section, the various members of the partnership have persisted in continuing interracial and international friendships and formal connections through ecclesial bodies. Over the years, the partnership has led to significant agricultural development in the Uganda parish, and the Wisconsin parishioners keep in mind their connection to their Uganda "twin" through annual celebrations of the partnership during Lent.

Cooperative Projects

In addition to ecumenical unity and mutual partnerships, another aspect of collaboration in mission is practical cooperation for specific projects and aims, including educational, charitable, social, and political purposes.[18] The missional collaborations in this section demonstrate that diverse groups of Christians often organize around a particular purpose or issue as a means of mission. Each of the studies represent cooperation between transnational and interdenominational groups for projects in a particular geographic location, area of social concern, or ecclesiastical domain. In the three case studies that follow, shared concern, a united vision for change, negotiated values (or differences), and mutual respect act as catalysts for missional action.

First, David Restrick's chapter charts the cooperation among local denominations, mission practitioners, and international associations and networks to develop tertiary theological education for the training of Mozambican leaders and seminary faculty. In the face of significant political restrictions, scant theological infrastructure in Portuguese, and remnants of colonial mission models, Restrick details how the need for theological education among evangelical and pentecostal Protestants in Mozambique was addressed by creative cooperation conceived by the *Faculdade Teológica Sul-Americana* (FTSA) in Brazil and Overseas Council International in the United States. Committed cooperation between the Nazarene and pentecostal Bible schools led to the founding of a Masters level programme in Portuguese and the *Instituto Superior Teológico Evangélico de Moçambique* (ISTEM). An example of cooperation and relationship building across difference for the shared purpose of improved and localized theological education, ISTEM operated from 2007–2019 and trained 71 women and men from 18 different denominations.

Stephen Allen's chapter looks at KAIROS' Indigenous Rights Program and the KAIROS Blanket Exercise as an example of cooperation that extends beyond the confines of the Christian church. Social justice, political advocacy, and healing and reconciliation for and with the Indigenous people of Canada have been powerful motivators for KAIROS members, diverse church partners, Canadian government officials, and participants in formative programmes that come together under KAIROS. The injustices and traumas experienced by Canada's Indigenous peoples at the hands of government and church policy and programmes, such as the Indian Residential Schools, unites concerned parties, many religiously affiliated, toward lasting change. KAIROS' Blanket Exercise, a role-play activity that illustrates the process and effects of colonization, has

---

[18] The term "cooperation" was the key word used in the early 20th century for different mission agencies working together for common goals. See John R. Mott, *Cooperation and the World Mission* (New York: IMC, 1935). By the 1940s, the term "ecumenism," with its implications of ecclesial unity, had largely supplanted the term cooperation as a keyword in global Protestant conversations. In terms of mission, however, cooperation remained a core idea.

significantly contributed to an increase in the understanding of Indigenous people among non-Indigenous people in Canada and around the world. And, as Allen notes in his chapter, KAIROS' commitment to decolonizing the Canadian church and society rests in mutuality fostered by cooperative partnerships.

The urgent need for cooperation to mitigate global climate change motivates the organizations in the final case study of this section. Tyler Lenocker explores how concerned North American evangelicals have responded to the ecological crisis by aligning with creation care networks like the Lausanne/World Evangelical Alliance Creation Care Network. Lenocker explores the history of the creation care movement in North America, its ties to traditional white evangelical parachurch ministries, and its predicament in an increasingly politically polarized and volatile evangelical subculture in the United States. Incorporating the experiences and work of evangelical creation care leaders in the United States, Lenocker demonstrates how North Americans committed to creation care as mission and witness find belonging and express agency through cooperation with global networks. And, while evangelical Christians concerned and active in creation care in North America remain on the fringe in the very churches and denominations they attend on Sunday morning, their concern for the wellbeing and flourishing of people around the world affected by the climate crisis holds the potential to mobilize many more to action.

Decolonizing Frontiers

The fourth descriptor for missional collaboration comes from the mid-20th century missiological framework of "frontiers," combined with contemporary emphasis on the necessity for North Americans to decolonize their own historical patterns of relating to perceived others. The term "frontiers" was used to denote boundary-crossing and risk-taking mission in contexts where the gospel was not fully present. "Frontiers of unbelief" was a concept used, for example, to denote mission among Europe's urban proletariat and in post-Christian secularized urban spaces. During the 1960s, the "frontier interns" programme of the World Council of Churches sent young leaders into challenging settings around the world for two-year immersions into the social and political – and often revolutionary – contexts of the day. Mission across frontiers was always shifting. It meant finding where God was at work in the world and joining in. Another use for the term among evangelicals was the idea, put forth in the 1970s, of "frontier missions" to refer to cross-cultural church-planting among "unreached peoples," ethnic groups lacking the gospel in their own cultures.[19]

In North America, despite the frequent use of the term across the theological spectrum of missional outreach, the idea of frontiers has also connoted expansionism and manifest destiny, including the displacement of First Nations peoples. Often a frontier was seen as empty space, when actually others were already there. In popular usage, frontier spaces were defined as needing to be

---

[19] On shifting definitions of frontiers in mission, see Dana L. Robert, "Mission Frontiers from 1910 to 2010. Part I: From Geography to Justice," *Missiology* 39: 2 (April 2011), 5e–16e, and "Mission Frontiers from 1910 to 2010. Part II: Unbelief, Unreached, and Unknown," *Missiology* 39: 3 (July 2011), 1e–12e.

filled by "civilized" Christians. In North America today, therefore, decolonization is an essential aspect of every collaborative mission, whether it be church-planting, holistic transformation, or social advocacy.[20] Decolonizing frontiers refers, then, to risk-taking mission that criticizes what has gone before, to witness to a better future. Decolonizing frontiers requires that self-criticism be intrinsic to sharing the gospel, especially in mutual relationship with those who have suffered abuse or neglect – even within churches themselves.

A key piece of decolonization in collaboration today involves commitment to interculturality. Even though the traditional idea of cross-cultural mission remains important, to move to a stance of interculturality implies the willingness to change oneself in relationship with the other. To be intercultural requires deep listening, humility, and openness to others' values and meanings. It means thinking of mission as "with" rather than "to." As Roger Schroeder notes, interculturality marks a shift from "international to multicultural to intercultural," with "mutual enrichment" as the assumption underlying relationships.[21]

Jonathan Schmidt, in his case study, analyzes the century-old pathway from Canadian mission as changing the "other" to mutual change in relationship, or interculturality. What began a century ago as the Canadian School of Missions has adapted over the generations from the context of imperial British Canada to a post-Christian nation that includes people of all faiths and no faith. Now known as the Forum for Intercultural Leadership and Learning (FILL), the old Canadian mission education movement is a "reference group" of the Canadian Council of Churches. FILL focuses on witness and solidarity among the diverse peoples of Canada, especially the First Nations who were shoved aside by European settlers. To be "just intercultural" means that justice issues are inseparable from interculturality.[22] "Peace be with you" (Lk. 24:36, Jn. 20:19) becomes the

---

[20] The agenda of decolonizing mission became prominent in ecumenical circles in the mid-20th century, in tandem with nationalist independence movements and the decline of European imperialism. For example, see Keith B. Bridston, *Mission, Myth and Reality* (New York: Friendship Press, 1965); Max Warren, "Introduction" to *Sandals at the Mosque: Christian Presence amid Islam*, ed. Kenneth Cragg, Christian Presence series (London: SCM Press, 1959); James A. Scherer, *Missionary, Go Home!: A Reappraisal of the Christian World Mission* (Englewood Cliffs, NJ: 1964). The urge to decolonize North American mission is a more recent movement that is directly related to awareness of the colonization of indigenous peoples by North Americans, the bias against immigrants, and Christian guilt and complicity in racism. See Mark Charles and Soong-Chan Rah, *Unsettling Truths: The Ongoing, Dehumanizing Legacy of the Doctrine of Discovery* (Downers Grove, IL: IVP, 2019); Love L. Sechrest, Johnny Ramírez-Johnson, and Amos Yong, eds., *Can "White" People Be Saved?: Triangulating Race, Theology, and Mission*, Missiological Engagements 12 (Downers Grove, IL: IVP Academic, 2018).
[21] Roger Schroeder, "Interculturality as a Paradigm of Mission," in *Intercultural Living: Explorations in Missiology*, eds. Lazar Stanislaus, SVD, and Martin Ueffing (Maryknoll, NY: Orbis Books, 2018), 173.
[22] Jonathan Schmidt, "A Prophetic Vision of Just Intercultural Community: The Canadian School of Missions and The Forum for Intercultural Leadership and Learning," in this volume.

touchstone for mission. FILL engages in anti-racism work, critiques white privilege, and seeks "revolutionary" interculturality, especially in relation to the shocking history of Indian residential schools, where churches collaborated to strip First Nations youth of their cultures. In order to challenge colonial mindsets and practices that continue to govern Canadian society and church life, FILL collaborates with its First Nations partners and also forms partnerships with migrants and people with disabilities. Along with his article, Schmidt shares FILL's principles of interculturality as an invitation to live into a new, peaceful, and just vision of the world.

Decolonization of mission has become an urgent issue for North American missionaries, and interculturality has become the new model of fresh possibilities. Using a Pauline image of the "body of Christ," Roger Schroeder describes a 3-year project on intercultural living undertaken by 20 Roman Catholic religious communities. In the era of world Christianity, with mission to and from everywhere, not only must religious communities navigate multiple cultures in their mission work, but their own communities have become intercultural. Therefore, how to live interculturally, in community, becomes a great and necessary challenge. Schroeder describes how this process requires knowledge, new practices, and the willingness to be "converted" from ethnocentrism. Teams from the religious communities undertook common learning, attended conferences, and developed action plans that included "reconciliation, cultural models of conflict resolution, practical suggestions for intercultural living, personality and culture, interculturality and leadership, and race and gender dynamics."[23] Schroeder reports impressive levels of participation by the communities, concrete improvement in the ability to live interculturally, and a helpful list of best practices. Speaking of the need for "respect and understanding," he concludes that interculturality is "a paradigm of mission."[24]

The third article on decolonizing frontiers is by Amanda Quantz. She explores outreach to LGBTQ+ Roman Catholic folks in San Francisco, beginning with the "Faithful & Fabulous Interfaith Drag Street Eucharist" held during Pride Week, 2021. LGBTQ+ ministry by Roman Catholic priests, sisters, and lay ministers decolonizes frontiers by reaching out to people specifically marginalized by the church's teachings and practices. Based on interviews with key participants in ministry to LGBTQ+ folks, Quantz's case study represents "a challenge and an opportunity to Roman Catholic missioners who wish to reach people who have been ignored or forgotten by the church."[25] Relying on the imagery of the millennial banquet described by Jesus, at which all are welcome, Quantz calls for building understanding and love through relating to people across gender identities. She movingly describes the struggles of LGBTQ+

---

[23] Roger Schroeder, "'Engaging Our Diversity: Interculturality and Consecrated Life': A Program of the Center for the Study of Consecrated Life (CSCL) at Catholic Theological Union at Chicago" p.168 in this volume.

[24] *Ibid.*, p.166.

[25] Amanda Quantz, "Ministry at the Margins: Outreach to the LGBTQ+ Roman Catholic Community in San Francisco" p.185 in this volume.

devoted Catholics to be accepted and to be in ministry. Quantz calls for decisive
action by the Roman Catholic Church to accept LGBTQ+ people as fully human
and "beautifully made" by their Creator: "Together, the faithful can practice
reflective listening, reevaluate views that we have perhaps formed uncritically,
and embrace those who, despite being marginalized or even rejected, choose to
remain in the church."[26]

Creative Collaborations as Missional Practices

Creative collaborations show that mission is alive and well among North
American Christians today. The case studies in this volume illustrate that the
practices of collaborative mission range across local and global networks. Old
distinctions between "home" and "foreign" mission do not make much sense in
an era of Christianity as a worldwide religion, especially when secularity, non-
belief, and shifting ecclesial terrain define North American religious realities.
Emphasis on locality, such as in city-wide church movements, Bethlehem
Centers, and Canadian Christian relationships with First Nations peoples,
coheres with consciousness of their grounding in global networks and with
Christianity as a migratory and worldwide community of faith. Whether the
shape of the collaboration is a cross-cultural missionary project, such as
theological training in Mozambique and walking with AICs, person-to-person
partnerships such as parish twinning and team visitations, or Latinx networking
for theological education, North American practices of missional collaboration
today exemplify the intersection of local, regional, and global networks.

The central importance of relationship-building as missional practice cuts
across all the case studies. Multiple case studies have emphasized being in
mission "with" others rather than "to" others, as the chief way to think about
North American collaboration in mission. The stated commitment to
interculturality on the part of multiple groups is at heart a cry for mutual
relationships in the body of Christ and beyond. Building relationships is both a
theological and personal imperative for the people involved in these case studies.
Spiritual growth and social justice overlap when personal relationships are a
compass for creative collaboration. People engaged in collaborative mission find
great spiritual satisfaction in their relational practices, even when activities are
challenging or difficult. For instance, the case studies illustrate perseverance in
mission despite self-criticism inherent in the KAIROS Blanket Exercise, the
constant sacrifices required for intercultural living, the rejection by the church
faced by LGBTQ+ believers, and the hurdles in building evangelical ecojustice
networks. Collaborative mission creates traction for the melding of personal
growth and social justice. Mission becomes not only a matter of finding the Holy
Spirit within; collaborating with others facilitates joining God for work in the
world.

We have explored four descriptors or touchstones for these case studies: 1.
Ecumenical Unity, 2. Mutual Partnerships, 3. Cooperative Projects, and 4.
Decolonizing Frontiers. Although some groups in the late 20th century critiqued

---

[26] *Ibid*, 196.

partnership as a model that did not truly prevent paternalism, today in North America a focus on partnership energizes networks of relationships. Today's partnerships strive toward the goal of mutuality across multiple kinds of boundaries – both the divisions within North America and across national borders. Mission, in its myriad forms, has been and continues to be the cooperative project of the church. The projects or issues that animate missional collaboration are endless. Global telecommunications and technologies that increase access and connection among disparate geographies, groups, and generations provide unlimited possibility for cooperation, network creation, and project development. Perhaps the most challenging goal of all is ecumenical unity – being one across ecclesial divisions. As the Roman Catholic case studies show, it is easier to partner on projects across ecclesial boundaries than to unite in evangelism and church-planting. Ecclesial aspects of mission are often competitive in nature. The self-criticism required by decolonizing frontiers presents North American mission with another challenging and painful task. In secular contexts, the deeper meaning of Christianity is no longer common knowledge among large swathes of the population, thereby making it easy to blame religion for social evils. North American Christians engaged in the process of self-criticism, therefore, must exemplify long-suffering humility animated by hope.

What is the meaning of creative collaboration for mission today? We have found that the courage to commit to collaborative practices across boundaries and divisions energizes theological commitment to unity, equality, peace, and justice under God. Collaboration encourages the faith needed to move forward in partnership, cooperation, and self-criticism with others. Living into hope for the future, and the ability to envision things as they should be, rather than as flawed and disappointing as they are, undergirds creative collaborations in mission among North Americans today. Risk-taking and sacrificial shared mission among Christ's followers, for the sake of the world that God made and loves, are core values for North Americans who seek unity, reconciliation, healing, and transformation.

Acknowledgements

The editors of this volume wish to acknowledge the support of the Center for Global Christianity and Mission at the Boston University School of Theology. The CGCM has underwritten the work of the editors. It has provided a home base for the North American study on missional collaborations launched in conjunction with the centennial of the International Missionary Council. We thank the leaders of the international study process sponsored by the Commission on World Mission and Evangelism of the World Council of Churches. We thank its representatives at Regnum Press for their assistance and willingness to answer our queries. We appreciate the participants in the study process, and particularly those who have produced the case studies for this volume. The interpretive framework for the volume is our own, subject to our own biases and limited perspectives. Finally, we acknowledge the dedicated people committed to creative missional collaboration throughout the world – the few represented by the wider study and the majority who continue their work far from public acknowledgement, but in faithfulness to God's mission.

The Editors

ECUMENICAL UNITY

Contemporary US Catholic Collaborative Mission

William P. Gregory

One hundred years after the founding of the International Missionary Council, Pope Francis is making missionary renewal the top priority of the Catholic Church. Since his election in 2013, he has continually urged Catholics to be more active in mission, more engaged with the brokenness of the world, and more committed to building structures of dialogue, fraternity, and cooperation across the divisions that separate people. As part of his call to action, he has also encouraged Catholics to act ecumenically whenever possible and to join with other Christians in common prayer, evangelization, and service to the poor. Speaking at the World Council of Churches in 2018, he proclaimed: "Walking, praying and working together: this is the great path that we are called to follow today."[1] Collaborative action, driven by "an increased missionary impulse," "will lead [Christians] to greater unity."[2]

> We think of what happened in Edinburgh at the outset of the ecumenical movement. It was truly the fire of mission that made it possible to surmount barriers and tear down walls which kept us apart and made a common path unthinkable. Together let us pray for this intention. May the Lord grant [...] a renewed impetus towards communion and mission.[3]

Francis's recent words advance the teaching of the Second Vatican Council (1962–65), which broke new ground in calling for all the baptized to both participate in the mission of the church[4] and "take an active and intelligent part in the work of ecumenism,"[5] through dialogue with other Christians, shared

---

[1] Francis, "Ecumenical Prayer: Address of His Holiness to Mark the 70th Anniversary of the Foundation of the World Council of Churches" (Ecumenical Pilgrimage, Geneva, 21 June 2018), https://www.vatican.va/content/francesco/en/speeches/2018/june/documents/papa-francesco_20180621_preghiera-ecumenica-ginevra.html.

[2] Francis, "Ecumenical Meeting: Address of His Holiness to Mark the 70th Anniversary of the Foundation of the World Council of Churches" (Ecumenical Pilgrimage, Geneva, 21 June 2018), https://www.vatican.va/content/francesco/en/speeches/2018/june/documents/papa-francesco_20180621_pellegrinaggio-ginevra.html (hereafter Ecumenical Meeting).

[3] Francis, "Address of His Holiness Pope Francis Commemorating the 50th Anniversary of the Meeting Between Pope Paul VI and Archbishop Michael Ramsey" (Rome, 5 October 2016), https://www.vatican.va/content/francesco/en/speeches/2016/october/documents/papa-francesco_20161005_vespri-canterbury.html (hereafter 50th Anniversary Address).

[4] Second Vatican Council, *Lumen Gentium* (21 November 1964), 33, https://www.vatican.va/archive/hist_councils/ii_vatican_council/documents/vat-ii_const_19641121_lumen-gentium_en.html.

[5] Second Vatican Council, *Unitatis Redintegratio* (21 November 1964), 4, https://www.vatican.va/archive/hist_councils/ii_vatican_council/documents/vat-ii_decree_19641121_unitatis-redintegratio_en.html (hereafter *UR*).

prayer, and joint promotion of the common good.[6] A generation later, Pope John Paul II reiterated these teachings in his 1995 encyclical *Ut Unum Sint*, highlighting the necessity of ecumenical cooperation in all areas of Christian activity:

> Relations between Christians are not aimed merely at mutual knowledge, common prayer and dialogue. They presuppose and from now on call for every possible form of practical cooperation at all levels: pastoral, cultural and social, as well as that of witnessing to the Gospel message.[7]

Cooperation between Christians, John Paul II asserted, is "a manifestation of Christ himself [...] a true school of ecumenism, a dynamic road to unity."[8] Its importance, therefore, calls for robust structures of organization, support, and formation. Bishops, parish priests, and all those involved in pastoral ministry must form the faithful so that "all Christians [are] animated by the ecumenical spirit, whatever their particular mission and task in the world and in society."[9]

Standing now two generations from the council, and to honour the work undertaken so memorably by the International Missionary Council, it is fitting for Catholics to pause and reflect on how well the church in the United States has been traversing along this cooperative path. How common is collaborative mission involving US Catholics today? What achievements are there to celebrate? What gaps, challenges, and issues attend the church's current progress? For a church of 80 million souls, 16,000 parishes, hundreds of religious orders, and a vast proliferation of intersecting agencies, institutions, and associations, gaining a comprehensive set of answers to these questions is obviously beyond reach. But by surveying a number of prominent Catholic institutions and ministries and incorporating the insights of knowledgeable observers, it is possible to discern the major trends. This plan was followed in one portion of the North American Missional Collaborations study process: a series of 16 interviews conducted from August 2021 to April 2022 with leading Catholic mission administrators and ecumenists. The major findings of that investigation, presented here, are divided into two parts. Part one sketches the major patterns that appear in contemporary US Catholic collaborative mission, and part two explores the positive values operative in these collaborations as well as their potential missiological and ecumenical significance.

---

[6] *UR*, 8–12.

[7] John Paul II, *Ut Unum Sint* (25 May 1995), 40, https://www.vatican.va/content/john-paul-ii/en/encyclicals/documents/hf_jp-ii_enc_25051995_ut-unum-sint.html (hereafter *UUS*).

[8] *UUS*, 40.

[9] Pontifical Council for Promoting Christian Unity, *Directory for the Application of Principles and Norms on Ecumenism* (25 March 1993), 58, http://www.christianunity.va/content/unitacristiani/en/documenti/testo-in-inglese.html (hereafter *Ecumenical Directory*).

Major Local and National Trends

A number of Catholic ministries have extensive footprints in dioceses across the nation. These include Catholic Charities, the Society of Saint Vincent De Paul, the pregnancy help movement, and the faith-based community organizations supported by the Catholic Campaign for Human Development. An examination of these ministries alongside several examples of Catholic institutions that operate on a national scale illuminates the major patterns that mark contemporary US Catholic collaborative mission.

The Catholic Charities network of agencies spans every US diocese. It is comprised of local bishops' organizations that pursue the corporal works of mercy within the boundaries of a given diocese, and Catholic Charities USA, which is the US bishops' official domestic disaster response agency. As a matter of policy,[10] Catholic Charities agencies routinely collaborate with ecumenical, interfaith, and community partners in providing youth services, affordable housing, counselling and addiction treatment, refugee resettlement, prison ministries, food pantries, and programmes for veterans, immigrants, and the homeless. Brian Corbin, Executive Vice President for Member Services of Catholic Charities USA, remarks that it is just the nature of on-the-ground justice and charity work that brings out this collaborative relationship:

> It would be a typical thing where a Catholic Charities agency would say, "Saint Robert's Lutheran Church, of course I need you! If you want to serve food every Wednesday at my food bank, please come." It's a no brainer. It's just practical, especially in the very specific social services work – food pantries, soup kitchens, the practical side of helping someone or doing advocacy together. There is a sense that, "Yeah, I know we have disagreements over there, but, as a Christian, Matthew 25! Outreach is critical to our work as Christians."[11]

The same thinking informs the work of the prominent lay Catholic association, the Society of Saint Vincent De Paul (SSVP), whose approximately 100,000 members are present in 30 percent of the nation's parishes.[12] While its groups pursue some ministries on their own (e.g., home visits and thrift store operations), its outreach often pragmatically partners with others in activities such as food distribution, post-incarceration services, support for single mothers and the elderly, and assistance with employment, fuel, and rent. "We'll work with anyone to help someone out of poverty," says David Barringer, Chief Executive Officer of SSVP's National Council of the United States. "We all see the same needs, and so it just makes sense to work together, because none of us have so much money that we can afford not to share with other people."[13]

---

[10] United States Catholic Conference, *In All Things Charity: A Pastoral Challenge for the New Millennium* (Washington, D.C.: United States Catholic Conference, 1999), 36–37.

[11] Brian Corbin, interview by William P. Gregory, 5 November 2021.

[12] International Confederation of the Society of St. Vincent De Paul, *Rule of the International Confederation of the Society of St. Vincent De Paul* (St. Louis, MO: National Council of the United States, SSVP, Inc., 2006), section 6.

[13] David Barringer, interview by William P. Gregory, 1 April 2022.

The same cooperative spirit also is evidenced in the pregnancy help movement, which gained momentum following the legalization of abortion in 1973. A predominantly lay women's effort and one of the most significant new examples of grassroots Catholic outreach to appear since the Second Vatican Council, pregnancy help centres offer an array of support services for women facing unexpected pregnancies, as well as abortion healing ministries, maternity homes, and other forms of assistance. Initially an entirely Catholic effort, the pro-life movement in general became jointly Catholic and evangelical beginning in the 1980s. Since then, the pregnancy help branch of the movement in particular has been a unique site of Catholic-evangelical encounter, involving not only collaborative activity, but faith-sharing, common prayer, and mutual discernment of God's will.[14] Heartbeat International, the largest affiliation of such centres, for example, has intentionally modelled inter-Christian unity since its founding in 1971. One of its founders, Lore Maier, was known to have repeatedly stated, "There can never be too many pregnancy help centres. There can never be any competition among us."[15] Heartbeat International's 1,850 US centres today bring together more than 40,000 Catholic, evangelical, and Orthodox staff and volunteers to ensure "that no woman ever feels that abortion is her only option."[16]

One final example to consider, having a large impact in dioceses across the nation, is the US bishops' Catholic Campaign for Human Development (CCHD). Established in 1969, CCHD awards $11 million annually to dozens of faith-based community organizations (FBCOs) working to alleviate poverty in areas such as housing and homelessness, immigrant and disability rights, criminal justice reform, small business creation, public safety, and neighbourhood improvement. Awarded projects have Catholic participation and diocesan support, but sponsored FBCOs are invariably ecumenical and interreligious in makeup, as well as racially, ethnically, economically, and generationally mixed. Building relationships among these diverse groups is a central value of the campaign, which sees its work primarily in "relational, not transactional"[17] terms. As CCHD Director Ralph McCloud notes:

> We encourage the organization of groups within themselves to be relational, to know each other, to understand each other, to walk with each other. We think that the money is just a very small part. We like to think of it helping folks sustain long-term relationships, long-term sustainability, self-determination. We have some resources, but relatively speaking, we're a small part of the puzzle.[18]

---

[14] Dr Peggy Hartshorn, interview by William P. Gregory, 12 April 2022; Margaret H. (Peggy) Hartshorn, *Foot Soldiers Armed with Love: Heartbeat International's First Forty Years* (Columbus, OH: Heartbeat International, 2011), 92–100.

[15] Peggy Hartshorn and Jor-El Godsey, *The Power of Pregnancy Help: The First Fifty Years* (Columbus, OH: Heartbeat International, 2021), 85.

[16] Heartbeat International, *Life Trends 2022 Report* (Columbus, OH: Heartbeat International, Inc., 2022). An excellent account of the pregnancy help movement is Laura S. Hussey, *The Pro-Life Pregnancy Help Movement: Serving Women or Saving Babies?* (Lawrence, KS: University Press of Kansas, 2020).

[17] Ralph McCloud, interview by William P. Gregory, 19 November 2021.

[18] *Ibid.*

Since its founding, CCHD has sponsored over 9,000 projects that have brought Catholics shoulder to shoulder with other Christians and community members in pursuit of shared dreams.

The consistent pattern we see among these four prominent examples indicates that, 60 years after the council, it is commonplace for Catholics to cooperate locally with other churches, religious groups, and community partners, especially in serving America's poor and vulnerable. In the numerous small-scale, hard-to-track grassroots efforts that are also taking place across the country, the pattern appears to be no different. Rev. James Loughran, SA, Director of the Graymoor Ecumenical and Interreligious Institute, expresses the observation of many interviewed in this study when he says that,

> The grassroots do a lot together on issues of social justice [...] It depends on the local pastors and the local non-Catholic rectors and ministers, and it is based a lot on personal relationships that have been built up over the years. But in mission you see a lot of local efforts going on of living out the gospel with other Christians, and even people of other religions. We do a lot together because of our faith-driven ideals.[19]

Dr Daniel Olsen, Director of the Office of Ecumenical and Interreligious Affairs of the Archdiocese of Chicago, concurs. Collaboration with other Christians and other religious organizations, he reports, is "what's baked into the system right now." Olsen notes that "some parishes work with Muslim mosques or Episcopal parishes down the street in soup kitchens. Those things are going on and the list is too long to go through."[20]

Two exceptions to this cooperative pattern stand out, however. The first is the low frequency of Catholic-evangelical cooperative efforts outside of pro-life activities. Alexei Laushkin of the Kingdom Mission Society notes this when he remarks that "the lay affinity [of evangelicals to Catholics] has not reached into or beyond abortion clinic, pregnancy crisis centre co-volunteerism. It hasn't really led to co-missional things in a substantial way."[21] Exceptions to this pattern exist, of course, for example, Glenmary Home Missioners work with evangelical and pentecostal churches in Appalachia and in a small number of evangelical Christian unity initiatives. But the general trend appears to be otherwise and is likely rooted in the widespread evangelical mindset that Catholics are not Christians, and it is best not to associate with them.[22]

A second exception to the collaborative pattern centers on the limited nature of the missional activities typically undertaken. In the classic binary, mission embraces both evangelism and social action. Yet a moment's reflection on the kinds of collaborations just described details an abundance of the latter yet little to none of the former in terms of focused engagements in proclamation,

---

[19] Rev. James Loughran, SA, and Aaron Hollander, interview by William P. Gregory, 6 October 2021.

[20] Dr Daniel Olsen, interview by William P. Gregory, 3 November 2021.

[21] Alexei Laushkin and Nathan Smith, interview by William P. Gregory and Allison Kach, 8 October 2021.

[22] *Ibid.*; Nathan Smith, interview by William P. Gregory, 12 August 2021.

evangelization, catechesis, and church planting. As Rev. James Loughran observes,

> There is very little mission in the more traditional sense of converting hearts to the gospel together. The more practical applications of working together on social projects locally is getting more headway than sacramental sharing or building churches together for the sake of the larger community.[23]

Some exceptions to this appear in the religious education provided by mixed marriage couples and in the occasional shared vacation Bible school.[24] But on the whole, the more overtly evangelistic the activity, the rarer it is for Catholics to partner with other Christians and vice versa, even though joint activities of this kind are envisioned in the church's ecumenical teaching.[25] Given the precipitous decline in religious affiliation in younger generations, one can only speculate what difference collaboration here might make. Regardless, Catholic collaboration in the United States is currently standing on only one leg.

These basic trends are also seen in national-level Catholic collaborative relationships. To illustrate the common patterns, what follows is simply a brief listing of major examples. The examples noted all center on outreach to the poor and vulnerable and are grouped into two broad categories: material support and advocacy.

In the area of material support, the Catholic Church is one of nine agencies designated by the US government for refugee resettlement and one of six agencies that allocate $120 million annually to poor communities through the Emergency Food and Shelter Program. The church's close partners in these ministries include the National Council of Churches, the Salvation Army, Church World Service, Episcopal Migration Ministries, Lutheran Immigration and Refugee Service, World Relief, the Jewish Federation, and the US Muslim community. In assisting victims of natural disaster, Catholic Charities USA and SSVP's Disaster Services work very closely with most of these same groups along with the Methodists, the Mennonites, the Church of the Brethren, and the Church of Jesus Christ of Latter-day Saints, among other partners.[26] In support of women facing unexpected pregnancies, the inter-Christian Leadership Alliance of Pregnancy Care Organizations (LAPCO) gathers the evangelical and Catholic lay leaders of the pregnancy help movement for national-level coordination.[27] Finally, in international humanitarian and development work, Catholic Relief Services (CRS) partners in 116 countries worldwide with local churches, governments, tribal leaders, and other public and faith-based organizations.[28]

Turning to public and legislative advocacy, CRS participates in several coalitions working to advance public policy for the common good. Two noteworthy examples are the Thrive Coalition, which advocates for US

---

[23] Loughran and Hollander interview.
[24] Olsen interview.
[25] *Ecumenical Directory*, 188, 207.
[26] Corbin interview; Barringer interview.
[27] Hartshorn interview; Hartshorn, *Foot Soldiers*, 96–97.
[28] Donald Rogers, interview by William P. Gregory, 26 October 2021.

government investment in global early childhood development, and InterAction, which pursues a range of priorities in international justice, peace, and sustainability.[29] On the domestic policy front, the church also helps staff Circle of Protection, a coalition of US churches that lobbies Congress to remember the poor and vulnerable in budget and appropriations.[30] In pro-life advocacy, meanwhile, the bishops' Secretariat of Pro-Life Activities works with the Lutheran Church – Missouri Synod, the Southern Baptist Convention, and the evangelical Family Research Council on a range of right-to-life and religious liberty issues. The Secretariat also teams with these same partners as well as with the Orthodox, the Assemblies of God, and the Church of God in Christ, among others, in joint national prayer initiatives for the unborn.[31]

Moving from the diocesan to the national stage, then, one sees the same patterns of cooperation centred on the church's social mission. Evangelicals and pentecostals cooperate most on pro-life issues while the other churches cooperate most in the other areas. One further point to note, though, concerns the apparent diffidence many evangelicals and pentecostals have in sharing a national stage with Catholics, as shown in their absence from the annual March for Life despite the shared commitment to end abortion.[32] Several of the Secretariat of Pro-Life Activities' official ties with evangelical and pentecostal leaders are relatively new compared to the more well-established grassroots relationships.[33] This indicates both the current dynamic nature of the pro-life arena and the fact that it may be easier for members of these groups to associate with Catholics as individuals and around a single social issue rather than on a more formal, church-to-church basis.

Interpreting the Trends

How are we to interpret these trends, particularly in light of Catholic teaching on missional collaboration? As noted at the outset, the Catholic Church's understanding of collaboration fits within its wider teaching on both mission and ecumenism and, specifically, within its teaching on the practical steps Christians need to take for separated churches to grow closer together. An important question, therefore, is: How well are these collaborations contributing to Christian unity? What is happening within them to bring the different communities of Christians closer? Answering this question requires us to do two things. First, we need to explore the different values animating and attending these collaborative relationships. This will enable us to appreciate more fully the potential contributions they are making to Christian unity. Second, we need to consider the prevalence of an ecumenical vision and spirit within them, or at least around them in the wider milieux of US Catholicism. For unless there is a vital

---

[29] Beth Knobbe, email message to author, 13 October 2021.

[30] Corbin interview.

[31] Thomas Grenchik and Greg Schleppenbach, interview by William P. Gregory, 9 December 2021.

[32] Laushkin and Smith interview.

[33] Grenchik and Schleppenbach interview.

impulse toward unity somewhere in the picture, it is hard to see how the various missional collaborations will be able to contribute to it.

A. Operative Values

What are some of the values motivating and informing contemporary US Catholic collaborative mission? Clearly, there are many. Perhaps the most basic one is the pragmatic desire to most effectively achieve the particular gospel purpose being pursued, whether that is to feed the hungry, uplift the downtrodden, or care for the sick. David Barringer of the Society of Saint Vincent De Paul expresses this value when he remarks that "For us I would say, it [collaboration] is not a goal, but more of a strategy, where what we really focus on is the corporal works of mercy."[34] This gospel-centred pragmatism likely factors into many collaborations, at least in part, for if one can fulfil God's will better through the help of others, then one should. But connections once established can also eventually come to be recognized as goods worth preserving in their own right, especially if they become generative of new and unanticipated joint activities. A pivotal interreligious gathering to protect local Muslims in Youngstown, Ohio, following the 9/11 attacks, for example, led to later efforts by the same group to reform local policing – a completely different issue. The formation of the group had created wholly new possibilities for social action.[35]

Stepping closer to the value of community, one also sees capacity-building in collaboration, where the goal is not just to get the job done, but to assist one's partners along the way. Donald Rogers, Global Church Engagement Advisor for Catholic Relief Services, describes how for CRS, "it was never a hesitation about the philosophy of an organization." They always had an open door to cooperating with different organizations. Rather, "it was always, could we rely on them to effectively manage? And if they couldn't, we still would work with them, but we would realize we would have to climb that mountain together."[36]

Beyond capacity-building, one sees other kinds of gifts exchanged between collaborators, sometimes very large ones. A dying Latter-day Saints church member willed $27 million to Catholic Charities USA because he knew and respected its work,[37] and the founder of a Catholic organization to reverse the effects of medical abortion handed over the running of the organization to Heartbeat International's evangelical president because of Heartbeat's deeply collaborative Catholic-evangelical culture.[38] Brian Corbin also recounts the following dramatic development from his time as president of a Catholic Charities housing corporation, which also exemplifies the anti-Catholic animus of many evangelicals referred to earlier:

> There was a group of evangelicals that started their own housing corporation. We were trying to figure out in the community what was the next step on housing, and I went to a meeting and one of them literally said to me: "I can't work with you and

---

[34] Barringer interview.
[35] Corbin interview.
[36] Rogers interview.
[37] Corbin interview.
[38] Hartshorn interview.

I really can't be in this meeting because he [pointing to Brian Corbin] represents the whore of Babylon." But, in time, because we all had to focus laser-beam on some housing issues, in time, he invited me to his house to talk about this. In time, he took me aside one day and said, "I guess you're not so bad, would you be interested in serving on my board?" I did. In time, they faced a crisis, and he gave his entire portfolio – $50 to $60 million of housing – to our Catholic Charities corporation because he trusted us and because he knew that we would do a better job than anyone else in the state.[39]

This episode also illustrates collaboration's power to break down social barriers, transform participants, and generate mutual respect and trust between groups of Christians who otherwise would not have interacted with each other. Ralph McCloud of the Catholic Campaign for Human Development similarly describes the unique relationships that are forged in the faith-based coalitions sponsored by the campaign. Once different groups in a coalition have had a chance to meet, pray together, and discuss the community's needs,

All of a sudden it becomes less important that they're Baptists [or Catholics, for example] and more important that they're human, they're neighbours, they're friends, they're colleagues. And the Baptists who would not have stepped foot in a Catholic church, all of a sudden they're saying "I didn't know Catholics were Christian" and then they have an appreciation for the faith [...] They're sharing meals together, they respect one another, they listen to one another, they realize they want the same things: the best lives for their children. It's something that is very beautiful to watch.[40]

In some cases, the Christian communion that emerges can blossom into an explicit spiritual ecumenism marked by the desire for the greater unity of the different churches gathered. Dr Peggy Hartshorn, president of Heartbeat International from 1993–2015, describes how she and other leaders of the pregnancy help movement discerned this very purpose of God at work in their collaboration.

I needed to watch and see what God seemed to be doing. Where is God opening the doors and where does he want us to go? And it was very clear to me – and I'm sure I'm not the only person – that what he was really blessing particularly was our coming together as Catholics and evangelicals. You could see the blessing on a personal level. Catholics were intrigued by the daily, hourly faith of the evangelicals. They really did make Jesus the centre of their lives and woke up at 5:30 in the morning to read their Bibles [...] So that was very challenging to some of the Catholics involved early on. It was attractive, and we respected their true commitment, that if they said they were Christians, that meant something and changed their lives. And also Catholics were challenged by the statements "When were you saved?" and it gave us an opportunity [...] to explain our concept of baptism and our relationship with the Lord. "What could bring you closer to the Lord than receiving his body and blood every day?" Evangelical Christians often were kind of wide-eyed: "Oh, well you really do believe in Jesus!" [...] So on a one-to-one basis we were really challenged, both the evangelicals and the Catholics, by getting to know each other, and we've obviously learned a lot from each other since we've been interacting so much through the years [...] And the

---

[39] Corbin interview.
[40] McCloud interview.

pro-life movement was also something that I began to see that God was using to bring the church together. God was not only using Christians of every stripe to come to enhance our pro-life efforts, but it was the pro-life movement he was using to bring his people together. All I know is we're getting together and loving each other and understanding each other and respecting each other through this work. So it's got to be his intention for the pro-life movement.[41]

One final, dual value to note is that any form of ecumenical cooperation that is public also witnesses on at least some level to Christian unity while also serving as a means of evangelization. Observers of church groups working together on issues such as refugee resettlement or environmental stewardship, for example, learn something about the importance of common witness for Christians, and come to see that Christians care about these things not despite but because of their faith.[42]

B. Missiological Significance

Clearly, contemporary US Catholic missional collaboration is informed and marked by many positive values, all of which should be gratefully acknowledged and celebrated. Coming together as God's people truly does create entirely new possibilities for accomplishing the many tasks of mission. But as we saw at the outset of this chapter, collaboration does not stand as an isolated phenomena in the Catholic Church's understanding of its calling. It fits within its wider ecumenical vision and programme and hope. This raises an important question: how fully are these collaborations serving as "a dynamic road to unity,"[43] in the words of Pope John Paul II, or tearing down the walls that keep us apart,[44] in the image evoked by Pope Francis?

The question matters because the cause of mission is not independent of the cause of Christian unity. As Rev. Thomas Ryan, CSP, Director Emeritus of the Paulist Office for Ecumenical and Interfaith Relations, explains, the church witnesses to the gospel not only in what it says and does, but just as importantly in what it *is* – in its *being* the one reconciled community Jesus intended.[45] But in being fragmented instead into thousands of opposed communities, the church's energies are turned against itself and its mediation of the gospel to the world is riven with strife. In other words, when unity fails, mission fails along with it to the extent that the church is weakened by its own internal wounds. Missional collaborations of any kind are certainly accomplishing a lot of good, as we have seen. But are they healing the church's wounds? Are they bringing the churches together, as Peggy Hartshorn describes? Or are they proceeding untouched by, and unconcerned with, matters of ecclesial identity and division and thus failing missionally on a more fundamental level?

Providing a general answer to this question is certainly not the best way of proceeding, for every particular case of collaboration deserves its own

---

[41] Hartshorn interview.
[42] McCloud interview.
[43] *UUS*, 40.
[44] 50th Anniversary Address.
[45] Thomas Ryan, CSP, *Christian Unity: How You Can Make a Difference* (Mahwah, NJ: Paulist Press, 2015), Kindle.

assessment. But the well-documented decline in the US Catholic Church's attention to ecumenism over the last few decades strongly suggests that many US Catholic missional collaborations today are not making the contribution to Christian unity that they could. The value they could offer of serving a healing function is very likely a rare occurrence.

To clarify this point, a brief description of the current US Catholic ecumenical scene will prove helpful. After Vatican II in the 1960s, the church established a number of institutional structures to promote local ecumenism and to form all the faithful in its ecumenical vision. But over the last few decades, those structures have been hollowed out: the required course in ecumenism is no longer taught in many seminaries;[46] required ecumenical officer positions are no longer meaningfully filled in most dioceses;[47] and throughout the US church, including in the episcopate, an attitude of indifference to this important conciliar priority has taken hold.[48] The picture is not all bad, of course. Several key institutional supports for ecumenism persist, including an invested group of committed bishops and religious orders, the USCCB Secretariat of Ecumenical and Interreligious Affairs, the Catholic Association of Diocesan Ecumenical and Interreligious Officers (CADEIO), and the National Workshop for Christian Unity.[49] But the activity of these entities, unfortunately, remains far too marginal to the life of the church. The result is that most Catholics today – including most priests, bishops, and mission collaborators – have little idea of the depth and seriousness of the Catholic Church's official ecumenical commitment and vision: the fact that the church sees itself as, in effect, engaged to be married with the rest of the Christian world, and that it believes fidelity to Christ requires every Catholic and Catholic institution to avidly contribute toward that eventual wedding day. As Daniel Olsen remarks, "I take it for granted that people don't know about this stuff."[50]

But if this is the ecumenical situation in the US Catholic Church today, then how much is missional collaboration actually contributing toward greater Christian unity? If we imagine missional collaboration to be like a ship's sail, then the ecumenical spirit and vision is like the wind that must fill the sail for the ship to move toward its proper destination. At present, the spirit of unity is not in the air, and so the ecumenical potential of most missional collaborations is likely not being realized. Even worse, in some places the spirit of division is actually in the air in the form of powerful cultural forces that are shaping many

---

[46] Katarina Schuth, OSF, *Seminary Formation: Recent History, Current Circumstances, New Directions* (Collegeville, MN: Liturgical Press, 2016), 31–32.

[47] Rt Rev. Alexei Smith, interview by William P. Gregory, 29 October 2021; Rev. Don Rooney, interview by William P. Gregory, 3 December 2021.

[48] Pontifical Council for Promoting Christian Unity, *The Bishop and Christian Unity: An Ecumenical Vademecum* (5 June 2020), http://www.christianunity.va/content/dam/unitacristiani/Documentazione%20generale/2020Vademecum/Vademecum-EN-GARAMOND.pdf.

[49] Rev. Harry Winter, OMI, email message to author, 25 July 2021; Rev. Harry Winter, OMI, interview by William P. Gregory, 3 September 2021; Loughran and Hollander interview; Rooney interview.

[50] Olsen interview.

Catholics' social imaginations around the divergent visions of America's two political parties, rather than around the church's unique social, moral, and missionary teachings, which cut across the political divide. Instead of working unitedly in the public sphere, consequently, many Catholics are increasingly pitted against each other and drawn into mutually-belligerent political missions.[51] The church's neglect in forming its own people both for unity and social mission has opened up a space that is now being filled with discord.

The point of raising these concerns is not to dismiss the many positive values obviously present in Catholic collaborative mission today. Nor is it to downplay the great strides that have been made in the decades since the council; truly, we are far from the era of rampant anathema-hurling. But it is important to be realistic about what missional collaboration today likely is and is not achieving for the inseparably linked causes of mission and unity. When collaboration does not stretch in any way toward its proper telos of greater Christian communion, that is a problem, as Rev. Thomas Ryan, CSP remarks,

> The concern is that this tension is not holding. And there are any number of lay-led movements for creation spirituality, economic justice, racial equality, peace. But when these are not identified in any way with concern for a renewed and united church, then the work of Christian unity is left to those few appointed by the institutions to advance the cause. That state of affairs is a death sentence for ecumenism because it must be in the end the result of the conversion of heart and mind *by the people* who make up the church, the body of Christ. This must be a work of the people and by the people and for the people for the sake of the credibility of the gospel and the life of the world.[52]

To conclude where we began, therefore, the present call for the missionary renewal of the church must be simultaneously a call for the ecumenical renewal of the church. Perhaps it will only be by walking together more in mission that we will rediscover that truth.[53]

---

[51] Laushkin and Smith interview.

[52] Rev. Thomas Ryan, CSP, interview by William P. Gregory, 16 November 2021.

[53] Ecumenical Meeting.

Missional Collaboration in North America's Global Cities: The Rise of City-Wide Church Networks

Dustin D. Benac and Christopher B. James[1]

> Is it possible for there to be a gospel city movement in the 11 counties, 256 cities of the Bay Area? Is that possible?
>
> *Nancy Ortberg, CEO, Transforming the Bay with Christ*[2]
>
> I think I get a lot of hope from city movements in the midst of the challenging times we're facing; it's encouraging to feel like I'm part of this movement that has a long history.
>
> *Kevin Palau, President and CEO, Luis Palau Association*[3]
>
> We unite diverse Christians for the flourishing of the city.
>
> *Kelly Fassett, Co-founder and Executive Director, UniteBoston*[4]

The rise of city-wide church networks is a distinctive feature of missional collaboration in North America.[5] In response to declining denominational structures and rising polarization in faith communities, this form of missional collaboration aims to connect Christians and communities of faith around a shared geography, the city, and a shared value: mission. The city is a place of both missional and mystical encounter. Ray Bakke, an early proponent of the city, observed on the eve of the 21st century: "Christ is with me in the midst of the slum, the neighbourhood is a slum no longer. For Christ lives in me, and his kingdom agenda confronts the neighbourhood."[6]

---

[1] The authors wish to acknowledge the thoroughgoing collaborative nature of this research and writing. Although academic conventions require listing first authors, the co-authors should be regarded as joint authors for this piece.

[2] Nancy Ortberg, interviewed 13 July 2021. All following attributions to Nancy Ortberg were also from this interview.

[3] Kevin Palau, interviewed 12 July 2021. All following attributions to Kevin Palau were also from this interview.

[4] Kelly Fassett, interviewed 12 July 2021. All following attributions to Kelly Fassett were also from this interview.

[5] We wish to express our gratitude to several organizations and individuals who supported this research. Louisville Institute provided funding to support the cost of interview transcription for this project. Two research assistants, Danielle Postma and Savannah Green, supported the research and analysis for this project.

[6] Ray Bakke, *A Theology as Big as the City* (Downers Grove, IL: InterVarsity, 1997), 37. Our interviews with leaders who support city-wide collaborative church networks identified a loose cannon of texts for city-wide church leaders. This library includes: Ray Bakke, *A Theology as Big as the City* (Downers Grove, IL: InterVarsity, 1997); Timothy Keller, *Center Church: Doing Balanced, Gospel-Centered Ministry in Your City* (Grand Rapids, MI: Zondervan, 2017); Eric Swanson and Sam Williams, *To*

Identifying cities as centres for Christian mission and ministry is not a novel formulation; however, the practice is growing in prominence and leaders are connecting diverse experiments in mission and ministry that are appearing across North America. The precise number of networks is hard to estimate, but the leaders of multiple national organizations indicate that anywhere from 36 to 100 different US cities are home to a city-wide church network. Among city networks, at least a dozen are fairly robust and influencing others. Cities with noteworthy networks include: Charlotte, New York, Houston, Boston, San Francisco, Portland, Phoenix, Austin, Columbus, and Denver. As a form of Christian witness, city-wide church networks have formed around a mission of bringing churches together to make a positive impact on the city.

City-wide church networks have a common commitment to serve the city and to promote Christian unity,[7] but their size, structure, composition, and leadership do not fit into a single template. Some leaders within networks work in their local neighbourhoods, seeking to connect Christians to felt needs. Some leaders coordinate pastors across their city, bridging historic divides and divisions. Others promote bridge-building leadership, equipping faith communities with the language and tools to understand and address systemic divisions that divide cities. Still others aim to resource and connect city-wide leaders across North America, convening conversations that promote collaboration and resource sharing. While those who lead in these networks do not all hold the same ministry position or denominational affiliation, they do share a desire to connect around the needs of their city. The instigators of these networks are predominantly white evangelicals, but there are also a notable number of African American, Asian, Hispanic, and multicultural churches participating. There are also a handful of networks that are rich with participation among mainline churches, some even with Catholic and Orthodox engagement. Collective impact is the primary goal animating these networks, but unity also plays an important role in their missiology. As the website for "City Gospel Movements," an initiative within the Luis Palau Association that resources and connects city networks across the country, proclaims: "We champion the citywide church because we believe the united church is the best witness to Jesus."[8]

In this chapter, we first introduce two city-wide church networks, noting their history, partners, key leaders, central programmes, and key similarities and

---

Transform a City: Whole Church, Whole Gospel, Whole City (Grand Rapids, MI: Zondervan, 2015); Kevin Palau, *Unlikely: Setting Aside Our Differences to Live Out the Gospel* (New York: Howard Books, 2015); Niel Powell and John James, *Together for the City: How Collaborative Church Planting Leads to Citywide Movements* (Downers Grove, IL: InterVarsity, 2019); Mac Pier, *A Disruptive Gospel: Stories and Strategies for Transforming Your City* (Grand Rapids, MI: Baker Books, 2016).

[7] Leaders across groups use the term "network" to describe a variety of connections and organizational structures. Accordingly, following Richard Scott and Gerald Davis, we define a network broadly as "a system of relationships among parts." Richard Scott and Gerald Davis, *Organizations and Organizing: Rational, Natural, and Open Systems Perspectives* (Upper Saddle River, NJ: Pearson, 2007), 280.

[8] City Gospel Movements, "Home," lasted updated 2022, https://citygospelmovements.org/.

differences.[9] While they share a number of features of other forms of missional collaboration (e.g., the local and global intersect, the priority of relationships and spirituality, attention to issues of justice and power), the particular form of missional collaboration evident in these two cases is reflective of a novel and noteworthy development. Emerging from two global cities, the missional collaboration present in city-wide church networks represent a wider movement in which the local and global converge in city-wide mission. We then turn from these two cases to consider the cluster of practices and broader conditions that enable this kind of missional collaboration to form and flourish across North America. Finally, we conclude by noting how this consequential missional innovation promises to provide a durable form of Christian witness. Drawn from interviews with 40 leaders and practitioners across North America, this work introduces city-wide church networks as a national phenomenon that invites ongoing attention from scholars and practitioners who wish to understand or support Christian thought and missional practice.

City-Wide Church Networks in Two North American Cities

The rise of city-wide church networks across North America displays a turn to local wisdom in order to advance Christian mission. Nevertheless, leaders across these two networks recognize the pervasive disconnection and lack of collaboration that characterize faith communities in the places they serve. Accordingly, city-wide collaborative church networks promote Christian unity in order to advance mission in their particular places. As two key leaders, Nancy Ortberg and Kelly Fassett, described their networks: we're "better together."

Our research studied two initiatives in missional collaboration that emerged independently in San Francisco, California, and Boston, Massachusetts. Separated by nearly 3000 miles and the particulars of each context, their work reflects a similar turn to the local in order to reground Christian witness and promote Christian unity. A brief introduction to these two city networks provides an opportunity for a comparison and consideration of their significance for missional collaborations beyond these two sites.

Transforming the Bay with Christ: San Francisco, CA

Transforming the Bay with Christ was co-founded in 2013 by Pat Gelsinger, a highly successful business executive, and a number of prominent Christian leaders in the San Francisco Bay Area. Gelsinger, a long-time Oregonian, was friends with Kevin Palau, Executive Director of the Luis Palau Association, which is based in Portland, OR. In 2008, The Palau Association had played a key role in bringing local evangelical leaders together and partnering with the mayor

---

[9] For an adjacent exploration of the growing role of networks in Christian leadership and practice, see Brad Christerson and Richard Flory, *The Rise of Network Christianity: How Independent Leaders are Changing the Religious Landscape* (Oxford: Oxford University Press, 2017).

to mobilize churches to serve the city.[10] The remarkable success of this partnership was written up in a 2008 *Christianity Today* article and was celebrated in Palau's 2015 book, *Unlikely: Setting Aside Our Differences to Live Out the Gospel.*[11] When Gelsinger arrived in the Bay Area to take the helm at VMware – a cloud computing company – he brought with him inspiration from having seen first-hand what had happened in Portland, so he invited a few venture capitalists and a few evangelical pastors to form a board and explore the possibility of starting a similar movement there.[12]

Nearly a decade later, Gelsinger is chairman of the board for TBC. Nancy Ortberg, a former teaching pastor at Willow Creek Community Church and, in the Bay Area, a former campus pastor at Menlo Church, became the CEO of TBC in 2015. As of 2021, TBC has three additional staff, each assigned to one of the three "strategic anchors" of their mission – Unify, Amplify, and Multiply.

TBC's Unify work is expressed primarily through their support of pastors' groups all across the greater Bay Area which, as leaders described it, encompass 11 counties and 256 cities, including San Jose, Oakland, and San Francisco. This area is home to more than 8 million people; and, as one staff person noted, close to 5 million of these are unchurched. One of the goals of TBC's Unify work is to have pastors' groups in 40 locations, so that every pastor in the region is no more than a 20-minute drive away from one. As of 2021, the Unify Director, Gary Gaddini, reported that TBC was connected to 28 networks of pastors in the Bay Area. Most of these groups are constituted by location, but a handful are specifically for leaders of ethnic communities – Latino, Indian, Southeast Asian, and African nations – and others are for female pastors, youth pastors, and lead pastors. By Gaddini's assessment, 19 of the 28 are currently viable and doing well, while the others need ongoing encouragement.[13] Prior to stepping into this role, Gaddini had been one of TBC's volunteer network leaders and lead pastor of an Evangelical Covenant church south of San Francisco. Local network leaders play an important, and uncompensated, role in the work of TBC, convening, inviting, and supporting the local pastors – a role which TBC staff referred to internally as "the bishop" of their local pastors' network.

In speaking about the importance of local unity among pastors, both Nancy Ortberg and another staffer referenced a quote attributed to philosopher and spiritual writer Dallas Willard: "The fundamental primary job of every pastor [is

---

[10] The Luis Palau Association is not alone in its initiative to "serve the city." For a partial list of related historical and theological reflections on the city, see footnote 6 in this chapter.

[11] Tim Stafford with Eric Pulliam, "Servant Leadership," *Christianity Today*, 31 October 2008, https://www.christianitytoday.com/ct/2008/november/13.42.html.

[12] The "few evangelical pastors" led large area churches of varying denominational affiliations, including two non-denominational churches and one each leading churches in the Evangelical Covenant Church and Presbyterian Church (USA) denominations.

[13] Gary Gaddini, interviewed 9 November 2021. All following attributions to Gary Gaddini were also from this interview.

caring for] the other pastors in his neighbourhood."[14] They described this outlook as a "kingdom mindset," focusing on a more expansive vision of the church than one's own local congregation.

This expansive vision of local unity is not without limits, however. TBC seeks to partner with, as Ortberg put it, "Jesus churches." But, as Gaddini said, "if there's a church that doesn't, let's just say agree [with] the deity of Christ, God bless them. I mean that. But we're not going to have unity [with them] because I'm not going to debate the deity of Christ with somebody." Based on their analysis, the Bay Area is home to 3,522 "Jesus churches." At their height before the pandemic, TBC reported connections with nearly 800 of these, although as of summer 2021 the number of active connections was down to around 440 in the wake of COVID-19. Of these, half are linked to TBC through their Unify work, the remainder through Amplify and Multiply efforts.

The large majority of churches currently involved in TBC's work are within the range of what sociologists classify as "evangelical." Ortberg was wary of the label, noting they have "Baptists sitting next to Pentecostals," but also expressed a desire for more connection with mainline and Catholic churches. While aspiring for an expansive unity, Ortberg acknowledges several challenges to this ideal, including the reality that Catholics have their own networks and charities and that, for many evangelical churches – although not for her personally – divisions over gender and sexuality questions are an obstacle to unity with mainline churches.

While unity efforts are fundamental to TBC's work – "everything is built off Unify" – they also have a role in making possible the impact of collective service which they seek to *amplify* and which serves the church's mission to *multiply* followers of Jesus. As Ortberg described her decision to take the position, she expressed her disinterest in being part of an organization with unity as its only goal: "I've never seen a unity movement do anything more than have a bad chicken salad once a year, pray together, pat themselves on the back and say, 'We did the unity thing.' It's a joke." What intrigued her, however, was TBC's holistic vision which included helping local pastors' groups move beyond relationships, prayer, and encouragement to collaborative vision around a shared cause.

TBC's Amplify work includes one-to-one conversations with church leaders about how they might become more externally-focused, how they might partner with other churches and faith-based organizations, and engage in more focused efforts to mobilize churches around three particular issues: education, foster care, and homelessness. These three are TBC's priorities, in part, because "there's hardly a church that isn't doing something" in one of them, and this fact paves the way for supporting and connecting churches in this work. As Gaddini described their vision: "We say this: 'we can't boil the Bay' but we can make a dent, I think, in those three areas."

---

[14] This quotation is from Nancy Ortberg's interview, but the idea was also referenced by Veronica Haniger, interviewed 19 July 2021. The original source, attributed to Dallas Willard, was not readily found.

Another way TBC seeks to amplify churches' impact is through telling the stories of what churches are doing and, thus, attempting to "change the narrative" many Christians have of the Bay Area as a spiritually dark and difficult context for ministry. As two staff members told us separately, engaging with TBC has catalyzed transformation of their own "leading narratives" of their context from, as Gaddini put it, "the Bay Area is a hard place to do ministry. It's hard soil," to "there are courageous women and men serving Jesus in his church all over the Bay Area, and it's a hard place to do ministry."

The Multiply work of TBC, focused on evangelism and church planting, is the least developed programmatically, but perhaps closest to the heart of TBC's mission. In 2018, Gelsinger was quoted in a CNBC video as having a vision of 1000 new churches and a million new believers in ten years. While Ortberg said that such unattainable goals undermine their credibility, they nonetheless suggest that the passion behind TBC's unity and service work is toward an evangelistic end. Indeed, Ortberg has been saying "service is the new apologetic," for at least a decade, and the staff member leading TBC's Amplify efforts cited it twice in our interview.

While TBC's work in both Unify and Amplify are ultimately understood to contribute to their evangelistic mission, Multiply is where they are involved in more direct efforts. Specifically, this component includes two initiatives. The first, in the area of evangelism, involves research underway to identify "the six to ten churches that are actually seeing conversion growth," to thank them and learn from them, and then "be like a bee and pollinate all around the Bay Area what [they]'re learning and then give people permission to adjust it, so that it could work for them." Their second Multiply initiative is to support church planting in the Bay Area. This includes efforts to annually, at least, convene the handful of churches and dozen organizations that are actively church planting in the Bay Area in order to minimize the "Christian competition" and to also cast vision for the possibilities of collaboration. Also important to TBC's involvement in church planting is their partnership with City to City, an organization that emerged out of the ministry of Tim Keller and Redeemer Presbyterian Church in New York City. This partnership in San Francisco took shape as a church planting incubator, a one-year programme for planters in their first three years of planting. Ortberg and TBC's Multiply Director, Toby Kurth, are on the faculty for the incubator. Drawing on the expertise of Kurth, a seasoned San Francisco church planter and data-driven leader, TBC has also developed a church plant assessment process. Thanks to a 5 million US dollar donation that Ortberg passed off to Stadia – an organization that works with church plant funding – those who pass TBC's assessment are given a matching grant for 20 percent of their church plant budget for the first three years. If they fail the assessment, however, they instead receive 1000 US dollars and coaching from TBC in how to strengthen their proposal the following year. As of 2021, 28 church plants in the Bay Area had received the grant.

Partnership is an important aspect of TBC's approach to all three strategic anchors. A number of the pastors' groups that TBC is supporting were already in existence before they began their work. Their Amplify work is centred on service areas where they can maximize collaboration between churches, and points churches to faith-based organizations such as Bay Shore Christian Ministries in East Palo Alto, which has been serving the community for 36 years with a major focus on education, tutoring, and afterschool care.

While it is evident that TBC could collect a significant amount of venture capital, Ortberg has made the strategic choice to keep the staff team small, indicating that at their current size they have all the funding they need. (TBC's 2019 revenue was 1.2 million US dollars.) As Ortberg explained,

> We will stay small on purpose for two reasons. The first is we work in a very small catalytic space [...] where you bring people together and collaborate, and something catalytic happens. If we get bigger, we're going to focus on starting things that actually compete with the very organizations out there that are doing the work that needs to happen. And then secondly, we don't want to be seen as a philanthropic organization. We've got to stay small, so we don't get bureaucratic, so we can stay [in] start-up mentality.

As TBC approaches its ten-year anniversary in 2023, it has a clearly articulated vision for missional impact. However, it also faces several missional horizons that demand care. First, the scale of TBC's work now includes an expansive area, with 256 municipalities and 8 million residents. Their re-imagination of this region as the Greater Bay Area stretches the limits of a place-based identity in a way that presses them to cultivate city-wide connection through two conjoined practices: 1) fostering local collaboration in 40 micro-regions, and 2) promoting regional collaboration with the San Francisco Bay Area metropolitan area at the centre. In doing so, TBC is experimenting with possibilities of scale that include complexities not found among other city networks. Second, TBC's penchant for data and metrics, along with the related expertise of their staff and board, may well yield tools that will ultimately be useful for other city networks. They now face the missional horizon of determining how to share insights derived from their contextual experiment to other city-wide networks that are shaped by other contextual, historical, and economic features. Third, like many other city networks, TBC now must consider whether it is feasible for them to effectively expand beyond their evangelical roots and existing networks into collaborative partnerships with mainline, Catholic, and Orthodox churches. The geographical size and ecclesial density of their delineated region may resist diversifying their partnership base. Many of the 3,522 "Jesus churches" they have identified are disconnected evangelical churches, and TBC will likely prioritize efforts to incorporate these congregations. TBC's relational approach and eagerness to make quantifiable gains seem likely to favour this growth over diversification. Fourth, and finally, the evangelistic heartbeat of TBC's mission may ultimately lead to significant realignment of their efforts if they do not produce the kinds of outcomes desired and envisioned by Gelsinger and others, in terms of conversions, church growth, and church planting.

UniteBoston: Boston, MA

Twenty-seven hundred miles away, a similar initiative to forge and strengthen church connections across a city is blossoming in Boston, Massachusetts. UniteBoston (UB) is an ecumenical "movement" that intends to "bridge historic divides among Christians from various denominations, races, and generations," all organized around a shared commitment to the mission and ministry in Boston.[15] Located in a historic and global North American city, UB's leaders are quick to describe the thick relational network that is possible between people of faith within this particular area. Boston's distinct cultural and ecclesial environment enables leaders to "form meaningful relationships [that] help [*sic*] foster unity movements," one board member observed.[16]

UB was founded following a series of seemingly accidental connections and conversations. Kelly Fassett and Mike Lloyd co-founded UniteBoston in 2010 in order to meet the physical and spiritual needs of the more than 700 congregations in the Metro Boston area. Fassett, who now serves as UniteBoston's Executive Director, recalls: "We saw, physically, we need to work better together. All of these churches have very similar mission statements and values and yet are working in isolation." This observation was matched with a personal sense of call: "I woke up and […] just really felt like God was telling me that I was here to unite the body of Christ. 'Unite my bride' is kind of the thing that I heard in prayer." Fassett notes that Jesus' life, Paul's witness, and the Holy Spirit's work throughout scripture are constantly "breaking barriers of race and ideology." "It was an emerging movement that we felt like God was already bringing forth," Fassett notes, "and we're just kind of joining in."

More than ten years later, Boston remains the unifying geographic centre and missional impetus for their richly contextual and collaborative work. The city provides a two-fold function for their city-wide mission. On the one hand, the city of Boston provides a clear geographical centre and shared identity that can unify collaboration across various forms of difference. Boston is, as one participant observed, "a major city [and] a large town." Particularly among faith leaders, it provides a geography that allows – and possibly compels – relational connection and collegiality. And, as a major city, Boston has historically been a centre for ideas and individuals that influence the "nation as a whole," as one leader noted. Early interest in their work from around the world demonstrated "the global reach of the Christian community here and the impact of increasing unity."[17]

On the other hand, Boston is also a cultural-ecclesial context that requires intentional work and witness for people of faith. In this "secular" environment, as multiple people described it, the life of faith and the ongoing organization of communities of faith requires a commitment, both in order to bear witness and to bridge the divides that separate people and congregations in the city. The overall mission of the organization is to "nurture Christian unity," one leader observed. Fassett then takes this mission one step further, saying her "vision for transformation is relationship."

---

[15] UniteBoston, "Join In," UniteBoston, http://www.uniteboston.com/help-ub/

[16] UniteBoston board member, interviewed 3 August 2021. In this chapter, the names of many focus group participants are withheld to protect anonymity.

[17] UniteBoston, "History," UniteBoston, last updated 2022, https://www.uniteboston.com/history/.

UniteBoston pursues its transformative work through four primary programmes. First, it curates and distributes a weekly newsletter that identifies local events, resources, and opportunities for partnership across congregations in the city. Much as switchboard operators once connected phone lines in order to enable conversation, UB's newsletter functions like a "switchboard" for congregations and faith leaders in the region, connecting otherwise disconnected individuals or projects around common concerns. Leaders estimate they have more than 3000 subscribers to their weekly newsletter. UB also hosts an annual Week of Prayer for Christian Unity that invites leaders from across the city to gather in prayer around the concerns they share and a common desire to see the city and Bostonians flourish.[18] As a public gathering of faith leaders from across the city, the Week of Prayer is a witness to the possibility of unity, even amid deep and historic differences. Interviews with board members and other UB participants also accentuated the importance of prayer as a unifying factor for their work. In several instances, individuals' early involvement with the Week of Prayer became the onramp for them to assume greater leadership.

UB also works to equip local leaders to mend the divisions that separate people throughout the city. To this end, they equip and resource Christians in their neighbourhoods to "find out where God is working and how churches can collaboratively serve together" in their "specific geographic locale."[19] These UniteBoston representatives are local instantiations of the unity UB hopes to cultivate across the broader city. Finally, UB hosts conversations and training events aimed at bridging the historic divisions caused by racial injustice and inequity in the city. While a commitment to justice is a longstanding value that unifies UB's work, it purposefully mobilizes leaders across the city around conversation and learning communities. These "Be The Bridge" groups express UB's abiding commitment to respond to the needs of the local faith communities through timely convenings and trainings.[20] Inspired by Latasha Morrison's book *Be the Bridge: Pursuing God's Heart for Racial Reconciliation*, UB described their goal for these groups in 2020 as allowing "Christians throughout the city to gain a shared and biblically-grounded understanding of the process of restorative reconciliation."[21] Each programmatic feature of UB's work aims to express and advance their central purpose: equipping followers of Jesus to practice Christian unity.

UniteBoston is a grassroots missional organization that aims to resource and partner with Christian leaders across the Boston metropolitan area. As such, its organizational structure, funding model, and local partnership reflect their commitment to promote Christian unity. Run on an annual budget of just over

---

[18] The Week of Prayer for Christian unity is the latest of many initiatives hosted by UB that aim to unify Christian leaders through worship and prayer.

[19] UniteBoston, "About Us," UniteBoston, last updated 2022, http://www.uniteboston.com/about-us/.

[20] The title for these groups, "Be The Bridge," is inspired by Latasha Morrison's book *Be the Bridge: Pursuing God's Heart for Racial Reconciliation* (Colorado Springs, CO: Waterbrook, 2019).

[21] UniteBoston, "UniteBoston's Fall Be the Bridge Group," last updated 2020, https://www.uniteboston.com/event/unitebostons-fall-be-the-bridge-group/.

100,000 US dollars, approximately half of their operating budget over the last three years came from individual donations. Their staff consists of three part-time employees and a broad volunteer base. Paid staff serve as the central hub for the resources, connections, communications, and coordination that advances UB's broader mission. A board that represents Christian leaders from diverse traditions and champions for UB's work also advances their collaborative work in the broader community. Finally, UB relies upon a broad base of volunteers to mobilize to promote unity through trainings, events, and local connections across the city. At every level of the organization, the individuals who have gathered around UB's work share a commitment to their vision to promote Christian unity through relational connections. For example, when volunteers or board members are asked about how they got involved with UB, they frequently note either participating in one of UBs events or their connection to Fassett, UB's Executive Director. While some of UB's leaders have a long history of service in the Boston area, others are recent transplants. This feature reflects a distinguishing feature of the Boston metropolitan area they intend to serve. In a global city with numerous educational centres, the people of faith who are working to reconnect Christians do not always come from the city; many come from elsewhere.

UB's vision to promote Christian unity has strengthened connections between leaders and congregations across the city. "I think organizations like UniteBoston almost give what I call the multiplier effect, because everybody's not going to be good at everything," one leader shared. "If we could use UniteBoston and other similar organizations as a connection piece, it allows churches to be authentically themselves. And then also take advantage of what's needed for holistic discipleship."[22] As noted here, unity, UB's particular organizational structure, and a vision for formation all combine to enliven individuals' involvement in this work. Drawing partners and participants from across the spectrum of Christianity, UB's prioritization of unity and ecumenism has fostered a constellation of relational partnerships. For example, UB's board includes both Protestant and Catholic leaders from across the city;[23] UB's "Be the Bridge" leaders include individuals who have served in predominantly white and predominantly Black churches; pastors and lay leaders are able to participate and support UB's organizing and connecting work; and volunteer leaders are drawn from various international communities who come to Boston for work or study. These diverse partners and participants are anchored by a shared commitment to Christian unity and a history of relational connection to key anchor institutions in the broader Boston area, e.g., Boston University, Gordon-Conwell Theological Seminary, and the Emmanuel Gospel Center. While UB purposefully works with partners and participants to promote unity and connection, they prioritize local connections as the primary medium to promote a more connected body of Christ. As one leader shared: "The beauty of the body

---

[22] UniteBoston Be the Bridge leader, interviewed 29 July 2021.
[23] Boston has a long history of Catholic thought and service. As one Board member noted: "This is a Catholic city."

of Christ is we all are in our silos, but together, we're better. Being able to create and facilitate that open dialogue in space is really a joy."[24]

As UB enters its second decade as an organization, it faces a number of missional horizons that require ongoing attention in order to continue advancing Christian unity throughout the city. First, their ongoing work requires capacity to meet the needs for connection and unity in an increasingly disconnected and polarized moment. The felt need that catalyzed UB's work nearly a decade ago has not abated; rather, the need for unity, connection, and collaboration for Christians within and beyond Boston has only grown. As UB continues to respond to this need, there remains a pervasive need for the kinds of connection, collaboration, and community they aim to promote. Second, consistency in leadership and participation will be important as they seek to build a more connected ecclesial ecology surrounding their work across Boston. As a purposefully small, grassroots organization, UB relies heavily on volunteers and part-time employees to advance its missional work. While this structure has the benefit of centring their work in local connections, it also renders their work dependent on a fluid set of relational connections and collaborators. With Fassett as a consistent feature of their work over the last decade, UB has had sufficient relational continuity to build and expand their network. Continuing this work into the next decade, however, will require similar consistency of leadership and relational connections throughout their network. Finally, the ongoing work of Christian unity in Boston will require resilience for UB's leaders and key partners. In the face of what one leader describes as the "deep divisions" that characterize Boston, the pursuit of unity requires resilience in order to continue in the face of historic and persistent fragmentation among people of faith in their city.

Convergent Spaces

These two missional collaborations share a number of distinguishing features. They also have several fundamental differences. Following Benac's reflections in *Adaptive Church*, each is a "convergent space," marked by a number of common practices that are expressed in contextually dependent ways.[25] We conclude this introduction to these two critical cases by outlining these similarities and differences in order to provide a glimpse into some of the variety present within "city gospel movements" across the US.

TBC and UB have a number of striking similarities. At the heart of both organizations is a missional desire to see the churches of their respective places bear a faithful and compelling witness in the largely post-Christian context in which they are located. This evangelistic telos is also reflected in the evangelical credentials of the organizational leaders, both women, and in the strong engagement of the evangelical churches. Importantly, however, both TBC and UB represent a revisioning of traditional evangelical approaches to Christian witness. Leaving behind revival meetings and Billy Graham-style crusades, TBC

---

[24] UniteBoston Be the Bridge leader, interviewed 29 July 2021.
[25] Dustin Benac, *Adaptive Church: Collaboration and Community in a Changing World* (Waco, TX: Baylor University Press, 2022).

and UB are pursuing evangelistic witness through church unity, informed by the vision of John 17.

The practices of unity present in TBC and UB include convening and storytelling. TBC supports dozens of pastors groups and hosts various other types of gatherings of Christian leaders of various traditions, largely for purposes of training. UB, similarly, has convened Christians of different traditions for worship gatherings and justice workshops. Storytelling as a unity practice is most evident in UB's newsletter, circulated widely, and in TBC's intentionality around "changing the narrative" about the church in the Bay Area through lifting up examples of transformative and effective ministry.

The unity that both TBC and UB strive for has limits, however. These boundaries are both doctrinal and geographical. Doctrinally, both networks point to the Nicene Creed as definitive but have also found the differences between churches on questions of sexuality and gender to be a point of challenge. Geographically, TBC and UB are each anchored in major global, coastal cities. In both cases, the particular cultural milieu of these urban areas is reflected in the ethos and practices of the city network.

One of the striking differences between TBC and UB emerges precisely because they each reflect the particular culture of their metropolitan areas. TBC manifests the venture capital and start-up culture of Silicon Valley, and UB reflects the prevalence of young adults and the high value on diversity characteristic of Boston – a city with 29 colleges and universities whose students make up 20 percent of the population.[26] Relatedly, TBC prioritizes engaging leaders both from churches and the marketplace, because, as Ortberg said, although "leaders aren't any better than anybody else [...] the work they do in culture is [that] they shift culture." UB, on the other hand, is more of a grassroots organization, both initiated by and largely composed of laity and young people.

Other points of difference are also noteworthy. While they are presented here in order to highlight contrasts, it would be a mistake to see the organisations as opposites in any of these regards.

One of the most substantive differences between TBC and UB is the composition of those who are engaged with their network. Participating churches in TBC are overwhelmingly from the evangelical stream. In this way, TBC is fairly representative of most US city gospel movements. UB, however, is engaged with a fuller ecumenical spectrum, including not only evangelical, pentecostal, charismatic, and mainline churches, but also participants in Catholic and Orthodox traditions as well as African American and Asian American churches. This priority for ecumenical and cultural diversity is evident on the UB Board and staff and was recently on clear display during the Week of Prayer for Christian Unity which featured seven nights of united prayer and worship in various settings and styles, including Korean, Catholic, and evangelical.

Finally, the names of these organizations provide important signals regarding their core objectives and what we have come to call "forefront practices." For

---

[26] Morgan Hughes, "Back-to-School by the Numbers," *Boston Globe*, 27 August 2018, https://www.bostonglobe.com/metro/2018/08/27/back-school-boston-numbers/g4d4Ix9PjW8x17HClmyA8J/story.html.

UniteBoston, unity is of primary importance, a conviction embedded in their tagline "Nurturing Unity Among Diverse Christians for the Flourishing of the City." For Transforming the Bay with Christ, it is missional transformation that is primary, with unity seen in part as a means to this end. Whereas UB dedicates its efforts to cultivating unity across Christians in all their diversity in the hopes that this unity will contribute to the city's flourishing, TBC is attentive to metrics for missional impact. For TBC, this impact encompasses both social and evangelistic impact.

Implications for Missional Collaboration

The history and structure of these two missional collaborations provide insight about the kinds of practices and broader conditions that support the formation and flourishing of city-wide collaborative church networks. The localized nature of such collaborative work means that there is not a replicable template for the collaborative work each pursues. Their combined work, however, expresses a form of practical wisdom and sense of possibility that guides their collaborative work. Hence, this cluster of practices and conditions may provide critical factors for city-wide missional collaboration, both within these two cases and in other efforts to promote partnerships that serve the city.

Clusters of Practices among City-Wide Networks

Placing these varied similarities and differences between TBC and UB alongside what we heard from other city network leaders brings a number of important clusters of practice into focus. While these practices come to expression in varying ways in different networks, they nonetheless appear to be characteristic of this new form of missional collaboration.

Above, we have already identified the varying practices of unity present in TBC and UB – convening, storytelling, and establishing the limits or boundaries of inclusion. We have also outlined their practices of missional impact, including service efforts, evangelism, and church planting endeavours, as well as the training and equipping of leaders. The ways that city networks across the nation take shape seem largely to depend upon how they engage in these two clusters of practices – practices of unity and practices of missional impact.

But other clusters of practice that we observed in UB, TBC, and other networks are also worthy of mention. First, city networks are engaged in the practice of reimagining and inhabiting localities. As geographically constituted organizations, city networks construct and communicate a sense of place (or places) through their narration both of the centre(s) and periphery/ies of their locale, as well as in their explication of its particular cultural and religious features. Simply put, city network leaders define and describe the place in and for which their network exists. This work involves constructing and communicating both a sense of parish as well as a sense of the unique challenges and possibilities therein.

Second, city network leaders are actively engaged in the practice of interpreting and appropriating scriptural and theological traditions to legitimate their work. Jesus' prayer in John 17 for believers to "be one [...] so that the world may know" plays a central role here in establishing a basis for unity. John 17 also provides a key logic to these predominantly evangelical organizations that proposes modelled unity and collaboration as a means to witness. This move represents a significant reinterpretation of the evangelical tradition's approach to mission, which has tended to emphasize proclamation of the gospel and personal evangelism over socially embodied forms of witness. Similarly, the call to "seek the shalom of the city" found in Jeremiah 29 provides a key precedent for prioritizing the urban environment, for approaching ministry holistically, and – as a command to exiles – for engaging in mission from a posture of cultural humility and with an openness to partnership with civic and non-religious entities. A third example of this appropriation of traditions is evident in the core ecclesiological claim represented by city networks – that the numerous and various churches of the place ought to be conceived of as "the city-wide church." The explicit scriptural rationale given is reference to Paul's practice of addressing epistles to the believers of a given city: "to all God's beloved in Rome" (Rom. 1:7), "to the saints who are in Ephesus" (Eph. 1:2), and "to all the saints in Christ Jesus who are in Philippi" (Phil. 1:1). A final example of this re-appropriation can be seen in the widespread use of "kingdom" language to express the important conviction that God's work exceeds that of any particular congregation. "Kingdom-minded" pastors, as suggested by leaders in multiple networks, are those with a vision that is bigger than the success of their own congregation. At times, kingdom language is also used to describe work that, while not explicitly religious in character, ought to be seen as contributing to building God's kingdom on earth. Both uses of the "kingdom" concept point to an expanded sense of God's work in the world – beyond the individual congregation and beyond soul-saving – and serve to reinterpret traditions that have located the kingdom variously in the church, heaven, and the future.

    Third, city networks are engaged in a cluster of practices of collaboration. This cluster includes not only their own practice of forging their own partnerships with leaders, congregations, and other organizations, but also their work of fostering and facilitating collaboration *between* congregations and other entities. Convening activities are integral both as a practice of unity and a practice of collaboration. As a practice of collaboration, convening takes place on multiple levels and in various ways. City networks most typically convene pastors to build trust and set the stage for collaborative work among churches but some also convene leaders across sectors – church, marketplace, non-profit – toward collective impact. Often city networks serve as backbone or bridge organizations that set the table for cooperation where competition might exist, for example, between church planting organizations engaged in mission across San Francisco. City network leaders are not only facilitating convening in their own local setting. They are themselves being convened with other city network leaders across the country – through Zoom, webinars, and retreats – by a handful of national and global networks attempting to connect, encourage, and resource these city network leaders with best practices and useful tools.[27]

---

[27] Our research identified several key nation-wide organizations supporting and convening city network leaders, including: Luis Palau Association's City Gospel

Conditions for City-Wide Church Networks

While the particular contextual features of each city shape these missional collaborations, we have identified seven conditions that support the rise of city-wide church networks in North America. Each is briefly introduced and summarized below.

1. **A post-Christian era**. The leaders who actively advance missional collaboration in Boston, San Francisco, and similar locations across North America identify the existence of a post-Christian era. Even as leaders may parse this era differently, interviewees identify the marginal position of Christian thought and practice as a defining feature. "We're a minority," one leader from Portland, Oregon, stated.[28] Or, as Kelly Fassett in Boston observed, "Being a Christian is not the norm." Leaders serving in post-Christian global cities (e.g., Boston, San Francisco, Portland, New York) unequivocally identified the rise and growth of their work as a consequence of a post-Christian society. For those churches with a commitment to an evangelistic mission, this perception of losing ground has served as a catalyst for collaboration and partnership around a shared mission.

2. **Crisis**. Leaders' acute encounter with crisis also motivates the turn to urban centres as an anchor for missional collaboration. While COVID-19 represents a recent and wide-spread crisis for many faith communities, collaborative mission efforts should not be viewed as an outcome of this single crisis. Leaders identified the way fires, school closures, shootings, and injustice all represent crises that had catalyzed their collective activity. As one leader who supports a network of city leaders observed: "I would say things that provoke churches toward a greater sense of unity and coordination are crises." Crisis has the capacity to catalyze collaborative mission.

3. **Trust**. Nevertheless, leaders must also trust one another in order to envision and pursue the various collaborative efforts that are arising in cities across North America. Trust is the essential condition for collaborative mission. Without trust, leaders cannot start and sustain the collaborations their work now requires. Guided by this fundamental insight, local and national leaders work to connect and convene individuals in order to build and strengthen the bonds of trust collaborative mission requires. "Trust is the central theme, the central need of any collaborative effort in a network of ministry people," one of TBC's Amplify leaders shared.[29] To this end, some individuals are working to build trust; others

---

Movements initiative; Lost Antler Ranch Leaders convened by Eric Swanson, who hosts monthly Zoom calls and annual retreats in addition to regularly checking in on a list of roughly 30 city leaders; Movement.org, which hosts a monthly global Zoom call and coordinates Movement Day; Parish Collective, which aims to reground missional witness in local neighbourhoods through convenings, conferences, and resources that promote place-based collaboration; and City to City, the global church planting effort that emerged from Rev. Tim Keller's Redeemer Presbyterian Church in New York City.

[28] Focus group participant, interviewed 13 July 2021.

[29] Transforming the Bay Area for Christ Amplify leader, interviewed 14 October 2021.

recognize the need to rebuild it; and still others are drawing upon this trust to engage in collaborative projects that serve their city.

4. **Shifting organizational structures**. Leaders also acknowledge how the organizational structures that support religious life in North America are shifting. Rather than grieving this shifting landscape, however, leaders engaged in city networks are working to build alternatives. "Folks are seeing their denominational structures being less relevant for helping figure out how to minister locally," one missional leader from southern Oregon observed.[30] In the vacuum created by this change, leaders are at once rediscovering their shared connection across denominational boundaries and are crafting convening organizations that can resource future work.

5. **Increasing polarization**. If unity is one of the chief goals of city-wide collaborative church efforts, polarization is the primary obstacle these collaborative efforts aim to overcome. Polarization presents in a variety of forms, but the consequence of heightened political and ideological division is the same: division, isolation, competition, and loneliness. "I think that one of the things we're trying to do in the cities […] is to not allow that polarization to divide the church unnecessarily," one national leader noted.[31] In the place of polarization, leaders are working to unify their community around a call to serve the city.

6. **The work of God**. Leaders are also quick to acknowledge the work of God in the rise of urban centres as anchors for missional collaboration and their participation in city-wide partnership. For many, this common work is a "movement" of the Spirit of God to re-establish the church in locality. For some, God called them to this work in surprising ways. "The Lord called me to it […] He just started highlighting the value of connection within prayer," a leader in Wilmington, South Carolina, shared.[32] For others, they can only bear witness to what God is doing by connecting people and calling them to their city. "I think God is bubbling up now […] I think there is a move of God to stir people's hearts for their city," a national convener of city-wide church networks reflected.[33] Still others note how they are simply joining in God's ongoing work in time and history. "We like to say we're joining what God is doing," one leader noted.[34] In each case, God's connecting, convening, catalyzing activity remains one unmistakable condition for urban missional collaborations.

7. **Catalysts**: Finally, the rise of city-wide church networks requires the convergence of three catalysts: relational connection, financial resources, and a renewed imagination for the city.[35] In the two cases profiled here, TBC and UB, these catalysts were present in different forms and different

---

[30] Focus group participant, interviewed 13 July 2021.

[31] Mark Reynolds, interviewed 18 August 2021.

[32] City Gospel Movements leader, interviewed 21 July 2021.

[33] Lisa Matthews, interviewed 28 September 2021.

[34] Interview 20 July 2021. The name of this participant is withheld to protect anonymity.

[35] Although leaders across these city-wide church networks rarely use the term "catalysts," their history and broader work illustrate how these three catalysts create the conditions for the missional collaborations they pursue.

economies of scale, but the combination of these catalysts enabled leaders to take the first step toward missional collaboration. Each emerged from a history of service in the region and drew upon existing relational connections. When social capital combined with financial capital, leaders were able to scale and expand their work. And from the very beginning, a renewed imagination for the city as a site for God's ongoing activity sustained their work. These three catalysts invite leaders to imagine how they can respond to God's ongoing activity through city-wide missional collaboration.

These seven conditions express a combination of catalyzing and enabling conditions that surround the formation and growth of city-wide church networks. Some conditions precipitate the formation of this particular form of missional collaboration, such as crisis, polarization, and a post-Christian era. Other conditions, such as trust, enable the formation and growth of city-wide church networks. The combination of these conditions illustrates the way environmental factors, human agency, and divine possibility coalesce around missional collaboration in each city. To form or support city-wide church networks requires acknowledging how many of these conditions cannot be managed or manufactured: leading and collaborating at this level requires discerning how to respond to conditions that cannot be controlled and prioritizing those that can enable collaborative work. As one city-wide leader reflected: "You can cultivate an ecosystem, but you can't control it."

"There's something happening"

Against a backdrop of several challenges facing US Christianity – religious disaffiliation, denominational decline, and polarization to name only a few – our research uncovered an unmistakable sense of dynamism and hope among city network leaders. With these two cases on opposite coasts as guides, we spoke with network leaders from New York City, Portland, Lansing, Chicago, Austin, Charlotte, and many other cities. Across these diverse contexts, leaders expressed relentless hope about what is possible when churches partner together across their city. Some of this optimism might be attributable to the newness of this organizational form being pioneered and the energy generated by such entrepreneurial efforts. But the prevailing sense we discerned among leaders was that their hope for the future of the church's witness was rooted both in a rich scriptural and theological imagination and in the glimpses of God at work that they had already seen as Christians collaborated for the good of their cities.

Many of the catalyzing conditions will not abate in the foreseeable future, and this new form of missional collaboration displays the kind of viability and flexibility that can sustain future ministry. Researchers and practitioners would do well to attend carefully to the conditions and cluster of practices this chapter has identified. Exploring the ways that these are uniquely expressed in particular local contexts may help to expand the church's imagination and toolkit for engaging in missional collaborations of various kinds in the decades ahead.

Whether one attributes the emergence of collaborative city-wide church networks in the US over the last 15 years to entrepreneurs responding creatively to changing conditions or to a fresh move of God to provide new wineskins for the church's mission – or both – the fact remains that these city networks reflect a new and promising form of ecclesial and missional collaboration in the United States. As one leader of a national organization serving city network leaders observed: "There's something happening."[36] As city-wide church networks continue to form and grow, this relentless hope can carry communities forward.

---

[36] Lisa Matthews, interviewed 28 September 2021.

Mission and Theological Education among Latinx Christians: Contributions of *La Asociación para la Educación Teológica Hispana*

Britta Meiers Carlson and Carlos F. Cardoza-Orlandi

Introduction

La Asociación para la Educación Teológica Hispana[1] (*AETH*) is a network of theological educators and institutions that seeks to provide connections, resources, and support for its members. Although theological education in the United States and Canada is not always associated with mission, we find that the work of *la AETH* is rooted in a missional imagination and that it serves to strengthen the capacity of Latinx leaders and churches to meet many contemporary challenges for mission. Additionally, the work of *la AETH* is intrinsically collaborative, crossing the boundaries of confessional and denominational backgrounds as well as cultural, racial, ethnic, geographic, and generational differences. As the United States and Canada undergo massive paradigm shifts in theological education, innovative organizations like *la AETH*, which represent the margins of the church, are leading the way, not only in education, but also in discerning God's mission in a world that is increasingly interconnected even in the midst of seemingly insurmountable divisions in society.

Our study is based on a series of ten interviews with current and former executive directors, board members, and network partners who have been connected with *la AETH* throughout its history. We conducted the interviews via Zoom during the summer and fall of 2021. Our observations, reflections, and questions below emerge from a series of conversations *en conjunto,* discerning how God is both inspiring and challenging the people of *la AETH*. We begin with a brief history and description of the organization, followed by a discussion of some of the unique contributions of *la AETH* to mission. We conclude the chapter with a series of questions that we believe will profoundly shape the organization moving forward.

A Brief History of *La AETH*

Two critical antecedents to the creation of *la AETH* were the Fund for Theological Education (FTE) and a particular interest and approach from a philanthropic organization to support the growing Latinx[2] Christian communities

---

[1] The Association for Hispanic Theological Education.
[2] The term "Latinx" refers to a diverse group of people of Latin American origin, including both recent immigrants from Latin America and people whose ancestry in

and their leadership formation. In 1989, the FTE provided financial support for the Hispanic Summer Program (HSP), which galvanized interest in the creation of an organization that would support theological formation at the grassroots. The dominant culture in theological education was hostile to Latinx Christian formation. For example, students who were admitted to theological schools found themselves dismissed when raising critical theological questions emerging from their Latinx contexts. Theological and ministerial curricula lacked the growing number of resources written by Latinx scholars. The HSP nurtured the marginalized and, in some cases, the previously mistreated students and faculty from institutions of theological education of both conservative and liberal character, including Protestant, pentecostal, and Roman Catholic scholars and institutions. The HSP, supported by the FTE, developed programmes and provided theological formation at the graduate level for Latinx Christian leaders. Furthermore, this community taught in and struggled with institutions of theological higher education to create certificate programmes for lay formation and ministerial ordination. The phrase "organic intellectuals" was used to illustrate a complex identity and vocation between communities of faith, theological institutes, and the academic profession in seminaries and universities – the latter with varying degrees of hostility to the Hispanic/Latinx theological vocation.

Based on a report commissioned by the FTE and completed by Justo L. González, the Pew Charitable Trusts showed interest in Hispanic/Latinx theological education.[3] A series of conversations between Latinx theological leaders, many who had connections to the HSP, and this philanthropic organization identified the critical need for theological formation among leaders in Latinx Christian communities. Critical to the conversation was the recognition that many Latinx Christians rarely encountered leaders from their own communities who had experienced theological formation in a higher education setting. Their leaders received theological formation from Bible institutes and other non-accredited programmes. Consequently, it was determined to have *un Encuentro de Educación Teológica Hispana*, later named *El Primer Encuentro*, under one very unique financial requirement: an allocation of $30,000 from Pew Charitable Trusts to be used in whatever *El Primer Encuentro* decided for the future of Hispanic/Latinx theological education. Pew Trusts agreed, and, in August 1991, *El Primer Encuentro* determined to organize *La Asociación para la Educación Teológica Hispana (AETH)*. In 1992, *la AETH* organized *El Segundo Encuentro* and celebrated its first biennial assembly. From its beginning, *la AETH* "always saw as part of its purpose to build relationships between all levels and programmes of theological education, and achieve that

---

what is now the United States precedes their home region's incorporation into the nation. We describe this group in more detail below, under the subtitle "Multi-Generational Mission."

[3] Justo González, *The Theological Education of Hispanics: A Study* (Decatur, GA: Fund for Theological Education, 1988).

not only the Latino community, but all areas of theological education, see the importance of our own Latino programmes."[4]

La AETH has continued to celebrate its biennial meetings addressing different topics in theological education and formation. For example, women in ministry and theological formation were key themes during the association's first decade. Equally important became topics related to the needs and concerns of Bible institutes, such as theological formation for Bible institutes' faculty, accessibility and publication of theological materials in Spanish, *tertulias* or small groups for theological and ministerial conversation, theological education for migrants, and second and third generation theological and ministerial needs, particularly among Latinx youth. *La AETH* also addressed difficult theological themes, namely, domestic abuse in Latinx communities, immigration and public policy, and sexuality in Christian Latinx communities.

During its first decade and a half, *la AETH* brought together different Christian traditions, thereby embodying one of the most ecumenical theological education organizations in the United States. It would surprise an outside observer to witness intense conversations regarding theological formation among Latinx Catholics, mainline Protestants, evangelicals, and pentecostals. While sharing meals and worshipping together, the interaction among Latinx theological educators flowed from committed laity to denominational leaders to professional theological educators and offered multiple avenues for the Christian mission of theological education. Whereas in many theological institutions the Latinx Christian communities' questions were dismissed or even ridiculed, the assemblies and conferences sponsored by *la AETH* provided the space *para conversar y discutir las preguntas teológicas de nuestra gente.*[5]

Since its beginning and as indicated above, *la AETH* persistently focused on a very important dimension of Latinx theological education: "to build relationships between all levels and programmes of theological education."[6] *La AETH* became and continues to be a critical interpreter of and for theological education within Latinx communities and in the broader context of theological formation in higher education settings of the United States and Canada. The Bible institute context – the primary source of theological formation for Latinx Christian leaders – was considered, at best, deficient and, at worst, ignored, ridiculed, and dismissed. *La AETH* never ceased to challenge theological organizations to recognize theological formation in Bible institutes as part of the grid of theological formation in formal educational contexts. In the last decade, *la AETH* worked for and achieved "affiliate status" with the Association of

---

[4] "La AETH vio siempre como parte de su propósito fue establecer vínculos entre todos los niveles y programas de educación teológica, y hacer que no solamente el pueblo latino, sino todo el ámbito de la educación teológica, vieran la importancia de nuestros propios programas latinos." Justo L. González, "3ELET: Trasfondo histórico, contexto teológico y realidad pastoral," conference presentation, 3er Encuentro Latino de Educación Teológica, Asociación para la Educación Teológica Hispana, online conference, 2–4 June 2021, 3. Paper shared via email with chapter author.

[5] González, "3ELET," 3, "to converse and discuss the theological questions of our people."

[6] González, "3ELET," 3.

Theological Schools (ATS – USA and Canada) and currently "promote[s] and certif[ies] the quality of Hispanic theological education programmes" in a partnership with the ATS.[7] Students with certificates from these institutes have a bachelor's degree equivalency that qualifies them for admission to ATS accredited Master of Divinity programmes in the United States and Canada.

La AETH's achievements surpass the many difficulties it faced and continues to face in its mission of theological formation for Latinx communities. *La AETH* depends on grants given by funding agencies and organizations that also limit the scope of its projects and purposes. While *la AETH* celebrates its ecumenical and intergenerational events and organizational culture, these gifts also bring internal challenges to *la AETH's* leadership. Yet, the association persistently nurtures an ecumenical, intergenerational, and intercultural environment grounded in its mission for theological formation. Broadening the scope of its constituency in a time of pandemic via online and digital structures, *la AETH* is a unique example of resilience in contexts of marginalization, hope in times of limited resources, humble success despite the resistance of theological institutions to grassroots theological formation of one of the growing populations of Christians in the USA and Canada.

Key Themes and Insights

Networks and Collaboration

La AETH is a network or, more precisely, a network of networks. These groups include ReDET (*Red de entidades teológicas*), which is composed of people and institutions dedicated to theological education in Latinx communities. According to one interview participant, ReDET members help *la AETH* in a variety of capacities, including recruitment, social media, thinking theologically, and imagining different models of church.[8] They also serve on the board and a variety of panels. *Las comunidades de práctica* are smaller networks composed of deans and directors from member organizations. These groups, which meet on a regular basis, provide accountability and strategic support as well as spaces for spiritual nourishment and theological reflection. Additionally, *la AETH* participates in a variety of informal networks resulting from workshops, lectures, conferences, and publications they have facilitated and from historic connections to the Hispanic Theological Initiative (HTI) and Hispanic Summer Program (HSP). These connections also lead to partnerships between association members. For example, a seminary in Michigan is partnering with a Bible institute in Puerto Rico to establish an online master's degree for the institute's professors.

La AETH's approach to collaboration is not merely utilitarian; it is relational and holistic. Several interview participants noted that the pastoral approach of *la AETH* allows them to form community despite theological and cultural

---

[7] "Who We Are," Asociación para la Educación Teológica Hispana, https://aeth.info/en/nosotros

[8] Interview with an AETH staff member, Zoom interview with the authors, 20 July 2021.

differences. One interviewee noted that intrinsic to *la AETH* is a sense that "we need each other [...] We could come together, we could meet the needs of one group, and then we could meet the needs of the other group and be a better reflection of the body of Christ."[9] Another participant noted that this approach helps Latinx teachers and scholars, who are often isolated from one another, to feel connected to their ecclesial roots and tuned in to the mission of the Latinx church in the United States.[10]

Teología en conjunto

In addition to ecumenical and cultural boundaries, one of the strategic goals of the organization from its founding has been to challenge the boundary between accredited theological schools and non-accredited Bible institutes. More recently, this goal has expanded to include other venues for theological education, such as community organizing networks and producers of online content. People trained for critical analysis in the academy and those who are deeply rooted in local congregations through Bible institutes are doing theology together. Said one interviewee, "you [academics] know the concepts. We [pentecostals] have the praxis."[11] This is one of the many strategies by which *la AETH* demonstrates a commitment to the tradition of *teología en conjunto*.[12]

As one interview participant so aptly put it, theological education does not only happen in graduate school. It "begins at the catechetical level; it begins in Sunday school, in local worship, and continues and should continue uninterrupted until a PhD degree."[13] Another interviewee offered that theological education "begins when the mother sings *coritos* to her child in her womb."[14] These testimonies also reveal that theology is living and embodied through the everyday practices of individuals and communities. "Theological education is more than just theology [...] theological education has to be about spiritual formation. And many persons have said we have left spiritual formation on the side. Theological education is, yes, about thinking critically and thinking theologically, but it's also about how we apply that thinking [...] theology [is] made out of the sweat and the blood of people in the community."[15] One member expressed deep gratitude for the way *la AETH* encourages safe spaces where participants can tell their stories, share their trauma, and witness to experiences of liberation. She perceives that this openness not only affirms the knowledge of

---

[9] Former AETH director, Zoom interview with the authors, 21 September 2021.

[10] Former AETH director, Zoom interview with the authors, 1 October 2021.

[11] Theological educator affiliated with *la AETH*, Zoom interview with the authors, 28 October 2021.

[12] *Teología en conjunto*, or "doing theology together," is a tradition and a concept with a long history in Hispanic/Latinx theological dialogue. For an overview of the tradition, see Rubén Rosario-Rodríguez, "Sources and En Conjunto Methodologies of Latino/a Theologizing," in *The Wiley Blackwell Companion to Latino/a Theology*, ed. Orlando O. Espín (Chichester, UK: John Wiley & Sons, 2015), 53–70.

[13] Former AETH director, Zoom interview with the authors, 1 October 2021.

[14] AETH staff member, Zoom interview with the authors, 20 July 2021.

[15] *Ibid.*

God that people have from their environments, but also leads to an expanded perspective on who God is in connection with the everyday lives of people.

Theological Education as Mission[16]

From its founding, *la AETH* recognized that theological education and mission are deeply intertwined, particularly in Latinx communities. As one interviewee stated, "it is not enough to understand things. We study not just to understand. We have to study theology to transform our own lives, our families, oriented by the values of God's reign. Theological education is missional, or it is something different."[17]

This sense of theological education as mission is carried out in that the very structure of *la AETH* and its programmes blurs the lines between church and academy. For example, a historic programme called *Las tertulias pastorales* facilitated spaces for pastors to gather, identified pressing questions of their ministries, and brought in resources that might address those questions. One leader from a member organization expressed that mission is central to the way her institute goes about strategic planning and, therefore, is a process that includes not only board members, but also faculty, staff, students, and alumni.[18]

La AETH also embraces a sense of mission in its publications. As one interviewee stated, many scholarly publications are "so heavily academic, so nuanced in every detail, so vigorously footnoted that for a student who comes to a Bible institute, who has gone through high school, and suddenly gets this 500-page book, it's very difficult." At the same time, "there are lots and lots of books that are very easy to read, but you probably shouldn't read them."[19] Therefore, *la AETH* commissions books that are "relevant for the community and at the same time [...] respectful of what scholarship knows about the questions." The association has published books in a variety of areas, from pastoral care and immigration in the church to a Bible commentary series.

Multi-Generational Mission

The umbrella term Latinx describes a diverse group of people, including those whose ancestors were living in the southwestern United States long before it was part of the United States and the most recently arrived immigrants from Central America and other parts of Latin America. The consistent waves of immigration mean that generational divisions that would challenge any community are exacerbated by differences in language, cultural hybridity, and levels of

---

[16] Although David Bosch does not name theological education as one of his paradigms for mission, the insights of our interview participants are consistent with Bosch's discussion of "teaching" as mission in the "Great Commission." For Bosch, teaching is not merely about intellectual formation, but about formation of the will. Bosch also describes missiology as an intersubjective enterprise. David Bosch, *Transforming Mission: Paradigm Shifts in Theology of Mission*, twentieth anniversary edition (Maryknoll, NY: Orbis Books, 2011), 67–68; 509.

[17] Former AETH director, Zoom interview with the authors, 11 November 2021.

[18] AETH board member and dean of a member school, Zoom interview with the authors, 9 December 2021.

[19] Former AETH director, interview with the authors, 1 October 2021.

education. One interviewee noted that the first generation often sees the church as a place for maintaining pieces of home and a haven from the trauma of immigration, while the second generation, having experienced discrimination, may desire a church that helps to strengthen and empower them to resist injustice.[20] Navigating these differences is vital to the church's mission in the United States.[21] As one interviewee put it, "young people are excellent missionaries," even to people who are not Hispanic.[22] The postmodern, postcolonial realities that so many churches are grappling with are embodied in the faith journeys of second and third generation Latinx Christians.

La AETH is meeting the challenge in creative ways. Mission Talk, an *AETH* member organization, seeks to address deep concern for racial and economic justice as well as the lack of immigrant rights that many young Latinx experience. The organization not only provides training for young leaders, but also seeks to help those leaders cultivate working relationships with pastors and bishops. Many first-generation immigrant pastors come from traditions that distrust the church's role in public advocacy. However, the pastors recognize that this work is an important concern of young people and, in response, have even gone so far as to participate in racial justice vigils and immigrant rights advocacy. World Outspoken, another network partner, approaches intergenerational mission as a challenge of intercultural competence. They train young leaders with the skills, knowledge, and emotional intelligence to navigate generational differences in approaching the relationship between faith and justice. Since 2016, *la AETH* itself has been working strategically to invite young people to participate in its biennial meeting and to sit on the board. Although multigenerational mission remains an unresolved challenge, nearly all of our interviewees mentioned it as a central, urgent concern that is worthy of significant effort.

Responding to Racism and Colonialism

Marginalization in the church, academy, and society was a concern of all of our interview participants. One individual put it bluntly: "I've been steeped in looking at many different forms that theological education for the Latinx community has taken place over many years. So, I have my scars from that history. I'm pissed off about some of the pieces about that history, which is not a surprise, right, because there have been many injustices that have taken place along the way. But I continue to believe that theological education is key to [...] the empowerment of Latinx communities in the United States and even beyond."[23] One strategy for addressing this injury has been to seek change within the existing academy. In view of this strategy, *la AETH* did not become a Latinx

---

[20] AETH staff member, interview with the authors, 20 July 2021.

[21] This kind of intergenerational tension is common among immigrant groups in general. The phenomenon is particularly complex among Latinx communities in the United States and Canada because of frequent travel to and from home countries as well as continuous waves of immigration from different parts of Latin America.

[22] Theological educator associated with *la AETH*, interview with one of the authors, 21 June 2021.

[23] AETH staff member, interview with the authors, 20 July 2021.

seminary at its founding. Although that idea was discussed in early conversations, according to two interviewees who were leaders at that time, a seminary would be easy to dismiss as a subpar institution because it did not fit the hegemonic norms of the academy. A network like *la AETH* could have a much broader impact. As mentioned above, *la AETH* now partners with the Association of Theological Schools (ATS) to certify Bible institutes that meet the association's standards. This certification process is just one of the many avenues through which *la AETH* has a broad impact on theological education in North America.

Others within *la AETH* are challenging the colonial norms of the academy by creating alternative channels for education. According to two of our interviewees, even the Bible institutes tend to mimic the "top-down" norms of the academy. One said that "they want to have a mini seminary in the Bible institutes following the patterns of the Eurocentric North Atlantic traditional curriculum."[24] These leaders have responded by seeking new models to do theological education, including blogs, podcasts, workshops, and trainings that are rooted in everyday spirituality and struggle, and addressed *en conjunto* with other leaders and educators.

Financial Paradigms

One leader of an *AETH* member organization noted that Latinx institutions tend to have limited financial resources. The resources are limited not merely because many Latinx communities have fewer resources to start with, but also because they are not visible to funders. Many organizations have the knowledge to provide services, but not to financially empower themselves. A frequent result, according to our conversation partner, is that people with passion and drive leave for Anglo organizations that offer more stability.[25]

La AETH has certainly struggled with its financial situation through the years. The organization is funded primarily through membership and conference registration fees as well as foundation grants. While they are grateful for these grants, the grants also complicate matters for the association. Said one interviewee, "foundations have become much more proactive than they used to be when we began. By that I mean the foundations decide we want this sort of thing, and then they go and ask for it."[26] *La AETH* has found repeatedly that, when a programme is successful, there is a desire from their network to continue it, even after grant funding ends. Meanwhile, staff must work on the projects connected to new grants. This means that the organization is stretched very thin. The same participant expressed that dependency on foundations is one of his deepest regrets about *la AETH*. He described it as a "new form of colonialism." To be free of this, he says, the association needs to figure out how to encourage more support from the grassroots.[27]

---

[24] Former AETH director, Zoom interview with the authors, 11 November 2021.
[25] Leader of a grassroots organization affiliated with *la AETH*, interview with one of the authors, 5 July 2021.
[26] Former AETH director, interview with the authors, 1 October 2021.
[27] *Ibid.*

La AETH and its network are seeking creative ways to address this challenge. The association accompanies network partners in discerning new strategies for financial sustainability. Member organizations are also working on the ground to provide training and resources for more fundraising sophistication.

COVID-19

As with so many organizations, COVID-19 brought opportunities and challenges to *la AETH* and its network. Most of our interviewees focused on positive outcomes. Conferences and workshops that were previously held in-person were now being hosted on digital platforms, making them accessible to a wider variety of people, including people in Latin America and around the world. One participant, however, pointed out that *la AETH* has been talking about digital forms of content delivery since at least 2017 as a means of reaching out to younger generations.[28] One network partner also reported that digital access to their courses has contributed positively to the participation of women in theological education. "For the first time in our history [our school] this semester will have a 62 percent women representation in their body, which is just amazing, and we're just even trying to figure out what that means to embrace this. And I think that part of it has been the women are now not just more available because it's virtual, right, and they can study in their own setting. They don't have to move out. You don't have to find babysitters." The same dean noted, however, that about 70 percent of her students struggle with computer use, so an all-digital programme does not seem to be the only answer to inequality in access.[29]

Las comunidades de práctica served a very important role providing holistic care for their members during times of isolation, according to two of our participants. As one of them reported, "I was able to get through a lot of the pandemic trauma that we were going through. We were Zoom tired, but we looked forward to the communities of practice on Zoom, even though we have [never] met in person."[30] Another suggested that this spiritual and emotional support also accelerated their ability to do theology together. "Especially coming through the pandemic, they have become caring communities and communities where we discuss what it means, who God is to us in this moment. And the spiritual formation pieces that we have found relevant or not in this moment."[31] How the association will draw from these lessons moving forward remains unclear, but the network's agile responses to this world-changing event have certainly opened up new and creative ways to perform mission.

---

[28] AETH staff member, interview with the authors, 20 July 2021.
[29] AETH board member and dean of a member school, Zoom interview with the authors, 9 December 2021.
[30] *Ibid.*
[31] AETH staff member, interview with the authors, 20 July 2021.

Questions and Challenges

Navigating Theological and Political Differences

As *la AETH* projects its next decade of missional work, there are some critical questions and challenges that it will face in its context of theological formation. First, in the last few years *la AETH's* confessional and denominational constituency has changed. Currently, there are fewer Roman Catholic and mainline Protestants, while the association experiences an increase in new Latinx evangelical groups and the diversity of pentecostal, neo-pentecostal, and non-denominational groups remains steady. This shift in the association's constituency presents some critical questions. For example, what ecumenical formation do the new groups have that might continue to nurture a collaborative environment created by previous generations of mainline Protestants and Catholics who had, and embodied, ecumenical commitments and formation?

Adding a layer of difficulty to questions about collaboration, *la AETH* also faces an intergenerational and theological challenge as an increasing number of third and fourth generation evangelical Latinx Christian leaders find themselves (1) struggling with the dismissal of their theological and ministerial questions and dilemmas in their evangelical theological institutions (similar to the early experience of theological leaders in *la AETH*), and (2) discovering that their theological formation is in tension with some of the predominant theological currents within *la AETH's* network, particularly theological commitments to social engagement and justice among young Latinx evangelicals. Will *la AETH* be able to navigate these theological complexities and tensions, and uphold its missional commitment to theological formation? What kind of theological formation will *la AETH* consider for certification? Will *la AETH* develop an institutional policy that will help it steer its missional commitment in a context of significant theological and political differences?

The above questions also have implications for the Latinx Christian communities. As the communities *copy* and are *shaped* by the tensions and divisions in the dominant US and Canadian contexts, will *la AETH* be able to offer a missional theological formation that, while guided by the context of the Latinx communities, will also broaden its horizon to include difficult theological conversations about such topics as sexuality, interreligious encounter and dialogue, racism, the role of women in ministry, immigration, ecology, and economic sustainability? For example, will the association foster conversations regarding the growing number of Latinx converts to Islam? Will *la AETH* create a safe space to address questions from Latinx youth regarding sexuality, immigration, and access to education? While most of our interviewees mentioned these issues only in passing, if at all, our younger participants and those who work closely with them were quite focused on these potentially divisive themes. We believe *la AETH* will need to develop strategies to help the church address such demands.

Cultural Diversity within the Latinx Community

Another issue that *la AETH* will increasingly face as it supports Latinx churches for quality theological formation is cultural diversity and power dynamics within

Latinx communities. Many of the leaders in the first decades of *la AETH*'s existence have been Puerto Rican, Cuban, or Mexican-American. As immigration patterns have shifted in recent years, the US and Canada have experienced large influxes of first Mexican, then Central American immigrants. *La AETH* is already experiencing this cultural diversity among its constituents and, to a lesser degree, among its leaders.

Carmen Nanko-Fernández writes that, as Latin@/Hispanic[32] people have become the largest ethnic minority in the United States, it has become necessary "to redefine ourselves as comunidad."[33] As Hispanic/Latinx theology was developing in the 1980s and 1990s, seeking common Latinx experiences was necessary for establishing a sense of community and political clout. *La AETH* was part of this effort. As the Latinx population continues to grow, how will *la AETH* honour its heritage and look to the future in a way that invites solidarity within the multicultural realities of Latinx Christians while still providing a theological education and formation appropriate for diverse contexts? What strategies will *la AETH* embrace to navigate the power dynamics between different cultural groups that are tied to race, citizenship and immigration status, and varying levels of cultural and linguistic agility?

The Sustainability of a Larger Constituency: Participation from Latin America
Now, if these are critical and difficult questions for the context of *la AETH* in the USA, Canada, and Puerto Rico, and among so many different ethnic groups and generations, imagine how these questions and challenges grow when *la AETH* includes the increasing Latin American constituency via online and digital platforms. What social, cultural, and theological criteria will the association develop to serve the growing demands of grassroots Latin American Christian groups while keeping its purpose of improving the quality of theological formation? Will *la AETH* be able to address the politically conservative social media platforms across the continent while promoting and creating spaces for theological formation that demand discernment, reflection, and social action?

Network or Institution?
La AETH exists as a network and, as described above, has resisted identifying itself as an institution of higher education. This stance has allowed the association to have a broad impact on theological education that might not otherwise have been possible. Resistance to institutionalization has also meant that *la AETH* is not closely connected with any particular location or denomination, which may contribute to the ease with which the association works across boundaries. However, as one participant put it, *la AETH* has never been able to feel "at home" and is at the mercy of host institutions for operating space. The association has had offices at seminaries in Georgia, Texas, Colorado,

---

[32] We use the term Latin@/Hispanic here to be consistent with the language used in the cited work. The term "Latinx" has emerged and become widespread since the publication of Nanko-Fernández's work.
[33] Carmen Nanko-Fernández, *Theologizing En Espanglish: Context, Community, and Ministry* (Maryknoll, NY: Orbis Books, 2010), 16.

and Florida, and it recently moved to Georgia once again. According to one interviewee, this nomadic existence has proven to be disruptive to *la AETH*'s efforts to build relationships with the churches and has contributed to association members experiencing themselves as outsiders in the theological academy.[34] This pattern of geographic uprooting is difficult for the staff of the association. Do they move in order to continue working for *la AETH* and developing its programmes or stay in the city where their families have put down roots?

How will *la AETH* continue to embrace and/or interrogate its status as a network on the margins of the theological academy? Its pilgrim existence certainly has the potential to give the association an epistemological perspective on the church and the academy that has great value for mission. On the other hand, it interferes with *la AETH's* ability to nurture institutional memory. We wonder how this tension will play out as new generations seek to nurture the mission of *la AETH* to promote excellent theological education for the church and the world.[35]

Conclusion

The questions and challenges above will likely have a dramatic impact on the work of *la AETH* moving forward. As our research has highlighted, the association has demonstrated incredible agility in the past as it faced denominational and generational diversity, racism and marginalization, and the ever-changing demands of funding agencies. Meanwhile, it has succeeded in maintaining responsive, relational connections with churches and grassroots networks. These connections are supported by an innate understanding, within the network of *la AETH*, that theological education is missional; at its best, it supports the church and its leaders as they respond to constantly evolving challenges for mission and ministry in the world.

La AETH has decades of experience in work that is now required of nearly all entities that seek to equip leaders for the church. Students are increasingly older and more racially and ethnically diverse; they experience more financial constraints and require more flexible educational arrangements such as part time, online, and intensive coursework.[36] As the North American church faces declining institutions, societal divisions that feel hopeless, and constantly evolving technological advances, theological educators could learn a great deal from the wisdom of *la AETH* in responding proactively and creatively to the Latinx churches' changing needs. After all, the association's constituents represent the theological, political, cultural, and generational diversity of one of

---

[34] Former AETH director, interview with the authors, 21 September 2021.

[35] The mission of *la AETH* is "to promote theological education of excellence and relevance of Hispanic leaders in their service to the church and the world." "Who We Are," https://aeth.info/en/nosotros.

[36] The ATS maintains comprehensive data demonstrating these trends. Association of Theological Schools, *Annual Data Tables,* https://www.ats.edu/Annual-Data-Tables. However, ATS data does not account for the increasing number of non-accredited options such as Bible institutes, denominational training pathways, and church-based programmes.

the US and Canada's largest and growing demographic groups. Of all its missional ventures, *la AETH's* commitment to Latinx Christian communities and theological formation seems to be what drives its ability to have such a far-reaching impact. It is a mission that is shaped in love for and by *la comunidad.*

MUTUAL PARTNERSHIPS

Sisterhood and "Sistering": Restating Relationships in the Cartography of Missional Collaborations – Dallas Bethlehem Center, A Case Study

Glory E. Dharmaraj

The ways in which women have organized for mission and the kinds of home mission institutions they have built have both changed since the 19th century, but their core mission of engagement with women and children has remained the same.[1] The story of United Methodist Women, now called United Women in Faith (UWF), and their mission institutions within the US, is a story of "sistering." Part of the evolving self-understanding of UWF, in their 153 years of engagement in mission, is the concept of "sistering." Being and becoming sisters in mission strengthened and expanded their collective identity of sisterhood. Sistering is also a process of securing and providing strength to the home mission institutions. Sistering lends itself to twin understandings in this mission endeavour. Firstly, women as agents of mission live as a sisterhood in mission. Secondly, sistering entails investment in the building, capital, and running intervention in the context of home mission institutions within the US. Women organized for mission built more than a hundred national mission institutions.[2]

One such story and one such space is the Dallas Bethlehem Center (DBC) in Dallas, Texas. It is also a story of adaptive and emergent missional collaborations as well as particular ways of being and doing in transformational spaces. The story of DBC is an outgrowth of a series of structural, dynamic, and emergent collaborations among the stakeholders such as the United Methodist Women, the Center itself, the neighbouring churches, and the community in order to address a seemingly simple and basic need: offering children pre-kindergarten education. The mission collaborations undertaken in offering this educational service constitutes a journey – a journey from local and national missional partnerships to a participatory communal movement. The educational service for the children is a lens to review and analyze the larger story of the place and placemaking.

The role of one of the Bethlehem Centers, namely the Dallas Bethlehem Center in Texas, is a quintessential American story of home mission against all odds imposed by the dominant structural inequities of the community. It is also

---

[1] I thank Dr Fred Jones, Fran Lobpries, Rev. Katherine Lyle, Dr Thalia Matherson, Harriett J. Olson, Ruth Robinson, Sharon Spratt, and Hortense Tyrell for their interviews. I thank Cynthia Rives for her interviews with the former presidents of North Texas UWF. I thank E. Frances Long, North Texas United Methodist Conference Archivist, for providing her expertise during my research process.
[2] Author's interview with Harriett J. Olson, CEO of the UWF, 22 January 2022.

a comeback story of "sistering" in building and sustaining collaborations, which is the focus of this case study.

Theological Underpinnings

Sisterhood has always been integral to women organizing for mission. For example, the first President of the Woman's Missionary Council of the Methodist Episcopal Church, South, Belle Harris Bennett, invoked "sisterhood" at the organization's outset, saying that Methodist women, "under the divine guidance," had already entered "into a great, loving sisterhood and established a work that to the end of the ages must make for righteousness [...]"[3] This memory of a just and inclusive future is worth recalling. Women engaged in mission have made the connection between impact and sisterhood over generations. Today, the prevailing memory is still sisterhood. "Impact, sisterhood, and personal commitment" are basic building blocks for women in today's mission.[4]

In addition to sisterhood, another underpinning theological concept is partnership. The ancient church imagined the triune God in a dance-like relationship of three persons. This image depicts the mystery of the godhead as a self-giving, life-affirming partnership – the community created in and by the triune God.

In the Wesleyan understanding of partnership, "God's mission flows from a threefold manifestation in God's prevenient, justifying, and sanctifying grace revealed in Jesus Christ and experienced in the hearts and lives of Christian believers."[5] The prevenient grace of the Creator bears, fosters, and nourishes the whole human family and leads us to recognize our shortfalls and sinfulness. God's justifying grace offers assurance of forgiveness and renews us with the core understanding of humans being made in the image of God. Sanctifying grace leads the redeemed community to be in mission with the neighbour, community, and the world.

Methodist women have based their understanding of missional relationships around the belief that all people are created "in God's image." The model for witnessing to this truth is the life and teaching of Jesus the Christ.[6] In building interracial relationships with marginalized communities, specifically with African Americans, another inspiring biblical concept has been the "kingdom of God." The women in mission saw themselves as "workers in God's kingdom,"

---

[3] Belle Harris Bennett, "President Message to the Woman's Missionary Council, 1911," in the *First Annual Report of the Woman's Missionary Council of The Methodist Episcopal Church, South, for 1910–1911* (Nashville, TN: Smith and Lamar), 96.
[4] Harriet J. Olson's address to the quadrennial Assembly of UWF on 22 May 2022, "CEO and General Secretary, Harriett Jane Olson, Speech: 'The Vision'," YouTube Channel: United Women in Faith, Uploaded: 14 June 2022, https://www.youtube.com/watch?v=Xu6gK5FwZ0s.
[5] General Board of Global Ministries of the United Methodist Church, "Partnership in God's Mission: A Theology of Mission Statement" (New York: General Board of Global Ministries, 1986), 8.
[6] Alice G. Knotts, *Fellowship of Love: Methodist Women Changing American Racial Attitudes, 1920–1968* (Nashville, TN: Abingdon Press, 1996), 261.

committed to extending the spatiality of God's kingdom,[7] especially to the communities who have been othered. To the UWF, in the spatiality of God's kingdom, there is no need to exclude any group.

Finally, women's mission work, especially among the marginalized within the US, is based on an ecclesial vision of the early church baptismal formula: "There is no longer Jew or Greek; there is no longer slave or free; there is no longer male and female; for all of you are one in Christ Jesus" (Gal. 3:28).[8] In 1901, the leader of the Woman's Home Missionary Society of the Methodist Episcopal Church, South (WHMS South), Belle Harris Bennett, inspired the leaders of administration with this bedrock conviction for starting work among the African American women and children.[9]

The Origins of Bethlehem Centers

During the days when women and children were legally classified as "chattel" and "non-persons," women organizing for mission raised money and pioneered work for women and children abroad and within the country, in the late 19th century and early 20th century, by establishing foreign and home missionary societies. In a segregated country with segregated spaces of living, the visions of founding the settlements known as Bethlehem Centers to serve the African American neighbourhoods were centred around interracial collaborations.

The earliest cluster of Bethlehem Centers started as settlement houses in Nashville, TN: Wesley House (1894), Centenary Center (1908), and Bethlehem Center (1911). The storyline of Bethlehem Center in Nashville traces its origin to an African American female, Sallie Hill Sawyer, a member of Caper Chapel Colored Methodist Episcopal Church, who had a dream of serving her people. A missionary called to serve her own people, Sawyer found a space in a Presbyterian church building and started a Bethlehem Center close to Fisk University in 1911. The Tennessee Conference Woman's Missionary Society adopted the programme, and Sawyer served as a house mother of the Bethlehem Center. The establishment of the centre is the result of ecumenical and interracial collaborations. Estelle Haskin, a white mission worker with the Methodist Training School in Nashville, served as a supervisor of the Bethlehem House. From its inception, the centre was run by an inter-racial advisory board and inter-racial staff for the programmes and planning.[10]

Southern Methodist women expanded this kind of ministry by establishing more of these types of centres. In order to distinguish the mission work already started in Settlement Houses among the immigrants and the indigent, these centres in African American communities were named Bethlehem Centers.

---

[7] *Tenth Annual Report of the Woman's Council of the Methodist Episcopal Church, South, 1919–1920* (Nashville, TN: Publishing House of the Methodist Episcopal Church, South, 1921), 179.

[8] Biblical quotations are from the NRSV.

[9] Noreen Dunn Tatum, *A Crown of Service: A Story of Woman's Work in the Methodist Episcopal Church, South, from 1878–1940* (Nashville, TN: Pantheon Press, 1960), 356.

[10] *Historical Development of National Mission Institutions* (New York: General Board of Global Ministries, The United Methodist Church, 2000), 2.

These centres continue to serve the marginalized African American communities in Nashville, TN (1911); Augusta, GA (1912); Winston-Salem, NC (1927); Spartanburg, SC (1930); Jackson, MS (1933); Charlotte, NC (1940); Columbia, SC (1945); and Dallas Bethlehem Center in Dallas, TX (1946).[11]

These centres are "expressions of faith"; a presence in brick and mortar in communities.[12] As the Women's Division of the denominational board of The United Methodist Church stated in 1976, the centres provide both advocacy efforts and direct services through their ministries *to* women and ministries *to* children, affirming that "institutions are a base for mission."[13] In 1998, the Women's Division updated this statement in its guiding document, the *Policy Statement: Ministries with women and ministries with children and youth,* with one of its core principles that the women's work is an affirmation of institutions as a base for mission.[14] The shift to the language of mission *with* (instead of mission *to*) speaks of participatory approaches to communal connectedness, interdependencies, and cooperative models and processes leading to mutuality in mission.

In founding the Bethlehem Centers, the leaders allied the vision and outcome of their ministries with "brotherhood" as a value for building a just future. "Adventuring in brotherhood" is how the ministry of the Bethlehem Centers was characterized. Deaconesses and missionaries, as ambassadors for Christ, have been into the task of building brotherhood in the communities across the country as they serve humanity in its needs, bringing diverse people together for the common good of communal flourishing.[15] It is still an unfinished task. Siblinghood is still a value to live into, working for racially integrated communities. In such a venture, those engaged in mission see glimpses of siblinghood or even experience it, as a reflexive impact.

---

[11] This group of Bethlehem Centers is one among many other groups of institutions such as Community Centers, Wesley Centers, Women's Residences, Neighborhood Houses, Residential Treatment Centers, and educational centres serving different populations across the country. Today, there are about 90 national mission institutions founded by the predecessors of the United Women in Faith.

[12] Betty L. Letzig, *National Mission Resources: Expressions of Faith* (New York: Mission Education and Cultivation Program Department, General Board of Global Ministries, 1987).

[13] *Ministries to Women, Ministries to Children: A Policy Statement* (New York: Women's Division, General Board of Global Ministries, The United Methodist Church, 1976), 3.

[14] *Ministries with Women and Ministries with Children and Youth: A Gift for the Whole Church. A Policy Statement of the Women's Division* (New York: Women's Division, General Board of Global Ministries of The United Methodist Church, 1998), 4.

[15] *The Coming Kingdom: Seventh Annual Report of the Woman's Division of Christian Service of the Board of Missions and Church Extension of the Methodist Church, 1946–1947* (New York: Woman's Division of Christian Service, Board of Missions, The Methodist Church, 1947), 124, 143.

Deaconesses and Lay Women in the Bethlehem Centers

The Bethlehem Centers emerged, during the era of segregation, from early collaborations between lay women organized for mission and the deaconess movement. From the time the Methodist Episcopal Church, South, recognized the fulltime lay vocation of deaconesses in 1902, the office of the deaconess came to be housed within the Woman's Home Missionary Society (WHMS). The WHMS opened ways to recruit, train, and send out deaconesses for service. The training curriculum was equipped with the latest sociological methods of collecting data systematically; these skills allowed the deaconesses to be "analysts of society," especially within urban settings.[16] WHMS placed deaconesses in Bethlehem Centers for their ministries to women and children through interracial boards.

The Dallas Bethlehem Center (DBC)

The origin of Dallas Bethlehem Center itself is a story of collaboration – local, communal, and national. First and foremost, an interracial board was formed with Mrs Luke Malone of First Methodist Church as president. Deaconess Alice McLarty, a white professional, appointed by the Woman's Division of Christian Service, began her duties in September 1946. She came from the Bethlehem Center in Augusta, GA, with its interracial board. She found an office space in St Paul Methodist Church in Dallas, TX, an African American church which was part of the Central Jurisdiction: a segregated jurisdiction for the African Americans in the Methodist Church. Many conferences and interviews were conducted with various agencies and churches, Council of Social Agencies, Community Chest, City and County Welfare, Health Department, Board of Education, school nurses, and individuals. Spearheaded by this study of the African American neighbourhood, the Child Welfare Division asked that a "spot study" be made to find out how pre-school children fared in crowded areas when their mothers were employed away from home. Therefore, with an aim to "build wisely and permanently," a survey was conducted using a form compiled by the Council of Social Agencies so that the Child Welfare Division would provide additional care for children.[17] In Methodist women organized for mission, wellbeing of children has been the litmus test for communal wholeness.

Commitment to ministry with children is a key principle undergirding the mission story of the UWF. Two of the former leaders of the United Women in Mission have defined it as a timeless question and a challenge. Theressa Hoover, the first African American lead staff from the segregated Central Jurisdiction of the Methodist Church, raised a diagnostic question for communal wellbeing:

---

[16] Mary Agnes Dougherty, *My Calling to Fulfill: Deaconesses in the United Methodist Tradition* (New York: Women's Division, General Board of Global Ministries, The United Methodist Church, 1997), 135, 170–71.

[17] *Thy Way Be Known: Eighth Annual Report of the Woman's Division of Christian Service of the Board of Missions and Church Extension of the Methodist Church, 1947– 1948* (New York: Woman's Division of Christian Service, Board of Missions, The Methodist Church, 1948), 45–46.

"How is the child developing?"[18] Thelma Stevens, a leader for social justice for the marginalized, summarized mission with children as entry into spaces of communal transformation. What "besets the children and the families" also "destroys their normal growth in the community."[19] Kindergartens, therefore, are spaces created and sustained by women's mission for the wellness of the communities.

Urban Planning and Its Impact on DBC

Mapping the Bethlehem Center collaborations requires looking into the placement and displacement of people where the centres are located. South Dallas, where DBC is located at 4410 Leland Avenue, Dallas, TX, 75215, embodies a layered history of broken places and broken dreams, crises of redlining, and racial discriminations. Facing this story of place involves facing the inherent structural disparities.

In *Mission Milestones of North Texas Women*, Frances Long and her co-authors offer a brief history of the DBC.[20] The authors compressed the surrounding history of the place into this haunting line: "The construction of Central Expressway had divided the Negro community."[21] While facilitating the movement between white suburbia and downtown where most of the jobs were available, the Central Expressway deprived the African American community of its cohesiveness. This move led to the tragedy of geographic displacement of the African Americans and its associated distresses, due to wilfully planned and systematically imposed inequities in the urbanscape. The resultant crisis of place is due to knotted disparities such as built-in infrastructure (including highways and freeways), segregated housing practices, redlining, and other economic discriminatory practices. Therefore, mission as place-making, that is, human flourishing in urbanscape, has run into deeply rooted structural impediments accumulated over the years.

The Woman's Division of the Methodist Board of Missions had already bought a building at 2921 Thomas Ave. for the DBC in 1948. However, it had to sell the property, since the city planners designated the area where the centre was situated as State-Thomas Historical District of Dallas. As a result, the lower-income African Americans were displaced further south of Dallas.[22] The immediate response of DBC to such an interlocking discrimination and lack of educational provision for the vulnerable population of pre-kindergarten children was to leave the place of injustices created by the dominant political, racial, and social forces. Further, Dallas was the largest city without a kindergarten

---

[18] Theressa Hoover, "History Rooted in Concern for Child," *Response* (New York: United Methodist Women, March, 1979), 4.
[19] Thelma Stevens, "'Thorns That Fester': An Oral Biography and Interview by Alice G. Knotts on December 5–7, 1983," from the personal collection of Ellen Kirby, former staff of the Women's Division of the General Board of Global Ministries.
[20] I thank Dr Thalia Matherson for referring me to this book and sending me a copy of the chapter on the DBC.
[21] Frances Long, et al., *Mission Milestones of North Texas Women* (Wolfe City, TX: Henington Publishing Company, 1984), 220.
[22] Ibid., 219.

programme in the entire country.[23] The need for pre-school and after-school care for children was urgent. Therefore, in 1955, the DBC also chose to move to the margins following the call to be in mission with those marginalized by forces of domination. Later in the 1970s, DBC moved into the current site at Leland Ave. "Place informs mission. Location is a way of corresponding to the neighbourhood," says the current CEO of the UWF, Harriett J. Olson, affirming the direct services offered by DBC, and accompanying those in the margins. Rev. Katherine Lyle, a member on the current board of DBC, says that if the services of DBC are no longer needed and "moving is necessary, we will move. We have moved once before. It is in our DNA."[24]

Situated south of I-30, even today, the surrounding neighbourhood and community of DBC is still a place where bank loans are nearly impossible for African American communities to obtain. It is a "credit desert."[25] The local media station has raised awareness of entrenched connections between banks and their lending practices to the community below I-30.[26] Coalitions for advocacy and livelihood have been created to address this problem.

Marginalized Zip Codes as Home Base for Mission

In 2013, North Texas Conference of the United Methodist Church (NTX Conference) launched what is known as Zip Code Connections. The goal of this initiative was to eradicate poverty in two high-poverty zip codes, one in urban south Dallas, home to 70 percent of African Americans where the DBC is located at zip code 75215. The other one is in rural northeastern Texas River, with missional focus on Clarksville, Red River County 75246.

The NTX Conference decided to work with partners already on the ground such as the DBC and collaborate with them in addressing poverty in the urban community in zip code 75215. A faith coalition of different churches was formed in order to offer breakfast and books to children. The coordinator of the programme from the North Texas Conference of the United Methodist Church was Rev. George Battle III, a former graduate student from the Perkins School of Theology, who had served as an intern and staff member at DBC during a period of fiscal crisis (referred to later in this study). He also worked from the centre on the zip code connection with the vision of DBC becoming an "act of renewal for the North Texas Conference in general."[27] Volunteers scheduled their time and offered tutoring to children. The ground-up efforts are from the

---

[23] Jim Schutze, *The Accommodation: The Politics of Race in an American City* (Dallas, TX: Deep Vellum, 2021), 40, 203, 222.

[24] Author's interview with Rev. Katherine Lyle, 9 February 2022.

[25] "Banking Below I-30," ABC News, Channel-8, WSAA, 28 February 2022. I thank Diana Masters for this reference.

[26] "Banks Own Many of Dallas' Low-Income, High-Crime Apartments – and They're Rewarded for It," YouTube Channel: WFAA-TV, Uploaded: 3 March 2021, https://www.youtube.com/watch?v=mVeSO9pVSes.

[27] Sam Hodges, "Dallas Center Experiences a Resurrection," United Methodist News Service, 17 April 2014, https://www.umnews.org/en/news/dallas-center-experiences-resurrection; author's interview with Fran Lobpries, 18 February 2022.

community itself.[28] Despite the collaborative efforts of the NTX Conference, the project did not bear much fruit within a quadrennium. The conference put together a resource using the lessons learned as a self-assessment, entitled *Important Learnings: A Guide to Ministry with Our Neighbors in North Texas*.[29] It offers invaluable lessons to those who engage in mission and explains how building long-term relationships and acting as guests are more important measures than implementing a top-down approach.

The dominant forces, which maintain entrenched inequities, have the power of conferring zip codes as destiny. In a deeper structural analysis of place, Collin Yarborough, a pipeline engineer who became a seminarian in Southern Methodist University, Dallas, TX, says that a "just and equitable city cannot be created with [...] one policy change or one grassroots campaign," for "it has taken many decades, policies, and actions to get to this point and will take many more to repair it."[30] It takes an "Incremental Development approach" that needs collaborations on multiple levels to repair and rebuild the city and community.[31] Any unjust system that was constructed incrementally has to be dismantled the same way that it was put up in the first place, slowly and systematically.

Health Care and Zip Codes

The DBC has deeply invested in childhood education, as its core commitment, while lifting up its voice for investing in the community to promote wellness at all levels. Studies have long shown the health inequities based on race and geography. A recent study has reaffirmed that there is a high correlation between lack of access to health care and low-income African American communities in Dallas, especially those who reside in the zip code 75215, where DBC is situated. The Dallas County health profile shows that the African American population has the highest percentage of deaths due to causes such as heart disease, diabetes, cancer, stroke, kidney disease, and Alzheimer's. Black Dallas residents and those living in southern parts of the city are more likely to be unhealthy and have less access to health care.[32] Dallas Bethlehem Center and the University of Texas Southwestern Medical Center have entered into a diabetic study this year. This partnership, along with the Parkland Hospital Service, is built around community wellness, according to Fred Jones, the Interim Executive Director of DBC.[33]

---

[28] "Dallas Bethlehem Center – Breakfast and Books to Go," YouTube Channel: Dallas Bethlehem Center, Uploaded: 15 August 2016, https://www.youtube.com/watch?v=TX4o9VdHkdA.
[29] North Texas Conference of the Methodist Church, "Zip Code Connection," https://ntcumc.org/missional-outreach/zip-code-connection. Click "ZCC Learnings" to access the Zip Code Connection Learning Guide, https://ntcumc.org/Zip_Code_Connection_Learnings_Guide.pdf.
[30] Collin Yarborough, *Paved a Way: Infrastructure, Policy, and Racism in an American City* (Coppell, TX: New Degree Press, 2021), 7–8.
[31] Ibid., 198–200.
[32] *Dallas County: Health Needs Assessment* (Dallas: Parkland Health and Hospital System and Dallas County Health and Human Services, 18 September 2019), 6, 42.
[33] Author's interview with Dr Fred Jones, Interim Executive Director of Dallas Bethlehem Center, 9 February 2022.

Laudable as this partnership is, the long-term wellness of the community depends on other factors such as childhood education, transportation improvement, criminal justice reform, and eradication of homelessness in order to break the cycle of ill health.[34]

Collaborations Forged under Climate Crisis

Collaborations often happen in emergencies. One such example is the story of Warren United Methodist Church in Dallas, an African American congregation seeking space in DBC for Sunday worship due to the impact of the snowstorm on their church building in 2021. At the surface level, it is a story of the centre offering a safe space for worship to a congregation whose building was under repair. Institutions bonding during natural disaster is no new story in mission.

However, a deeper strand of the story is the impact of natural disasters and the duration of power outages in the most vulnerable communities. In the Texas winter storm of 2021, when the power grid was cut off, the two most vulnerable communities severely and adversely affected were two counties: Dallas and Houston.[35] The most at-risk populations in these counties are racial minorities. DBC, with its zip code 75215, is predominantly situated in an African American community. Warren United Methodist Church in South Dallas is a congregation of African Americans. While the USA is disparate climatologically, the impact of extreme weather on the socially vulnerable is severe. Context, intersectionality, and geography often determine emergent on-the-ground missional collaborations.

Media as Megaphone

Dallas Bethlehem Center was in serious fiscal crisis in 2011 due to a confluence of unforeseen factors including the recent recession. News flashed across the local newspaper, *Dallas Morning News*, "South Dallas Nonprofit Dallas Bethlehem Center to Close Doors."[36] "Give us a deaconess," said Ruth Robinson, the former president of the North Texas UWF, to the National Office of the organization, in order to restore the services of DBC. Robinson refused to accept that the DBC was on the threshold of shuttering its doors. For her, deaconesses stood for community welfare and resilience.[37]

With an emergency grant from the National Office, DBC was able to hire Fran Lobpries, a skilled fundraiser, as a consultant. She later became the executive

---

[34] *Dallas County: Health Needs Assessment,* 6.

[35] Joan A. Casey, "Consecutive Hours with 10,000 + Customers without Power in Texas, February 10-24, 2021," in Harvard Radcliff Institute, "Next in Climate Change," hybrid programme on 4 March 2022. It was part of a series of studies on climate change and its impact on health and wellbeing organized by Harvard Radcliffe Institute. "Blackout | Next in Climate Change | 4/6 ‖ Harvard Radcliffe Institute," YouTube Channel: Harvard Radcliffe Institute, Uploaded: 14th March 2022, https://www.youtube.com/watch?v=0XAB4vYzr4w&list=PLTt9bwjR4BIetInjrJETmkl u4xz_vLAYi&index=4.

[36] Mark Norris, "South Dallas Nonprofit Dallas Bethlehem Center to Close Doors," *Dallas Morning News,* 15 December 2011.

[37] Author's interview with Ruth Robinson, 18 January 2022.

director. Unfortunately, when the building was closed for a period in December 2011 to 2013, it could no longer operate under the grandfather rule that safeguarded the building codes. Reopening now meant complying with current building codes and safety ordinances, including the instalment of a sprinkler system all through the building and renovating children's classrooms to meet current safety standards. The estimated cost for the sprinklers alone was 100,000 US dollars. Lobpries decided to get the story out quickly, because "if you need help, you need a megaphone."[38] She picked up the phone and called the *Dallas Morning News*, expressing the urgent need of DBC. Columnist Steve Blow made an appeal, recounting the lasting impact of DBC to the community.[39] Donations poured in, and the centre reopened in 2013. Soon after, the church media covered this news in faith language: "Dallas Center Experiences a Resurrection."[40]

Emergent Collaborations

Coalitions for service took a new turn. The ChildCareGroup in South Dallas was looking for a larger building for its operation. As a provider of childcare, this group fit well within the historic work of DBC, so the DBC has allowed ChildCareGroup to use its facilities. Such a partnership for a common goal is a "God thing." The Crossroads Community Services provides food, since the place is a "food desert," and the First United Methodist Church of Dallas coordinates the food delivery system with volunteers from the community itself. Dallas Police Athletic League for Youth Athletics is another agency housed in the new building.[41] The centre is a platform for continuing its witness by providing space and facilities for non-profit work. Neighbourhood groups for advocacy and community volunteers for meal distribution are other local partners.[42] Many of the collaborations for direct services and livelihood are forged locally, while UWF, the national organization of women organized for mission, has offered sistering in terms of capital, building, and grants.[43]

Virtual Tea Party and Real Time Visit

During the COVID-19 pandemic, when face-to-face meetings were not possible, Barbara Weaver, the president of the Dallas Metro District UWF, North Texas, felt a pull during the long and often scary time of lockdown. She decided to host a Metro District Virtual Mother's Day Tea to lift the hearts of the women and benefit a local organization involving women and children by raising funds. Weaver hosted a tea party on Zoom, and she said the pandemic brought new

---

[38] Author's interview with Fran Lobpries, 18 February 2022.
[39] Ibid.
[40] Hodges, "Dallas Center Experiences a Resurrection."
[41] Author's interview with Sharon Spratt, 10 February 2022. Author's interview with Thalia Matherson, 3 January 2022.
[42] Cynthia Rives' interview with Ruth Robinson, 11 April 2022. Interview shared with the author.
[43] Author's interview with Harriett Olson, 28 January 2022.

learning opportunities to her.[44] DBC became the main recipient of the funds raised.

Further, all 99 units of the North Texas UWF raised Thanksgiving baskets of food in 2020. One participant, Mary Campbell, visited DBC after 61 years after her initial visit to the place as a young girl. She came back personally with her friend and delivered 87 bags of sugar, 150 cans of jellied cranberry sauce, and 166 cans of green beans. Such stories are instances that strengthen the ties to the place as well as expanded sisterhood among the networked women in mission.[45]

Institutionalizing Collaborations: Caring Connections

Mapping missional collaborations is not a mere charting of an even flow of partnerships. The thematic sequence is marked by forced disruptions, discontinuities, and sometimes restorations as part of a historical reality. One such instance is the forced merger of the Woman's Division with the denominational board due to an unforeseen and abrupt restructure in 1964. All the national mission institutions including DBC, owned by the Methodist women organized for mission, were brought under the denominational board without the ratification of the Woman's Division. But the women kept at their "sistering" role by managing to retain the control of the property and finances, and they made annual appropriation to the denominational board for sustaining the mission institutions.[46]

"Caring Connections" is a missional collective initiated by the UMC denominational board in the mid-1990s among 102 national mission institutions. It aimed to bring together all the UMC national mission institutions, including the Bethlehem Centers, and build a national network whereby institutions could help each other. An initiative called Sharing Partners Action Network (SPAN) strengthened the institutions through financial and technical resources offering peer-to-peer networking opportunities, mentoring, capacity building, and staff professional development. DBC was part of this network.[47] In 2010, all the

---

[44] "Attention to Dreams, To Lift the Hearts," in *United Women in Faith Annual Report* (New York: United Women in Faith, 2020), 2.

[45] "Sharing Thanks: Past, Present and Future," North Texas Conference of The United Methodist Church website, 11 November 2022, https://ntcumc.org/news/sharing-thanks-past-present-and-future.

[46] All the national mission institutions owned by the Woman's Division were brought under the denominational board in 1964. This structural arrangement continued until 2010, when the board returned the women's national mission institutions back to the women. Robert J. Harman, *From Missions to Mission: The History of Mission of the United Methodist Church, 1968–2000* (New York: The General Board of Global Ministries, The United Methodist Church, 2005), 187; Barbara E. Campbell, "Turning Prayer into Deeds," *New World Outlook* (General Board of Global Ministries, Fall 2018), 28.

[47] Author's interview with Hortense Tyrell, Director of National Ministries, UWF, 27 October 2021. Also, from "Caring Connections" records in the archives of Global Ministries, Atlanta, GA.

national mission institutions were returned to the original owner, the Methodist women organized for mission.

Cartography of Missional Collaborations

A mapping of collaborations as mission can be mentally visualized as a spiral-shaped, open-ended transformative mission model. Stories of the place and challenges to the mission work in the sites lead the reader to "see" patterns of dominance and resistance and collaborations forged and sustained. This process ensures on-going mission. These collaborations come under two broad categories: collaborations for direct service and those for advocacy. The latter involves prevailing memories, submerged memories of place and mission, and work for justice. These stories lead to incremental collaborations incorporating new insights, accrued wisdom, and new partnerships. It is an open-ended process repeated over and over with the accrued wisdom. It is a means by which DBS constantly becomes and bears witness in the community as church in the world.

Dallas Bethlehem Center is a quintessential story of collaborations as a way of *being* and *becoming*. It is a story of coalitions for service and advocacy, neighbouring and witnessing for community connectedness and a collective new future.

"A Rare Encounter in Mission History": The Story of Partnership between African Independent Churches and North American Mennonites

James R. Krabill

In the late 1970s, mission historian Andrew F. Walls made the rather startling assertion that Africa's independent churches (AICs)[1] – with their enthusiastic embrace of the Word of God – should perhaps be considered Africa's Anabaptists. He noted that

> the independents have been marked above all by a radical biblicism – daring Christians in effect to live by what the Bible says. The Word is even visibly present when the charismatic person speaks, led by the free Spirit. Its visible presence is exalted even among groups who can barely read it; and more than one notable spiritual man has been anxious to demonstrate that, although illiterate, he can quote the Bible accurately and appositely. In some ways, the radical biblicists among the independents may be compared to the Anabaptists in Western Church history: the same wild variety, the same strong cohesion as "people of God," the same insistence on following the Word as they hear it.[2]

Walls' claim came exactly 20 years after North American Mennonites – a successor branch of the 16th century Anabaptists – first made contact with West African independent churches and began exploring partnership relationships. In this essay, I will trace the origins and history of those relationships and describe some of the joint ministries carried out between the partners over 6 decades and in 12 sub-Saharan African countries. I will conclude by analyzing what lessons for the global faith family might be learned from these relationships, which the Princeton-based Overseas Ministries Study Center executive director, Thomas John Hastings, has qualified as "a rare encounter in mission history."[3]

---

[1] The acronym "AIC" has been variously used in academic circles to represent African *Independent* Churches, African *Initiated* Churches, African *Indigenous* Churches, African *Instituted* Churches, and at the suggestion of Jehu Hanciles more recently, African *Immigrant* Churches. We will employ a variety of these terms throughout the course of this essay.

[2] Andrew F. Walls, "The Challenge of the African Independent Churches: The Anabaptists of Africa?" *The Occasional Bulletin of Missionary Research* 3: 1 (April 1979), 50. Walls' article cited here was eventually reprinted in a collection of his writings, *The Missionary Movement in Christian History: Studies in the Transmission of Faith* (Maryknoll, NY: Orbis Books, 1996), 111–18.

[3] These comments by Hastings were offered in the context of his endorsement for the book *Unless a Grain of Wheat: A Story of Friendship Between African Independent Churches and North American Mennonites*, ed. Thomas A. Oduro, Jonathan P. Larson, and James R. Krabill (Carlisle, Cumbria, UK: Langham Global Library, 2021), i. The book chronicles 60 years of AIC-Mennonite relationships.

How the Story Began

In 1958, Mennonite Board of Missions (MBM), headquartered in Elkhart, Indiana, received a letter of invitation to visit a group of unaffiliated congregations in eastern Nigeria who had listened to *The Mennonite Hour* – an MBM internationally transmitted radio broadcast – and were interested in learning more about Mennonites. Mission workers Edwin and Irene Weaver were appointed the following year to begin a ministry with these churches and eventually discovered scores of other similar movements scattered throughout Nigeria and all along the coast of West Africa in Dahomey (Benin), Togo, Ghana, Côte d'Ivoire, Liberia, and Sierra Leone.

Few Westerner observers in the 1950s knew much about these emerging movements. "Anthropologists had studied the exotic Cargo cults in the South Pacific and the Peyote religion practiced among Native Americans," noted Mennonite missiologist Wilbert R. Shenk. "But mission scholars saw no reason to devote time to the study of nativistic, syncretistic, or other movements reacting to Christianity. Such phenomena were generally not recognized as being of direct relevance to Christian missions."[4] The indigenous churches sprouting up all across sub-Saharan Africa during this period were founded by leaders wanting to avoid foreign control in order to develop patterns of worship and theological understanding that comported with an African worldview and culture. Instead of asking what they might learn from this widespread indigenous phenomenon, most Western missions and their churches reacted strongly against AICs.

Mennonite mission workers arriving in southeastern Nigeria in the late 1950s were quickly plunged into a world completely unknown to them. In subsequent years, scholars like Harold W. Turner would engage in serious study of African and other new religious movements and discover that wherever in the world Western Christianity confronted traditional, "primal" worldviews, a wide range of religious activity resulted. Some groups emerging from this encounter typically chose to remain close to the tradition and never really qualified – by their own intent and desire – as "Christian churches," properly defined. Other groups made radical breaks with the past, but had little interest in reproducing Western forms of Christianity on their way to New Testament faith.[5] But none of these studies by Turner and others had yet appeared in 1959, leaving the Weavers to do their own research and make their own discoveries.

What the missionary couple *did* encounter were other Western mission agencies working in the region that were generally critical and hostile to local

---

[4] Wilbert R. Shenk, "A Short History," in *Unless a Grain of Wheat*, 9.

[5] One of Turner's earliest attempts to identify this spectrum of "neo-primal," "synthetist," "Hebraist," and "independent church" reality appeared in V.E.W. Hayward, ed., *African Independent Church Movements* (London: Edinburgh House Press, 1963), 84–94. Other important works include David B. Barrett, *Schism and Renewal in Africa* (Nairobi, Addis Ababa, Lusaka: Oxford Press, 1968); and M.L. Daneel, *Quest for Belonging* (Harare: Mambo Press, 1987). For a complete listing of Turner's contribution to this field of study, see the bibliography compiled by Jocelyn Murray in A.F. Walls and Wilbert R. Shenk, eds., *Exploring New Religious Movements: Essays in Honour of Harold W. Turner* (Elkhart, IN: Mission Focus, 1990), 207–15.

indigenous movements. Occasionally, an experienced missionary showed sympathy and would encourage the Mennonites to continue developing relationships with these marginalized groups. But, for the most part, the long-established missions were united in their advice to the Weavers: "Leave!"

Notwithstanding this consensus, the Mennonites felt compelled to stay. Clearly, this place was an unconventional "mission field." A rethinking of strategy would be required. It was discerned that the most promising posture was dialogical interaction between the indigenous churches – who had no structures bringing them together – and the long-established missions, with their inter-mission council. This initial approach proved effective.

Gradually, leaders in all the groups agreed to meet periodically to get acquainted. Such encounters required honest conversation where grievances and misunderstandings were acknowledged and dealt with. Negative stereotypes of "the other" were named and repudiated, thus clearing the way for respectful listening to one another. Gradually, a basis for relationship was established and the mission-founded churches cooperated in staffing a Bible school that served AIC needs for training their leaders. Remarkably, five different projects emerged over a several year period from the Weavers' creative initiative and persistent leadership – a scholarship study programme, the Inter-Church Team, the United Independent Churches Bible School, the Inter-Study Group, and the Independent Church Fellowship.[6]

"Each of these projects," notes Wilbert Shenk, "was practical and focused on acknowledged needs. Each one brought together people and groups who otherwise would not have cooperated with one another. The goal was to lay the foundation of trust and respect while meeting concrete needs."[7]

---

[6] See James R. Krabill, "Evangelical and Ecumenical Dimensions of Walking with AICs," in *Evangelical, Ecumenical, and Anabaptist Missiologies in Conversation*, eds. James R. Krabill, Walter Sawatsky, and Charles E. Van Engen (Maryknoll, NY: Orbis Books, 2006), 244; Wilbert R. Shenk, "Mission Agency and African Independent Churches," *International Review of Mission* 63: 252 (October 1974), 482–85, and Wilbert R. Shenk, "'Go Slow Through Uyo': Dialogue as Missionary Method," in *Fullness of Life for All: Challenges for Mission in Early 21st Century*, edited by M.L. Daneel, Charles Van Engen, and Hendrik Vroom (New York: Editions Rodopi, 2003), 337–39; and Edwin Weaver and Irene Weaver, *The Uyo Story* (Elkhart, IN: Mennonite Board of Missions, 1970).

[7] See Shenk, "'Go Slow Through Uyo,'" 336. The broader context of the Mennonite experiment in West Africa and its impact on the initial group of Nigerian leaders requesting Mennonite involvement are described more fully in R. Bruce Yoder, "Mennonite Mission Theorists and Practitioners in Southeastern Nigeria: Changing Contexts and Strategy at the Dawn of the Postcolonial Era," *International Bulletin of Missionary Research* 37: 3 (July 2013), 138–44; and R. Bruce Yoder, "The Challenge of Multiple – and Sometimes Conflicting – Stories," in *Unless a Grain of Wheat*, 136–38. See also his unpublished PhD dissertation, "Mennonite Missionaries and African Independent Churches: The Development of an Anabaptist Missiology in West Africa: 1958–1967" (Boston University, 2016).

Partnerships Expand on Multiple Fronts

The Biafran War in Nigeria erupted in 1966 and disrupted all areas of life. Foreign staff had to evacuate, and all programme activity was suspended. Even though the Mennonite mission presence in the region was scheduled for reduction and phasing out, the war forced an immediate cessation. Unable to return to Nigeria, the Weavers travelled up and down the West African coast to gain a better grasp of the indigenous movements in each country. Following the pattern of ministry developed in southeastern Nigeria, this process meant seeking out leaders of both independent and mission-founded churches. Their findings paralleled those they had discovered earlier – mutual distrust and animosity, absence of relationship and communication, lack of appreciation for "the other," and little desire or vision for doing anything differently. Many leaders, however, acknowledged deep-seated conflict within the Christian community; and from the AICs, the Weavers heard repeated requests for help in training.

In four of the countries visited by the Weavers – Liberia, Côte d'Ivoire, Ghana, and Dahomey (Benin) – relationships were established and programmes emerged. In both Benin and Ghana, leaders from a wide assortment of AICs came together to form Bible study groups. The Good News Theological Seminary on the outskirts of Accra, Ghana, grew out of the Weavers' initiative and, in 2021, celebrated 50 years of uninterrupted service and theological training with AIC leaders.[8] Several dozen AIC and mission-founded denominations in Benin's Marxist-imposed Interconfessional Protestant Council entered into conversation with the Mennonites, requesting partnership in three specific areas, in health services, agricultural development, and Bible training for church leaders. That relationship, now spanning 40 years, has resulted in the creation of Bethesda Hospital, a micro-loan initiative, a community development and environmental sanitation programme, and the Benin Bible Institute that, since its inception in 1994, has trained nearly 1,500 graduates currently serving in leadership roles in 70 denominations and other institutions throughout the country.[9]

---

[8] Thomas A. Oduro, "The History and Pedagogy of the Good News Training Institute in Accra," in *Ministry in Partnership with African Independent Churches*, ed. David A. Shank (Elkhart, IN: Mennonite Board of Missions, 1991), 132–60; Thomas O. Oduro, "Healing a Strained Relationship between African Independent Churches and Western Mission-Founded Churches in Ghana, 1967–2017: The Role of Good News Theological Seminary, Accra, Ghana," in *African Instituted Christianity and the Decolonization of Development*, ed. Phillipp Öhlmann, Wilhelm Gräb, and Marie-Luise Frost (Abingdon: Routledge, 2020), 227–39; Edwin Weaver and Irene Weaver, *From Kuku Hill: Among Indigenous Churches in West Africa* (Elkhart, IN: Institute of Mennonite Studies, 1975).
[9] Rodney Hollinger-Janzen, "A Biblical Teaching Program by the Interconfessional Protestant Council of Benin with Mennonite Cooperation," in *Ministry in Partnership with African Independent Churches*, 161–70; Saturnin D. Afaton and Marianne Goldschmidt-Nussbaumer, "Activités Sanitaires du Conseil Interconfessionnel des Églises Protestantes en République Populaire du Bénin," in *Ministry in Partnership with African Independent Churches*, 381–94; Nancy Frey and Lynda Hollinger-Janzen, *3-D Gospel in Benin: Beninese Churches Invite Mennonites to Holistic Partnership* (Elkhart, IN: Mennonite Mission Network, 2015); Victor Gbedo, *Histoire des pères fondateurs de*

In Côte d'Ivoire, things developed very differently with the Harrist Church – the largest and historically-predominant indigenous church in the country. There, Mennonites responded to the call from the head of the church, John Ahui, to "help me water the tree" by carrying out research on the prophet-evangelist William Wadé Harris,[10] offering public lectures, creating a resource centre,[11] and partnering with Harrist Church leaders among the Dida people to establish a village-based Theological Education by Extension (TEE) Bible study programme[12] and collect and publish over 500 indigenous hymns composed by local musicians.[13] Considerable effort was also invested in building bridges between the Harrists and Western mission-founded churches in the country, the Roman Catholics, mainline Protestants, evangelicals, and pentecostals.[14]

While Mennonite and AIC relationships were developing in West Africa, there was increasing interest in exploring whether similar partnerships might be welcomed in the southern part of the continent. Beginning already in 1968, fact-finding trips were made to Swaziland (now Eswantini), Lesotho, Botswana, and South Africa.[15] Pilot projects were launched in three of these countries, but placing workers in South Africa at that time proved problematic.[16]

In the end, Edwin and Irene Weaver, having completed their West African tour, were requested to travel to the region and develop a working strategy for partnership relationships between Mennonites and AICs. The couple established residence in Gaborone, Botswana, from January 1975 to May 1977, and interviewed multiple potential AIC leaders and partners.[17] "But there was no

---

l'organisation non-gouvernementale Bethesda en République du Bénin (Cotonou: ONG Bethesda, 2016).

[10] David A. Shank, *Prophet Harris: The "Black Elijah" of West Africa*, abridged by Jocelyn Murray (Leiden: Brill, 1994).

[11] David A. Shank, "The Work of the Group for Religious and Biblical Studies in West Africa (GERB)," in *Ministry of Missions to African Independent Churches*, ed. David A. Shank (Elkhart, IN: Mennonite Board of Missions, 1987), 13–32.

[12] James R. Krabill, "Ministry among the Dida Harrists of Côte d'Ivoire: A Case Study," in *Ministry of Mission to African Independent Churches*, 33–55; Modeste Lévry Beugré, "Like in Marriage There Is a Profound Mystery That You Can't Explain," in *Unless a Grain of Wheat*, 171–73.

[13] James R. Krabill, *The Hymnody of the Harrist Church among the Dida of South-Central Ivory Coast (1913–1949)* (Frankfurt am Main: Peter Lang, 1995); James R. Krabill, "Hymn-collecting among Dida Harrists," *Ethnodoxology: Global Forum on the Arts and Christian Faith* 2: 1 (April 2014), A20–A36; Alphonse Kobli Beugré, "When I Was Chosen as a Preacher, I Wanted to Understand More of God's Word," in *Unless a Grain of Wheat*, 69–71.

[14] David A. Shank, "A Decade with God's Mission among African-Initiated Churches in West Africa," *Mission Focus Annual Review* 11 (2003): 85–104.

[15] Don Jacobs and James Bertsche, foreword to "Southern African Study" (unpublished manuscript, 1970), iii; James Juhnke, "A Collection of Writings by Mennonites on Southern Africa," reproduced and edited by Vern Preheim (unpublished manuscript, 1972), 53.

[16] Shenk, "A Short History," 19.

[17] James E. Bertsche, *CIM/AIMM: A Story of Vision, Commitment and Grace* (Elkhart, IN: Africa Inter-Mennonite Mission, 1998), 443–590.

grand strategic blueprint," writes Wilbert Shenk. "The culture of each country was unique – shaped by its history, ethnic groups, languages, natural resources, economy, and political system."[18]

A wide variety of ministries between AICs and Mennonites throughout the region took the shape of what was already being experienced in West Africa – ministries of worship encounters,[19] Bible study and training,[20] historical research,[21] marriage enrichment seminars,[22] the development of AIDS resources,[23] intercultural learning,[24] and the building of deep friendships.[25]

In addition to these more localized or regional initiatives, Mennonites also worked with AICs to foster friendships and conversations across the continent of Africa. Efforts of this nature included hosting pan-African conferences with scholars, mission workers, and church leaders serving in academic institutions and various grassroots ministries. Two such gatherings – in Abidjan (1986) and in Kinshasa (1989) – brought together several dozen partners and produced over 40 published case studies of relationships being established.[26] An occasional newsletter, *The Review of AICs*, was also produced and widely diffused for nearly 15 years (1990–2004) with materials by and about AICs, Mennonites, and

---

[18] Shenk, "A Short History," 20.

[19] Nathan Dirks, "Sounds of Singing Soaked the Wooden Ceiling Beams, Wafting a Sweet Aroma," in *Unless a Grain of Wheat*, 149–51; Phil Lindell Detweiler, "God-Centered Prosperity," in *Unless a Grain of Wheat*, 31–33.

[20] Bryan Born, "Reading the Bible through the Lens of the Spirit," in *Unless a Grain of Wheat*, 49–52; Veliswa Mbambo, "The Sweetness of Unity in Christ," in *Unless a Grain of Wheat*, 83–84; Reuben Mgodeli, "Bible Study Has Increased Our Confidence and Our Standing with Other Christian Churches," in *Unless a Grain of Wheat*, 155–57.

[21] Rachel Hilty Friesen, "I Soaked in the Memories of the Prophet of the Land," in *Unless a Grain of Wheat*, 90–92.

[22] Rudy Dirks, "It Is Impossible for a Man to Be Faithful to One Woman," in *Unless a Grain of Wheat*, 76–78.

[23] Sherill Hostetter, "A Tribute to Umfundisi Hlobisile – A Model for Women in Church Leadership," in *Unless a Grain of Wheat*, 98–100.

[24] Sandi McLaughlin and Elinor Miller, "'These Are No Ordinary Clothes, but Special Clothes for Divine Work,'" in *Unless a Grain of Wheat*, 124–27; Moreno Rankopo, "We Have Learned Together about Worship, Marriage, Prophecy, and Burnt Offerings," in *Unless a Grain of Wheat*, 110–12.

[25] Thompson Mpongwana Adonis, "They Came to Work *with* Us," in *Unless a Grain of Wheat*, 127–29; Tim Bertsche, "I Shared a Long Journey of Discovery with Rev. Philip Mothetho, Friend and Brother," in *Unless a Grain of Wheat*, 160–62; Sharon Dirks, "The Silent, Invisible, and Mysterious Ways That God's Kingdom Grows," in *Unless a Grain of Wheat*, 180–83; Darrel Hostetter, "In Honor of Isaac Dlamini – My Partner, Colleague, Language Teacher, and Best Friend," in *Unless a Grain of Wheat*, 112–15; Jonathan P. Larson, "Sacred Oil, Rustle of Robes," in *Unless a Grain of Wheat*, 176–78; Isaac Moshoeshoe, "Mennonite Affirmation of Us Ended Our Feeling of Aloneness," in *Unless a Grain of Wheat*, 115–17; Joseph Motswaosele, "Friendship Flowered between Us as We Prayed for Each Other," in *Unless a Grain of Wheat*, 119–21; Albert Maphasa Setumo, "There Was Nothing That Separated Our Spirits," in *Unless a Grain of Wheat*, 162–63.

[26] Shank, ed., *Ministry of Missions to African Independent Churches*; Shank, ed., *Ministry in Partnership with African Independent Churches*.

a few other Western expatriate missionaries and scholars.[27] More recently, a collection of over 60 testimonials from both Mennonites and AIC partners have been compiled and published for the purpose of documenting personal accounts of events, encounters, conversations, or discoveries arising from various partnership experiences and casting light on the nature, texture, and significance of those experiences.[28] Reflecting on the stories recounted in this collection and the long relationship between Mennonites and AICs, Boston University's Dana Robert qualifies this partnership, expressed in multiple and diverse forms, as "one of the greatest stories of Christian mission in the twentieth century."[29]

Looking back on 6 decades of Mennonite relationships with AICs in 12 countries of sub-Saharan Africa, Wilbert Shenk has identified some of the guiding principles which have shaped mutual partnership ministries:

1. Mennonite agencies go only where they are invited into a working relationship with AICs.
2. Having heard AIC leaders in West, Central, and Southern Africa call for assistance in equipping their people to understand the Bible more adequately, Mennonites regard their main contribution to be encouraging and enabling study of the Scriptures.
3. Mennonite workers will focus on equipping church leaders through training appropriate to the background of the leaders and the needs of their churches.
4. Workers will facilitate constructive inter-church relations, both among AICs and between AICs and the traditional denominations.
5. Mennonite agencies will avoid providing subsidies for capital projects or supporting operating budgets for churches or institutions.
6. It is not the goal of Mennonite agencies to establish Mennonite churches alongside AICs. If such churches should emerge, it will be the result of local initiative, not the foreign agency.[30]

Qualities Contributing to a Partnership Stance

In 1974, 15 years into the Mennonite-AIC experience, David A. Shank reflected on some of the qualities that might enable Mennonites to relate to African-initiated churches. His conjectures, among others, included these:

- We have a believers' church stance that does not require institutional identity with American Mennonitism as a precondition for work within

---

[27] This publication, compiled and edited by Stan Nussbaum, Mennonite mission worker with AICs and erstwhile director of the Centre for New Religious Movements at Selly Oak Colleges, Birmingham, UK, featured book reviews, teaching curricula, ministry accounts, obituaries, project proposals, requests for assistance, trip reports, and much more (see the Nussbaum reference in Oduro, Larson, and Krabill, eds., *Unless a Grain of Wheat*, 198).

[28] Oduro, Larson, and Krabill, eds., *Unless a Grain of Wheat.*

[29] Ibid., back cover.

[30] Shenk, "A Short History," 20.

and/or for a movement, or as a necessary consequence of missionary endeavour.

- We are latecomers to the scene in West Africa and do not have to overcome a stigmatizing history of colonial involvement; the believers' church stance is one of non-identification with the powers that be, colonial or otherwise.
- Our history of rejection – sometimes oppression – by mainline Christianity gives us a measure of credibility to movements that have the same experience.
- Our history of being a "third way" as compared to the Catholic or Protestant options in the sixteenth century, to the liberal or fundamentalist options, and the service or evangelism polarizations of this [20th] century, helps us understand those who do not fit the usual – even Western – ecclesiastical categories.
- We have a tradition of biblicism as compared to philosophical theology.
- Our tradition of distance from and critique of Western culture from within makes us open to others who from their own tradition maintain distance and critique from without.
- Our tradition of ethical guidelines – often perceived as legalism and moralism – gives us understanding of movements that lay down explicit life patterns in an attempt to give guidance through the maze of cultural confusion.
- Our tradition of congregational consensus and discipline gives us an openness to collective patterns of life that are often far removed from the individualistic faith and spiritual life patterns of much of Western Christianity.
- Our history and tradition of lay leadership and evangelism make us open to leadership patterns that are less acceptable to hierarchically or institutionally controlled ecclesiologies.
- Our nonresistant tradition differs from most missions that have been tied to the Western powers. Some independent movements – the Kimbanguists in Zaire [Congo] and the Harrists in Côte d'Ivoire – share this stance.
- The small size of our church keeps us from being a threat to others.
- Our struggle to be a confessing church under the pressures of ethnicity gives us understanding and insight into ethnic movements working toward mature faith.[31]

Some of these characteristics no doubt predisposed Mennonites to change course in mission strategy in the early 1950s – just a few years prior to the AIC encounter in West Africa – when Mennonite workers serving in northern Argentina chose to shut down their mission compound with store, school, clinic, and chapel, designed as an outreach ministry *to* indigenous peoples of the Chaco region, and instead work *alongside* emerging grassroots Christian churches

---

[31] David A. Shank, *Mission from the Margins: Selected Writings from the Life and Ministry of David A. Shank*, ed. James R. Krabill (Elkhart, IN: Institute of Mennonite Studies, 2010), 337–38.

cropping up throughout the area.[32] Such decisions have likewise been foundational and direction-setting for Mennonite ministries over many years in "partnering with grassroots African-initiated churches, encouraging the growth of home-grown messianic faith communities in Israel, in nurturing locally-inspired Anabaptist networks in the UK, South Korea, Australia, New Zealand, and South Africa, and in developing North American urban programs in which participants are challenged to 'see the face of God in the city,' rather than importing their own personal passions, purposes, or programs."[33]

Four Emerging Principles for Developing Partnerships

A number of guiding principles have stood the test of time for Mennonites in developing ministry partnerships. Among them are the following:

1. Partner Contexts Shape Relationships and Ministries

None of the partnerships Mennonites have worked with over the years are identical to others, since all are shaped by the specific histories, personalities, and socio-religious contexts which give birth to them. This fact means that, while one does gain valuable experience from prior relationships, each new encounter requires starting the careful listening and negotiation process all over again to avoid the trap of making assumptions about new partners who may hold values and agendas quite different from anything previously encountered.

2. Identifying Willing Partners Involves a Process of Discernment

In 2013, Mennonite Mission Network determined that virtually all of its ministries had derived over the years from four primary sources: *individual calling, US constituency, international partners,* and *agency priorities.* This procedure enabled the agency to eliminate the multiple requests coming from other origins and to focus instead on nurturing those which had proven to be most valuable in producing lasting, fruitful partnerships. This system also required of the agency a commitment to balancing the requests and aspirations of *all* partners so that the power, financial resources, and loudest voices did not override or drown out other partners of equal importance and value.

3. Partners Must Define Expectations and Articulate What They "Bring to the Table"

The diagram below appeared in a 27-page booklet produced by Mennonite Mission Network, entitled *Walking Together: Following God's Call to Reconciliation.*[34] In this publication, the agency articulated who it was and what

---

[32] Wilbert R. Shenk, *Changing Frontiers of Mission* (Maryknoll, NY: Orbis Books, 1999), 60–64; Willis Horst, Ute Paul, and Frank Paul, *Mission Without Conquest: An Alternative Missionary Practice* (Carlisle, Cumbria, UK: Langham Global Library, 2015).

[33] James R. Krabill, forward to *Mission Without Conquest*, x.

[34] Mennonite Mission Network, *Walking Together: Following God's Call to Reconciliation* (Elkhart, IN: Mennonite Mission Network, 2013; rev. ed. 2017).

it "brought to the table" for potential partners to consider. Chapters included, "What is our context?" "Who are we and where did we come from?" "Where are Anabaptist Christians today?" "What is our calling?" "What do we believe about mission?" "What are the values that support our organization?" "What sources inspire and give birth to our ministries?" and "What is our commitment?" The booklet was translated into several languages and used in many places around the world as a starting point for discussions with groups, organizations, or national churches interested in exploring possible partnership relationships with the agency.

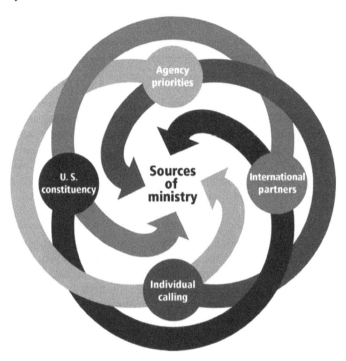

4. Knowing Where One Is Situated on the "Partnership Relationship Continuum"
Is Helpful in Avoiding Misunderstanding and Reducing the Risk of Failure

During the 1990s, Mennonite Mission Network developed an instrument to help partners on all sides discern what they expected from a potential partnership. Referred to as the "Partnership Relationship Continuum," it identified three levels of potential engagement: Cooperation, Coordination, and Collaboration.

An accompanying text of case studies provided practical illustrations of various choices made and generated fruitful conversations between potential partners prior to entering into commitments they might in the long run be unwilling or unable to honour.

The Partnership Relationship Continuum

Cooperation	Coordination	Collaboration
• Interaction happens as needed.	• Interaction is around the specific project.	• Organizations are fully committed to long-term project and relationships.
• No need for united vision overall.	• Overall goals of partners must be compatible.	• Common new mission and goals are created.
• No joint planning is required.	• Planning is project specific.	• Comprehensive planning and joint strategies are needed.
Cooperation	**Coordination**	**Collaboration**
Cooperation	**Coordination**	**Collaboration**
• New relationships occur within existing roles.	• Roles are negotiated, but function relatively independently.	• New organizational structure and/or clearly defined roles are created.
• Authority rests solely with individual organizations	• Authority rests with organizations, but decision. making is coordinated.	• Authority is distributed to partners to balance ownership and accomplish joint purposes.
• Resources are kept separate.	• Resources are shared for project purposes.	• Resources are jointly secured or pooled and jointly managed.

© Mennonite Mission Network

Concluding Reflections: Caution, Honesty, Realism, Humility

Careful planning and the best of intentions do not mean that partnerships turn out the way they were designed or imagined. In his sobering 400-page volume *Power and Partnership: A History of the Protestant Mission Movement* (2013), Jonathan S. Barnes reveals that the history of partnerships has not been a particularly glamorous one. The term "partnership" itself, according to Barnes, originated during the colonial period and was often employed by the white minority in power to secure their ongoing and future control and influence. Closely aligned with the idea of trusteeship, the term was carefully designed to communicate an "eventual levelling of power dynamics in relationships," while remaining "just short of autonomy and independence."[35] Freedom and autonomy would someday come, but in the meantime, "it was the West's 'sacred trust' to lead others in the process of becoming enlightened and civilized."[36]

Barnes does not jump quickly to happy endings on this matter. "Although today we rightfully celebrate living in a post-colonial age," he warns, "unless churches are willing to acknowledge that inherited issues of Global church power, paternalism, and control are still lived out in our present ecumenical relationships, partnership will be impossible to realize."[37] Chastened understandings and fresh terminology are today employed to capture the goodwill and finest intentions of all parties concerned. But "regardless of what terms are used to describe these relationships, or what theologies are used to undergird them," says Barnes, "if they are to lead to solidarity and mutuality,

---

[35] Jonathan S. Barnes, *Power and Partnership: A History of the Protestant Mission Movement* (Eugene, OR: Pickwick Publications, 2013), 3–4.
[36] Ibid., 406.
[37] Ibid., 416.

inherited legacies of colonialism, neocolonialism, and differentials of power must be acknowledged and addressed."[38]

It is likely too early to undertake a full evaluation of the six decades of partnerships which have developed between North American Mennonites and AICs in a dozen sub-Saharan African countries. It is indeed gratifying and humbling to hear others describe these relationships as "a rare encounter in mission history" or even more as "one of the greatest stories of Christian mission in the twentieth century." But partnerships have always been complicated endeavours, fraught with all the human and institutional failings which Barnes so accurately names. If, however, the Mennonite-AIC story can contribute to incremental steps toward a day of new and transformed relationships, then "it may be possible," in Barnes' own words, "for a new ecumenical World Christianity to emerge – an ecumenical Christianity where we can be not only partners, but friends."[39]

---

[38] Ibid., 422.
[39] Ibid., 423.

The Missional Collaboration of The Pentecostal Church of Chile and the United Church of Christ: The Holy Spirit Moving People and Congregations across Borders

Christopher P. Ney

In the second half of the 20th century, the word "partnership" was adopted widely to describe relationships among churches in the global community. Explaining the historical context for the use of this term, Dana Robert says, "among mainline Protestants, self-criticism of paternalistic mission practices led to new mission theories of 'partnership' from the 1960s onward."[1] Despite its common usage, the term is contested because of the challenge of navigating relationships across lines of difference – including nationality, ethnicity, language, and culture – and unequal resources.[2] Seeking to promote more authentic relationships, missiologist Andrew Kirk provides a theological and ethical definition for the ideal type for Christian partnership:

> Within world Christianity, "partnership" expresses a relationship between churches based on trust, mutual recognition and reciprocal interchange. It rules out completely any notion of "senior" or "junior", "parent" and "child", or even "older" and "younger". It is a term designed to show how different parts of the Church belong to one another and find their fulfilment through sharing a common life.[3]

But human relationships are messier than ideal types. Whether in the local church or global mission, faith is lived in complex relationship networks.[4] This case study represents the nearly 40-year history of partnership between the Pentecostal Church of Chile and the United Church of Christ as told through the stories of faithful people who responded to God's call to cross borders for the gospel. Whatever the missionary impulse means for Christianity, it is carried by individuals in community and the relationships they form. Examining the practices of partnership as they have been lived reveals the complexity of these relationships, even between two denominations with deep ecumenical commitments.[5] Nonetheless, this history shows growth in the understanding and practice of partnership as faithful people strive toward authentic relationship across lines of difference.

---

[1] Dana L. Robert, *Christian Mission: How Christianity Became a World Religion* (Malden, MA: Wiley-Blackwell, 2009), 71.
[2] For an extensive review of the history of this term in ecumenical conversation, see Jonathan S. Barnes, *Power and Partnership: A History of the Protestant Mission Movement* (Eugene, OR: Pickwick Publications, 2013).
[3] J. Andrew Kirk, *What Is Mission?: Theological Explorations* (Minneapolis, MN: Fortress Press, 2000), 184.
[4] Bonnie J. Miller-McElmore, "Revisiting the Living Human Web: Theological Education and the Role of Clinical Pastoral Education," *Journal of Pastoral Care and Counseling* 62: 1–2 (Spring–Summer 2008), 3–17.
[5] Nancy Ammerman, "Rethinking Religion: Toward a Practice Approach," *American Journal of Sociology* 126: 1 (July 2020), 6–51.

The Holy Spirit in the Global South

Unlike many mission relationships that were established primarily through the action of churches in the North Atlantic, the partnership between the Pentecostal Church of Chile and the United Church of Christ began through the agency of Christians in the Global South, thanks to the ecumenism of the founder of the Pentecostal Church of Chile, Bishop Enrique Chávez Campos.[6]

Pentecostalism in Chile traces its roots to early 20th century revivals in Valparaiso, Chile, led by the Rev. Dr Willis Hoover, a missionary from the United States. Hoover led his congregation to experience the "gifts of the spirit," but Methodist authorities ordered him to cease the worship that led to ecstatic practices. Hoover and his congregation trusted the power of the Holy Spirit, rejecting denominational authority and forming the Methodist Pentecostal Church instead.[7] Chilean Pentecostal theologian Juan Sepúlveda explains that the loss of external financing and theological education required the new church to become self-financing and self-directing in its pastoral practice. "Thus," Sepúlveda says, "Chilean Pentecostalism became the first example of an autonomous Protestantism."[8]

In 1946 1947, Enrique Chávez Campos, a pastor of the Methodist Pentecostal Church in Curicó, Chile, broke away from the parent Pentecostal denomination in a conflict involving finances, forming The Pentecostal Church of Chile (IPC).[9] Curicó is a provincial city in Chile's agricultural heartland. Missionary and missiologist Carmelo Álvarez identifies Chávez as one of four early leaders in the Latin American Pentecostal "ecumenism of the spirit," and he had a global vision of the church. Based on interviews he conducted, Alvarez reports that Chávez always respected ecumenical leaders. He tried to establish a relationship with the Pentecostal Holiness Church in the United States, a denomination with Methodist roots. But Chávez found that they were too conservative for the Chileans.[10] In addition to his personal convictions, Chávez also responded, both positively and negatively, to factors that sought to influence Chilean Pentecostalism and world Christianity.

---

[6] Carmelo Álvarez, "La Vocación Ecuménica de Los Pentecostales," in *Historia de la Iglesia Pentecostal de Chile*, by C. Álvarez, P. Correa, M. Poblete, and P. Guell (Santiago, Chile: Ediciones Rehue, n.d.), 7.

[7] Willis Collins Hoover, *History of the Pentecostal Revival in Chile: The Famous First-hand Story by the Founder of the Pentecostal Work in Chile*, trans. Mario G. Hoover (Santiago, Chile: Imprenta Eben-Ezer, 2000), 82–97.

[8] Juan Sepúlveda, "Theological Characteristics of an Indigenous Pentecostalism: Chile," in *In the Power of the Spirit: The Pentecostal Challenge to Historic Churches in Latin America*, ed. Dennis A. Smith and Benjamin F. Gutiérrez (Louisville, KY: Presbyterian Church USA, 1996), 2.

[9] Carmelo Alvarez, "Joining the World Council of Churches: The Ecumenical Story of Pentecostalism in Chile," in *Pentecostalism and Christian Unity: Ecumenical Documents and Critical Assessments*, ed. Wolfgang Vondey (Eugene, OR: Pickwick Publications, 2010), 38.

[10] Carmelo Alvarez, "Sharing in God's Mission: The Evangelical Pentecostal Union of Venezuela and the Christian Church (Disciples of Christ) in the United States, 1960-1980," (PhD thesis, Vrije Universiteit, 2006), 49.

In the 1950s, the US fundamentalist pastor Carl McIntire promoted his campaign against the World Council of Churches (WCC) to the IPC. Seeking to exploit the anti-Catholic sentiments held by many Chilean Pentecostals, McIntire claimed that the WCC would lead Latin American *evangélicos* back to Rome. Invited to speak at an annual assembly of the IPC, McIntire even associated Roman Catholicism with paganism and claimed it was a sign of the anti-Christ. Chávez questioned these extreme claims and travelled to the United States to learn more about the ecumenical movement himself and meet with representatives of the WCC. Upon his return to Chile, he reported what he had seen and heard and asked the church to begin the process of affiliation with the WCC.[11] Then, in 1960, Chile suffered a devastating earthquake, creating a national need and opportunity for pentecostal churches to cooperate with each other and international partner churches. A new organization, *Ayuda Cristiana Evangélica* (Evangelical Christian Aid) was formed to support relief and recovery efforts.[12] Although Chávez faced opposition from other Chilean pentecostal church leaders and from within the IPC, he led the IPC to join the WCC in 1961, together with two other Chilean Pentecostal denominations. These groups became the first Pentecostal churches to join the global body, an important contribution to the history of global Christianity. By fostering relationships with other churches, Chávez crafted an ecumenical pentecostalism.[13]

Then in 1968, Chávez sent Rev. Gerardo Valdivia to New York City as a missionary to establish the Pentecostal Church of North America. Valdivia's presence led to the relationships that formed the mission partnership between the IPC and the United Church of Christ (UCC). Valdivia's memoir, *Misión en Libre Asociación,* describes the challenges that he faced in this assignment and his commitment to honour his bishop's wishes and do God's will.[14] A pivotal moment in Valdivia's ministry – and the history of the IPC-UCC relationship – took place, strangely enough, in Brooklyn, NY. In 1980, Valdivia drove a church van through central Brooklyn to gather people for worship. He stopped at a parishioner's home in Sunset Park, next to a small brick church. A man emerged from the church and, upon seeing the sign on Valdivia's van, asked if they were pentecostal. Valdivia, not realizing he was speaking to that church's pastor, responded affirmatively. Then the man asked if they would like to buy the church building. A friendship formed between Valdivia and this man, Rev. Eino Salo, pastor of a UCC Scandinavian Congregational Church.[15] A letter from UCC conference minister Rev. Thomas Boates to the UCC mission secretary helps to explain the motivation of the UCC to develop this relationship – denominational officials saw the changing demographics of urban neighbourhoods and the

---

[11] Alvarez, *Historia de la Iglesia Pentecostal de Chile*, 45.
[12] Alvarez, "Sharing in God's Mission," 52.
[13] Alvarez, *Historia de la Iglesia Pentecostal de Chile*, 46.
[14] Gerardo E. Valdivia, *Misión en Libre Asociación: Relatos del trabajo misionero del Pastor Gerardo E. Valdivia Reyes en la ciudad de Nueva York, y los orígenes del Acuerdo Fraternal entre la Iglesia Unida de Cristo y la Iglesia Pentecostal de Chile* (Concepción, Chile: EEEP Ediciones, 2013), 69–70.
[15] Valdivia, *Misión en Libre Asociación*, 129–30.

worldwide growth of Pentecostalism. In this case, the neighbourhood around
Salo's church had changed dramatically with the arrival of Spanish-speaking
families, and Boates noted that greater understanding of the appeal of
pentecostalism might help the UCC reach new communities.[16] Eventually, these
pastors reached an agreement that the Pentecostal Church of North America
would use the church at 733 44th Street In Brooklyn for worship services. More
importantly, they made first contact between the IPC and the UCC.[17]

In a letter to Bishop Chávez, dated 15 October 1980, Valdivia described the
UCC as one of the most important denominations in the United States and the
possibilities that ecumenical relationship between the denominations might
offer. At the time, Valdivia worked for the National Council of Churches and
had relationships with officials in the WCC after travelling to Geneva with
Chávez as a translator. Both organizations had offices at the Interchurch Center
in Manhattan, which also housed the national offices of the UCC. Physical
proximity facilitated meetings and relationship-building with the director of
Overseas Ministries, the Rev. Dr Jeffrey Utter.[18] Five years later, a partnership
between these two denominations was celebrated and affirmed at the 15th
General Synod of the UCC held in Ames, Iowa, and at the annual meeting of the
IPC in Curicó.[19]

Initially, the goals of the partnership were broadly defined as "sharing
fellowship through visits to Assemblies of each other's denominations,"[20]
together with building mutual understanding and showing shared support for
social, educational, and theological work in each country. As a next step, Pastora
Eriqueta "Kety" Chávez Reyes (daughter of Bishop Chávez), two male pastors,
and a lay person travelled from Chile to the United States. Significantly, this first
Chilean delegation was led by a woman, reflecting the commitment of the IPC
to women's ordained leadership of local congregations. Before the advent of
digital communication, international travel was one of the few means to develop
bi-national relationships. Expense and other factors limited travel to a small
group of people, but the willingness to overcome these obstacles underscores the
commitment these churches made to partnership.

In 1989, the relationship developed through a series of "encounters" between
IPC pastors and UCC leaders. The IPC accepted a mission intern through the
United Church Board for World Ministries (UCBWM), the predecessor to
Global Ministries.[21] In that same year, stewardship of the UCC side of the

[16] T. Thomas Boates, Jr, letter to Sandra Rooney, Secretary for Mission Education and
Interpretation, United Church Board for World Ministries, 26 November 1991. Archive
of the Chile Mission Partnership, Global Ministries, Indianapolis, IN, copy in author's
possession.
[17] Valdivia, *Misión en Libre Asociación,* 137–38.
[18] Ibid., 141.
[19] Ibid., 197–99.
[20] Minutes of the Fifteenth General Synod United Church of Christ, 29 June 1985, 29.
Available at ResCarta Archive, United Church of Christ,
http://rescarta.ucc.org/jsp/RcWebBrowse.jsp
[21] Timeline of the Massachusetts Conference United Church of Christ Partnership with
IPC, 1985–1997, archive of the Chile Mission Partnership, in author's possession.

relationship began to shift from national to regional, as representatives of the Massachusetts Conference of the United Church of Christ (MACUCC), with leadership from conference minister Steve Gray, began to explore an international mission relationship. These discussions were interrupted by the death of Bishop Chávez in January 1991. The death of their founder was deeply unsettling for the IPC. However, in April of that year, the terms of a covenant between the IPC and the MACUCC were established, and a delegation from Massachusetts visited Chile with representatives from UCBWM. This new covenant built upon the initial agreement, outlining four areas of cooperative ministry: representation at the annual meetings of each group, educational exchanges in the form of delegations to each country, camps in Chile consisting of equal numbers of Chileans and North Americans for communal work, and mutual education through communication among pastors and lay people.[22] The initial commitment to this covenant was established for five years; it has been renewed and revised several times, but the basic elements remain.[23] In June, the newly-elected president of the IPC, Ulises Muñoz, attended the annual meeting of the MACUCC.[24]

A Missionary to Massachusetts

A major next step happened in 1995–1996 when IPC Pastor Oscar Aguayo, his wife Sara, and two daughters spent a year in Massachusetts as "a missionary-in-residence." The programme was described thus:

> In the spirit of partnership, the Missionary-in-Residence will come as a Christian ambassador from the Pentecostal Church of Chile to the Massachusetts Conference to broaden our faith and religious experience, share gifts, and minister to us and interpret the faith and culture of the Pentecostal Church of Chile.[25]

Preparation for the Aguayos' missionary service in Massachusetts took years of planning. The partnership archive includes significant correspondence among leaders of the UCBWM, the IPC, and the MACUCC. Topics included the work of the Chilean missionary, provisions for housing and other needs, school for the family's children, and preparation for cross-cultural immersion. Alison Buttrick, the UCBWM Mission Intern in Chile, and Myriam Hernandez Jennings, a UCC lay leader who had immigrated from Chile to Massachusetts years earlier, helped facilitate communication among these groups. Eventually, a delegation from Massachusetts to Chile provided the opportunity for a face-to-face meeting. The Aguayo family was commissioned for service at the IPC cathedral in Curicó.

---

[22] "Covenant of the Partnership in Mission Between the Pentecostal Church of Chile and the Massachusetts Conference, United Church of Christ, USA," archive of the Chile Mission Partnership, in author's possession.
[23] "Background Paper for Covenant in Koinonia between the Pentecostal Church of Chile and the Massachusetts Conference of the United Church of Christ October 2005," archive of the Chile Mission Partnership, in author's possession.
[24] "Brief History, 1985-1997," archive of the Chile Mission Partnership, in author's possession.
[25] "Fact Sheet," archive of the Chile Mission Partnership, in author's possession.

When the Aguayos arrived in Massachusetts, they met with pastors and church leaders and offered presentations about Chile and Chilean Pentecostalism to as many as 150 congregations![26] Everywhere they went, people were moved by their witness – the joy and humility they demonstrated in their shared ministry, the gift of music, and their teenage daughter's willingness to describe how faith in God helped her overcome abuse of drugs and alcohol. Many people noted the cultural difference and admired the Aguayos' ability to inspire reserved New Englanders to show emotion and religious fervour. One pastor noted that Oscar is a "loving critic of our bureaucratic pastorates to the neglect of the people in our charge."[27] Another pastor wrote that Oscar reminded his congregation "that especially in worship, the Holy Spirit is not to be fettered." The Aguayo family lived in Wellesley and developed deeper relationships there; nevertheless, needs in Chile continued to call to them. Oscar visited the city dump regularly and salvaged children's toys, sending them to Chile monthly with help from a Chilean flight attendant. Martin Copenhaver, former pastor of one of the Wellesley churches, wrote, "We know that the Lord sent you here. Otherwise, why would you come to a place like this?" He explained that the Wellesley community is sometimes inhospitable because it is "rich in things but poor in soul." Copenhaver added,

> By their presence, the Aguayos witnessed to the enormous scale and scope of what it means to bear the name of Christ – the demands that are entailed, the willingness to trust that is required, the sustaining strength that is promised.[28]

Similar comments were expressed by clergy and lay leaders at other churches, and many expressed a greater awareness of the Chilean context as a result. They also noted approvingly that the Aguayos showed great interest in learning about ministry in North America. At the same time, some North Americans expressed scepticism about pentecostalism, the lasting impact of hearing only one presentation, and the relevance of ministry activities in very different contexts. A highlight of the year-long missionary in residence programme included a forum held on 17 April 1996, featuring the Rev. Dr Mary Luti, Dr Harvey Cox, IPC President Ulises Munoz, and Pastor Oscar Aguayo. Unfortunately, the event was not recorded.

The MACUCC and UCBWM conducted extensive evaluation meetings with the Aguayo family and leaders of the missionary-in-residence programme.[29] Yet these evaluations were not shared with IPC leaders in Chile. The one-page reflections on the Aguayo's church visits were assembled into a bound booklet

---

[26] "Reflections on the visit of the Aguayo family to Massachusetts, 1995–1996. Missionary-in-Residence to the Massachusetts Conference from the Pentecostal Church of Chile" (a booklet of evaluations of the Aguayos' visits to local churches). Also, "1995 Report" and "1996 Report of the Mission Partnership," newsletter of the Massachusetts Conference United Church of Christ, archive of the Chile Mission Partnership, in author's possession.

[27] "Reflections."

[28] Martin Copenhaver, in "Reflections."

[29] Minutes of the Mission Partnership Committee, "Missionaries in Residence Evaluation, Framingham, April 29, 1996," archive of the Chile Mission Partnership, in author's possession.

for the archive and as a memento for the Aguayo family.[30] When I visited the family in Chile in 2017, they immediately showed me the booklet and talked about the events of that year as if they had only just happened. Yet they lamented that no one in Massachusetts had translated the collection. The failure of UCC officials to translate and share information in Chile represents missed opportunities for mutual growth and learning.

While different languages and cultures created challenges for the Aguayos during their year in the US, their re-entry to Chile was fraught with conflict and hard feelings. Some members of the IPC believed that the Aguayos had benefitted financially from their service in the United States. During their year in missionary service, the MACUCC provided housing, health and life insurance, transportation, and a monthly stipend of 1000 US dollars.[31] This clergy compensation package was not extravagant by US standards. But it is easy to understand the possibilities for confusion, especially because the majority of Chilean Pentecostal churches cannot provide a living wage to clergy. There was also confusion about re-entry support from the MACUCC for the Aguayo family upon their return to Chile and the Aguayos' pastoral assignment and living arrangements in Concepción, Chile.[32] These difficulties reached a critical moment in January 1997 when Pastor Aguayo resigned from all leadership positions within the IPC. Correspondence from President Ulises Munoz to the MACUCC affirmed that Pastor Aguayo's status was an internal concern of the IPC but that the conflict the family experienced was related to their work as missionaries to the United States. The letter showed sensitivity to personal and professional boundaries, expressing regret that the IPC had not participated in the evaluation process at the conclusions of the Aguayos' service. But it reaffirmed the commitment to a healthy relationship between the denominations.[33] Further correspondence from January 1997 shows that Aguayo rescinded his resignation after consultation with church leaders, and he was restored to pastoral leadership.[34]

While the Aguayos faced these re-entry challenges, missionary Elena Huegel was assigned to serve as a liaison, based in Curicó, Chile, between the IPC and the MACUCC.[35] Her tasks included communication, translation, administration, and hosting delegations.[36] Huegel is a third-generation missionary in the

[30] "Reflections."
[31] Stephen Gray, Associate Conference Minister, letter to Pastor Oscar Aguayo, 3 January 1995, archive of the Chile Mission Partnership, in author's possession.
[32] David A. Vargas, Executive Secretary, letter to Stephen Gray, 2 May 1996 and response by Stephen C. Gray to David Vargas, May 6, 1996, archive of the Chile Mission Partnership, in author's possession.
[33] Ulises Munoz, letter to Stephen Gray, 18 January 1997, archive of the Chile Mission Partnership, in author's possession.
[34] Ulises Munoz, letter to Stephen Gray, 30 January 1997, archive of the Chile Mission Partnership, in author's possession.
[35] "Brief History," archive of the Chile Mission Partnership, in author's possession.
[36] 1998 Report of the Mission Partnership, newsletter of the Massachusetts Conference United Church of Christ, in author's possession.

Christian Church (Disciples of Christ) in Latin America.[37] Raised in Mexico, Huegel began her missionary service in Paraguay and then worked in Chile for 20 years. Her background includes Christian education and outdoor ministry. As a result of the Aguayos' service in Massachusetts, the Mission Partnership launched a programme in 1996 to establish sister church relationships between local congregations in each country. As many as 15 congregations in each country participated to grow in understanding of their partners' lives.[38] Facilitating communication among these congregations was one of Huegel's first assignments. The programme lasted for several years, but eventually Huegel took on other responsibilities to support the partnership.

The two churches remained committed to building relationships among their members, trialling a number of programmes to overcome the challenges involved in any cross-cultural relationship. In 2004–2005, Huegel led a youth choir exchange that took place with a group of approximately 12 young people from each country, touring both Chile and the United States. Lasting two years, it included performances in churches, recording two CDs, faith formation, and cross-cultural friendship building.[39] Many of the young people who participated in the choir remain in touch with each other. Two North American participants later married, while another participant returned to Chile as a mission intern.

While serving in Chile, Huegel enrolled in the peacebuilding and trauma healing programme of Eastern Mennonite University. She combined these interests with her training in outdoor ministry to establish Centro Shalom, a peace and environmental education centre of the IPC. Located in the foothills of the Andes near the small town of Vilches, Centro Shalom reflects Huegel's commitment to creation care and social justice. Like most of Chile, the land had been clear cut and planted with non-native species. Slowly, church volunteers have helped indigenous plants and trees to reclaim the land. At the same time, the programme of Centro Shalom reflects appreciation for the indigenous people of South America. Hymns and prayers are offered not only in Spanish but also Mapudungun and Guaraní, languages spoken by indigenous communities in Chile, Argentina, and Paraguay.

When the work of Centro Shalom began, periodic camps from the US helped build cabins and other structures, creating a new form of cross-cultural exchange. This effort developed into the CONPAZ programme for youth from Massachusetts and the Ohio Conference of the Christian Church (Disciples of Christ) to join with youth from a Chilean church for a ten-day experience of service, faith-formation, and cross-cultural learning. Today, Centro Shalom is led by a Chilean director, Patricia Gomez Torres, and Chilean Board of Directors, plus a team of 25 to 30 people who volunteer as counsellors, medics, storytellers, and song leaders. Centro Shalom, a product of the partnership,

---

[37] Elena's parents and grandparents served as missionaries in Mexico for the Disciples of Christ. In 2019, the family celebrated a 100-year commitment to global ministry.
[38] "Sister Churches, March 2003," archive of the Chile Mission Partnership, in author's possession.
[39] "Evaluation of the MACUCC Youth Choir Exchange to Chile, July 2004/2005," archive of the Chile Mission Partnership, in author's possession.

remains an important place of encounter with creation, God, neighbours, and self.

CONPAZ Programme as Cross-Cultural Encounter

In many ways, the CONPAZ programme is the result of the decades of collaboration and the many shared activities that took place between these two denominations. The programme, a ten-day cross-cultural encounter between young people from Chile and North America, is a brief immersion experience.[40] Yet, the skills that are developed through the entire process seek to equip participants for other cross-cultural experiences. In this way, the programme reflects Elena Huegel's lifetime commitment to mission and building mutual care and understanding among people from different nations. It is worth examining the programme in detail to understand the ways in which it nurtures these skills and values.

Chilean participants come from the same local church, while US participants come from multiple congregations of their conference. The Chilean participants have often participated in other Centro Shalom programmes, while most North American participants have had other camp experiences in the US. Among both groups, CONPAZ represents a faith-based, cross-cultural immersion. The programme schedule seeks to respond to the challenges of acclimating to a foreign environment and building cross-cultural friendship.

For US delegations, a typical schedule begins with an overnight flight to Chile on Friday.[41] After arrival and processing through Chilean immigration, the travellers travel by bus to the Centro Shalom office in Talca, about 160 miles south of Santiago. The first day involves rest, orientation, getting settled into dormitory rooms, and preparing for travel to Centro Shalom. On Sunday afternoon, the group attends worship with a local IPC congregation, often including a procession with band instruments and choir. For most North Americans, it is a first experience with pentecostal worship. Monday's schedule includes a tour of Talca, the provincial capital, and a trip to Centro Shalom by public bus after lunch. The trip is only 60 miles, but the trip can take as long as two hours as the bus makes regular stops on a rural highway. When the delegates arrive at the Centro Shalom stop, they walk on a dirt road to the gates of the camp property. The 20-minute walk is dusty and hot, adding to the fatigue of weary travellers. But the natural beauty is invigorating, and the walk marks a significant transition from one space to another – a border crossing that might be more significant than an overnight plane ride.

The afternoon at the Shalom Center involves more orientation, including safety rules, sleeping arrangements for the cabins, shared tasks for meals, personal hygiene, and service work. On Tuesday, the first full day at Centro

---

[40] The author has participated in CONPAZ camps as a group leader and as a chaperone for youth and adults from Massachusetts. These reflections are based largely on those experiences.
[41] Itinerary for a Massachusetts UCC CONPAZ Delegation, February 2019. Author's records as a delegation leader.

Shalom, the itinerary includes reflection on the theme of the week, time for prayer or journal writing, a hike or games, work on the property, and chores. On Wednesday, the Chilean youth arrive in the late morning. Two or three North American youth walk back to the bus stop to greet the Chileans and accompany them on the dirt road. For the next three days, the two groups follow the schedule established on Tuesday of work, devotional time, shared meals, and games.

The wilderness experience at the Shalom Center is foreign to both the North Americans and the Chileans. The North Americans have been immersed in a foreign culture since arriving in Santiago, while the Chileans are not accustomed to camping or to sharing so much domestic labour. But the North Americans are in a more unsettled position, so the schedule allows the North Americans to arrive first and learn camp practices, which creates a sense of agency. When the North Americans greet the Chileans, those who have been guests become hosts.

Relationships are built over meals, card games, chopping or piling wood, and scrubbing toilets. When the time at the camp ends on Saturday, the Chileans and North Americans walk the dirt road to the bus stop together. The Chileans return to their homes, and the North Americans return to the office in Talca. The North Americans prepare for a home stay with the families of the Chilean youth from camp. A warm shower is a luxury after four days of dip baths with cold water! In groups of two or three, the North Americans spend Saturday night with Chilean hosts, sharing meals and local activities. Together, they attend worship on Sunday afternoon, followed by a meal for the entire congregation and their visitors. The local churches typically offer extravagant hospitality, a Chilean feast for their international guests. Then, the North Americans return to the office in Talca and prepare for departure. The final day in Santiago includes sightseeing and shopping. A final gathering happens at the airport, as campers and Shalom Center staff sit on the floor for a closing reflection. As the North Americans pass through the airport security gates, the Chileans wave goodbye.

Just as the staff of Centro Shalom prepare the camp, the North Americans also prepare for travel as an important part of the learning process. Typically, orientation takes place during three or four meetings, using printed materials from Global Ministries and a booklet created by Huegel titled "Pilgrimage to Holy Ground: A Preparation Manual for Overseas Journeys." It includes her original writing together with material from other sources.[42] Travellers also receive a journal with devotional material and blank pages for personal reflections. The camp programme provides time each day for devotions and journal writing as spiritual practices. Through CONPAZ, North Americans and Chileans meet at Centro Shalom and practice the camp's core values of cultural awareness, peace, and creation care.

---

[42] Elena Huegel, *Pilgrimage to Holy Ground: A Preparation Manual for Overseas Journeys* (Curicó, Chile: Centro Shalom, Pentecostal Church of Chile, 2004). The manual contains Bible study, devotional materials, reflections on cultural differences (including an explanation of the individualism-collectivism continuum), culture shock and reverse culture shock, the meaning of September 11 in Chile and the US, background of partner churches, and practical matters like common vocabulary, packing lists, and travel tips.

The practices of the CONPAZ programme are grounded in a community covenant that is based on faith in Jesus. The words of the covenant are painted on a large board in the worship space. Below the placard is a notebook for each participant in Centro Shalom to sign as an act of affirming the covenant.[43] The covenant says,

> We, the participants, supporters, motivators and facilitators of Centro Shalom commit ourselves to this covenant with the help of our Lord Jesus Christ to strengthen healthy human relations in our community. We agree
> - to work together for health and physical, emotional, spiritual, and social well-being,
> - to participate in all activities, to respect and accept each person for their needs and their gifts,
> - to use language and tone of voice in a positive way,
> - to resolve conflicts without violence through conversation or with outside help,
> - to care for the equipment, common spaces, and personal property,
> - to respect the schedule and special times,
> - to enjoy and respect the ecosystem,
> - to walk only on the paths,
> - to throw trash in the appropriate receptacles,
> - to remain in designated zones,
> - to take only memories and to leave only footprints.

The CONPAZ orientation materials identify culture as an invisible companion that guides our actions and recognize that different cultures are neither good, nor bad, but different. The community covenant and the manuals for staff and participants establish explicit norms for the shared time Centro Shalom. These norms reflect the values of partnership and the importance of embodying these values in individual's lives. The Shalom Center is a product of the partnership between the IPC, the Global Ministries of the UCC, and the Christian Church (Disciples of Christ). Its programme reflects the values of cross-cultural encounter and how participants in the partnership have grown in their understanding of cross-cultural friendship.

Conclusion

Despite the remarkable endurance and vitality of the partnership between the IPC and the MACUCC, the relationship faces significant challenges. Some of these concerns are common to most cross-cultural mission relationships. Different views of human sexuality have become more prominent because of cultural changes in Chile and the United States. Longstanding issues of language, culture, church practice, and unequal access to resources continue to be obstacles to mutuality. Both the IPC and the UCC churches have struggled to avoid patterns of paternalism or romanticism in their relationships. Both churches have worked to ensure that the relationship is maintained by the denominations, and supported

---

[43] Author's photograph of Centro Shalom, 21 February 2017.

through Global Ministries, so that it represents more than individual relationships. Yet institutions, like individuals, change.

In the aftermath of the 2009 earthquake in Chile, the churches of the MACUCC provided significant funding for a housing campaign for families in the IPC. This campaign followed a long pattern of the MACUCC providing financial resources for special projects in Chile. The response to the earthquake was so strong that a new sister church effort was created, but it lacked the institutional support that Huegel had provided to the earlier sister church project. During her final years in Chile, her assignment expanded to include outdoor ministries in Paraguay and Puerto Rico. At the same time, staff and organizational changes in the MACUCC reduced resources for the partnership.

The death in 2013 of long-time MACUCC staff member Sue Dickerman meant the loss of connection between the women's ministry of the two churches, as well as the loss of the last staff member to remember the founding of the partnership. As a testimony to the strength of Sue's connection to Chile, during the final days of her life, a delegation travelled through the area that was most damaged by the earthquake. In each community, members of the IPC lifted up prayers for *Hermana Susana*, which was a beautiful example of the power of relationships formed by this collaboration.

In February 2020, the IPC elected a new bishop, Pastor Sergio Veloso, following the retirement of Pastor Ulises Muñoz from the bishop's role. Responsibility for the partnership resides with the bishop's office, so this change is significant. In 2017, the MACUCC merged with the conferences of Connecticut and Rhode Island to establish a new Southern New England Conference of the United Church of Christ. The place of historic global mission relationships remains unclear in the structure of the new conference.

The mission partnership between the IPC and the UCC shows that missional collaboration relies on both individual and institutional actors. It requires these actors to have certain skills and attitudes, such as language and cross-cultural competency, combined with a theology of ecumenism. Put more simply, the collaboration requires values of humility, openness, and curiosity to learn about difference. Missional collaboration, like all ministry, cannot take place without people who are willing to serve. But this kind of ministry depends upon resources that institutions can best provide.

From a chance encounter in Central Brooklyn to the creation of permanent institutions and ministries of the Pentecostal Church of Chile, the mission partnership between the United Church of Christ and the Pentecostal Church of Chile represents a powerful example of two churches seeking a relationship across miles of distance and many kinds of difference. Hundreds of lives have been touched by these cross-cultural encounters, offering brief reminders that there are Christians on the other side of the globe who know about us and care for us, a living symbol of God's care for all of creation.

Twinning Relationship and Missional Collaboration: A Catholic Parish in Uganda and in the United States

Angelyn Dries, OSF

In the last half of the 20th century, Catholics in the Archdiocese of Milwaukee, Wisconsin, had many ways to learn about, finance, or engage with world mission. They sent money to pontifical mission societies, such as the Propagation of the Faith, or directly to a missionary or mission community with whom a family might be familiar. The Catholic Students' Mission Crusade was active in some Catholic high schools, colleges, and the archdiocesan seminary. Catholic Relief Services, appealing to donors' compassion to respond to others' needs, provided multiple opportunities for families and individuals to make a difference in food sources, nutritional care, and the education of children in countries abroad. Catholics who saw becoming a missionary as their vocation joined a religious congregation whose primary focus was overseas mission. One intention of missionary work was conversion to Catholic life and practice.

This chapter will explore another form of mission: the collaboration of "parish twinning," as experienced between two Catholic parishes with the same faith tradition but with different contexts. St Eugene parish is in the United States; Our Lady Queen of Apostles parish is in Uganda. In 2022, they celebrated 20 years of their twinning relationship. I have been on the St Eugene twinning committee for half of that period. I am grateful to the committee that kept records of their meetings and letters to and from the parishes.

Background

Learning a Twinning Frame of Mind

In 2000, the World Mission Office in the Archdiocese of Milwaukee offered a way to reflect upon the twinning process in a day-long reflection process, "Key Perspectives for a 'Twinning-Frame-of-Mind.'"[1] By this time, over 90 parishes in the Milwaukee Archdiocese had a relationship with another parish. Elements of the process included mutual communication, listening to people's experience, and sharing concerns, joys, and faith among parishioners of all ages.[2] The archdiocese noted that "the *relationships* that are created and nurtured among the members of both twinning parishes are more important than the funds distributed. Have faith that the money raised will be spent responsibly by the

---

[1] "Key Perspectives for a 'Twinning-Frame-of-Mind'" [title of the reflection day event], Office for World Mission, Archdiocese of Milwaukee, [c. May 2000].
[2] *Ibid.*

recipients."[3] American parishes needed to remember that the relationship "avoids dependency and paternalism toward their twin." "The bridges of faith offer as much to US parishes as their partners [...]. We are evangelized and changed as we help other communities of faith."[4] That energy has been reflected in the experience of the Fox Point, Wisconsin, and Nkokonjeru, Uganda, parishes.

The US Catholic Bishops' 1997 "Called to Global Solidarity. International Challenges for US Parishes" is a backdrop for support of a different form of mission, parish twinning. Two Catholic parishes in different parts of the world "collaborate."[5] In other words, they "work together" toward common goals and, in the process, enlarge their role and understanding of "Catholic" and of mission. Catholics are members of a "universal Church that transcends national barriers," the bishops said. "A parish reaching beyond its own members and beyond national boundaries is a truly 'catholic' parish."[6] This understanding of "catholic" was a newer emphasis, reflective of Pope John Paul II's attendance at the Africa Synod.[7]

Another document informing the case study presented in this chapter is the US Catholic Bishops' 2021 "Call to Solidarity with Africa," which addressed this continent's experiences and issues, such as apartheid, efforts toward an end to abduction and enslavement of children in Sudan, and responsibilities of companies and governments involved in African oil development.[8]

In 2022, Our Lady Queen of Apostles parish, Nkokonjeru, Uganda, and St Eugene parish, Fox Point, Wisconsin, celebrated their 20-year twinning relationship. Although geographically distant from each other by 7,750 miles, on different continents, with varied experiences and challenges related to their contexts, parishioners have come to know, interact with, learn from, and pray for each other through their sustained engagement over time. What does the relationship look like? What makes them "twins," and in what ways do they resemble each other? How are their interactions a missional collaboration? With some background of national and international events, papal encyclicals, and local leadership as embodied in the experience of the two parishes over 20 years, we will explore the development of a twinning relationship between parishioners

---

[3] See also, Fr William Nordenbrock, CSSP, "The Whys of Parish Twinning: Rooted in the Gospel and Manifested in and through Social Justice," presentation at USCMA Annual Conference, 25 October 2001.

[4] "Key Perspectives for a 'Twinning-Frame-of-Mind.'"

[5] USCCB, "Called to Global Solidarity. International Challenges for US Parishes," 12 November 1997, https://www.usccb.org/resources/called-global-solidarity-international-challenges-us-parishes.

[6] *Ibid.*

[7] President Mandela remarked to Pope John Paul II, "You delayed your visit to this country [South Africa] because you viewed with disdain a system that treated God's children as lesser beings." Donald G. McNeil, Jr., "Pope's South Africa Visit Honors 2 Vows," *New York Times*, 17 September 1995, 12. During his papacy, he visited Africa 16 times.

[8] USCCB, "Call to Solidarity with Africa," 14 November 2001, https://www.usccb.org/resources/call-solidarity-africa-november-2001.

in Nkokonjeru (Diocese of Lugazi), and those in Fox Point (Archdiocese of Milwaukee). First, I provide some context for each parish.

Nkokonjeru, Uganda

Our Lady Queen of Apostles Parish, Uganda, is the older of the two parishes. In November 2022, they celebrated 125 years as a parish and a centennial of their church's physical building.[9] The parish began in the 19th century after the Mill Hill missionaries arrived in the region. Fr Herbert Vaughan founded the missionary congregation in North London in 1866. He did not consider his group to be British alone, so he drew priest candidates from other European countries and from the United States. Some Mill Hill missionaries made their way to the eastern part of Africa, with some arriving in Uganda in 1895.[10]

By that time, the British had colonized Kenya (1888), Uganda, and Buganda (1890). Mill Hill missionaries worked among people of various tribes and languages. The Little Sisters of St Francis from England arrived later in Uganda. They opened schools for girls and started a small hospital, especially for women and children.[11] Anglicans also had missionaries and parishes in the area.

Raids by Islamic groups in the 19th century led to the capture of young boys. The northern region of Uganda had experienced the terror that led to the death of 23 Anglican and 22 Roman Catholic young men, executed during the persecution of Christians under ruler Mwanga in Buganda (now part of Uganda), between 1885 and 1887. Mwanga perceived that in introducing the English language, Christian churches were agitating insurrection against his regime. The martyrs' lives and sanctity are celebrated at the National Shrine of the Uganda Martyrs in Namugongo, Kampala. Although Catholics and Anglicans were somewhat competing with each other for converts, martyrdom was the first shared missional experience between them in the region. One of the martyrs, St Pontian Ngondwe, a soldier, is patron of the Catholic Lugazi Diocese. Martyr's Day, 3 June, is a national public holiday in Uganda. In 2015, Pope Francis was the third Pope to visit the Anglican Martyrs shrine in Namugongo. The Episcopal News Service reported that the Pope was strongly moved by the experience and remarked that the shrine "testifies to the ecumenism of blood."[12]

The country endured another war in northern Uganda, starting in August 1986. The conflict was between the Lord's Resistance Army (LRA), largely funded by the government of Sudan, and other groups. Part of the issue was the economic inequality between northern and southern Uganda. By the 1990s, the LRA had become a terrorist group, backed by Sudan. LRA killed, maimed, and

---

[9] Archbishop of Milwaukee Timothy Dolan and St Eugene pastor Fr Kenneth Knippel joined the Ugandans for the celebration.

[10] St Joseph's Missionary Society Mill Hill Missionaries, "Our History: Part 7: The Africa Mission," https:/millhillmissionaries.com/part-7-the African mission/.

[11] In 1923, Irish-born Mother Mary Kevin Kearney (1875–1957) founded an indigenous community, Little Sisters of St Francis, for mission in Africa. Their motherhouse is in Nkokonjeru, Diocese of Lugazi, where she is buried. This community is one of the largest indigenous communities in the region.

[12] "Pope Francis Visits Martyrs' Shrine," Episcopal News Service, 30 November 2015, https://www.episcopalnewsservice.org/2015/11/30/pope-francis-visits-martyrs-shrine/.

disfigured large numbers of people. Children were kidnapped, sold, and some of them used as sex slaves or bondservants. Some were even ordered to kill relatives.[13] The Acholi region bore the brunt of these attacks.[14] Uganda was not the only African country to suffer the long-term effects of colonialism.[15]

Papal Recognition of the Catholic Church in Africa

In early 20th century Uganda, Catholics were the largest Christian community in the area. Following many stages of meetings beginning in 1969, Pope John Paul II convened a synod in Rome with the African bishops.[16] Their conversations were reflected in *Ecclesia in Africa*, which summarized the issues, values, strengths, and challenges for Catholics of that continent. Africa now stood collectively and visibly as an "adult" church among other Catholic churches in Europe, the Americas, and Asia.

The Africa Synod underscored the social and cultural elements of life and the deleterious effects of colonialism. As conversation continued over the weeks, the bishops indicated that "primarily there should be places engaged in evangelizing themselves so that subsequently they can bring the Good News to others."[17] African Catholics "should be communities which encourage the members themselves to take on responsibility, learn to live an ecclesial life, and reflect on different human problems in the light of the Gospel."[18] Catholic life had social consequences.[19] "Above all, these communities are to be committed to living Christ's love for everybody, a love which transcends the limits of the natural solidarity of clans, tribes or other interest groups."[20] The statement was particularly germane, given the effect of Sudanese groups, which had taken over northern areas of Uganda, and situation of the Ugandans, who lived with the consequences of French and English colonial policies. While not all the bishops at the gathering were from Africa, the bishops symbolized in a collective and public way the presence of the African church.

---

[13] USCCB, Department of Social Development and World Peace, "Background on Northern Uganda," February 2007. https://www.usccb.org/issues-and-action/human-life-and-dignity/global-issues/africa/uganda/upload/Background-on-Northern-Uganda-2007-02.pdf

[14] The Acholi people are a Nilotic ethnic group in southern Sudan and northern Uganda.

[15] Catholics were not necessarily all of one mind in relation to how the new government would work. See J.J. Carney and J.L. Earle, *Contesting Catholics: Benedicto Kiwanuka and the Birth of Postcolonial Africa* (Havertown, PA: Casement Academic, 2022).

[16] John Paul II, *Ecclesia in Africa*, 14 September 1995. https://www.vatican.va/content/john-paul-ii/en/apost_exhortations/documents/hf_jp-ii_exh_14091995_ecclesia-in-africa.html.

[17] *Ibid.*

[18] *Ibid.*

[19] For development of the Uganda situation, see Carney and Earle, *Contesting Catholics.*

[20] Kiwanuka, the first black Chief of Justice in Uganda and a Catholic, was 50 years old when he was kidnapped from his court chambers and assassinated on 22 September 1972.

Fox Point, Wisconsin, USA

The other "twin" is St Eugene Parish, founded in 1957. The parish is situated in a northern suburb of Milwaukee in the planned village of Fox Point, Wisconsin. Sunday Mass was celebrated in the first years at the old town hall. The beloved founding pastor, Fr William H. Mackin, remarked, "Since we started from scratch together, we became a family."[21] A church was soon built, and a grade school was erected on property purchased earlier by "the labour priest," Fr Peter Dietz (1878–1947).[22]

Fr Kenneth Knippel was appointed pastor of St Eugene Parish from 1996 through 2008. When beginning the process of parish twinning, the parish's Human Concerns Committee first sought a partner in the archdiocese with whom to be in a twinning relationship, but to no avail. The Milwaukee Archdiocesan Mission Office provided a workshop for parishes interested in connecting with Catholics beyond the United States. At the time, mission opportunities in Central and Latin America had gained the attention of people in the United States, especially in the 1960s and 1970s.[23]

By the 1980s, more US Catholic parishes expressed an interest to "twin" with a parish outside of the United States. As the US Catholic bishops later wrote, "an important role for the parish is to challenge and encourage every believer to greater global solidarity."[24] This perspective had less emphasis on mission as Christian conversion to a specific denomination. Rather, mission highlighted the social and the structural – that is, "incarnational" consequences of religious faith.

Search for a Twinning Parish

The St Eugene Human Concerns Committee searched for four years to find a local parish with whom to "twin." After several attempts bore no fruit, Ed Ricker, Chair of the Twinning Committee, contacted the Milwaukee Archdiocesan Office for World Missions. He and Knippel invited the Missions Director, Sr Frances Cunningham, SSSF, to explore some options with the parish committee. She and Sr Rosemary Huddleston, OP, had visited the newly formed Diocese of Lugazi, Uganda, in December 1999. The diocese was about 100 miles from the country's capital, Kampala. Bishop Sskamanya Matthias[25] and Chancellor Father Mulinda Lawrence gave them a tour through the sprawling new diocese, some of it accessible only by boat.

---

[21] William H. Mackin, quoted in "St. Eugene Forges Family in Its Short History," *Catholic Herald*, 27 March 2018. https://catholicherald.org/catholic-herald/general/st-eugene-forges-family-short-history. The cornerstone for a new church was laid in 1958.
[22] Dietz was associated with Fr John A. Ryan and William Kerby, who urged US bishops to address a pastoral letter on the "labour question."
[23] For more information on the overall development of mission interest in how US parishes interacted with parishes mainly in Latin and Central America, see Kim Lamberty, "Toward a Spirituality of Accompaniment in Solidarity Partnerships," *Missiology: An International Review* 15: 2 (April 2012), 181–93.
[24] USCCB, "Called to Global Solidary."
[25] Uganda names are indicated in this sequence.

Our Lady Queen of Apostles Parish in Nkokonjeru was divided into 24 sub-parishes with 26 schools. The population of 11,145 was dispersed among 17 villages. During the American visitors' tour, the English Little Sisters of St Francis, who had opened grade schools in the area, indicated to the visitors that parish schools and social service agencies would welcome a relationship with a US Catholic parish. Having this information, the St Eugene committee discussed the Uganda possibility, as well as options in Mexico, Central America, and Asia.

Decision about Location

After further conversations with newly appointed Bishop Ssekamanya in Nkokonjeru, Knippel and the St Eugene Human Concerns Committee chose to twin with Our Lady Queen of Apostles. One factor in the location decision was that Knippel had offered a room at the rectory to Fr Ntege Peter Richard from the Lugazi Diocese when he was pursuing doctoral studies in education at Marquette University, Milwaukee. Through the priests' interactions at the rectory, Knippel took an interest in the people and experience of Ugandans. He travelled to Uganda with Ntege and experienced something of their culture and expression of Catholic life in a situation new to him. Knippel contacted Fr Athy Kaferro at Our Lady Queen of Apostles to get the twinning process moving. In retrospect, the twinning grew initially from the expression of hospitality Knippel offered Ntege in St Eugene's rectory.[26]

In 2008, Fr Jerry Herda was appointed to St Eugene, remaining pastor for nine years. In his time, the Twinning Committee grew, as did parishioner interest. He made two trips to Uganda with parishioners. This tradition has continued, as did St Eugene's welcome of Ugandan priests and laity to the Fox Point parish.

Learning from Experience

St Eugene's Committee's first endeavour in twinning taught them what not to do. Having contacted Our Lady Queen of Apostles parish and school about what they might need, the St Eugene committee bought 435 boxes to fill and ship to the Uganda parish. Parishioners brought basketballs, soccer balls, school supplies, clothing, and "all sorts of things," including three computers to ship to the Uganda parish, all items requested by Our Lady Queen of Apostles parish and school.[27] With space available for more items, someone knew of hospital bed frames being discarded and thought a Uganda hospital could use them. In the end, St Eugene Parish Twinning Committee sent everything in a shipping container to Uganda, although they could not fill all 435 boxes. Months passed with no response from Uganda. The Fox Point parish discovered that the shipped items were still in the Kampala port, far away from the parish. The Uganda parish would have to pay a tax at the port and pay for a truck to haul the container to the parish. The boxes needed to be unloaded from the containers. The items (minus the three computers) ended up stacked in the pastor's small house for

---

[26] Bishop Ssekaanya visited St Eugene Parish in 2003.
[27] Both parishes had a school.

weeks. Determining how to get things to people who needed them became a huge logistical problem, especially given the physical distance between the parish areas.[28] These first "gifts" ended up being a burden for the Uganda pastor and the parish!

Archdiocesan Assistance to Parish Twinning

In the early stages of parish twinning, some Eugene committee members attended a day of reflection and input provided by the Milwaukee Archdiocesan Office for World Mission. About 90 parishes in the archdiocese had a relationship with a parish, many of these in Latin America. The day focused on parishes seeking or engaged in a sister parish relationship. Participants had conversations around the topic "Key Perspectives in a Twinning Relationship: Communication, Prayer, Learning Experience." With the idea that every local church is both mission-sending and mission-receiving, participants named how the "twins" were accountable to each other and ways to keep twinning alive over the years. What did solidarity look like in their parish relationship? Participants were asked, "If we visited your parish today, how would we know that you are in a Twinning relationship?"[29]

St Eugene Parish Twinning Committee identified their mission. "First, develop and sustain people-to-people relationships between the two parishes. Second, grow mutually in awareness of the cultural commonalities and differences of both parishes. Third, grow together in faith and share the spiritual riches of the gospel and the gifts each possesses."[30]

Annual Event for Financial Support of Parish Twinning

Every year, St Eugene raises funds during Lent to support the twinning relationship. At the end of the Sunday liturgy, a Parish Twinning Committee member gives a talk about some aspect of life in Uganda in relation to the year's theme. Prayer cards are distributed to parishioners to remind them to keep Uganda parishioners in prayer. Video updates from previous Lenten Projects are shown in the narthex. St Eugene School children are involved by raising money through "No Uniform Days," listening to a parishioner who has visited Uganda speak of the experience, and prayer. Some students and adults have prayer partners with a student or parishioner in Uganda.

Parish funds since 2005 have helped Our Lady Queen of Apostles Parish develop sustainable agriculture projects, which were successful for the Ugandans both individually and collectively. Since then, annual themes around sustainable

---

[28] Fr Knippel, notes from Parish Twinning Homily. He was celebrant for Sunday liturgies on 12 and 13 March 2022 for the 20th anniversary of the twinning relationship.

[29] USCCB, "Partners in Mission: Guidelines for Solidarity and 'Twinning' Relationships." At this point, about 57 Archdiocese of Milwaukee parishes were engaged with twinning relationships, including seven in the Lugazi Diocese.

[30] St Eugene Parish Twinning Files, undated document prepared after the archdiocesan meeting. The Parish Twinning Files are located at the church at 7600 N. Port Washington Rd., Fox Point, WI, 53217.

agriculture are pictured on the prayer card distributed at Mass. For example, the card from the year with the theme "Cultivating Faith and Raising Hope" featured parishioners engaged in various aspects of their Sustainable Agriculture Program. The 20-year prayer card bore the image of the Parish Twinning Banner with the phrase on the back, "One in the Lord. God is Good! All the Time!"

Impact on St Eugene Parishioners who Went to Uganda

The twinning relationship sometimes impacts parishioners in new ways. Jenny Kopetsky, chair of the Twinning Committee since 2014, has been to Nkokonjeru twice, once with her husband and once with her daughter. She noted, "I experience a sense of mission each time we do the kickoff weekend. Since we have been in the relationship for 20 years, the majority of our parishioners have made the Lenten Project part of their Lenten Journey. We are connected through prayer and friendship."[31] Jenny reflected that her daughter's interactions in Uganda gave her a sense of mission when she went to college and participated in non-profit groups that help with home building and repair.[32] Thomas E. Jenkins, PE, was in Nkokonjeru leading an Engineers Without Borders project with University of Wisconsin students. He observed that in Nkokonjeru, "there is not the sharp division between the secular and religious aspects of life we in the US are accustomed to." Village council meetings opened and closed with a prayer – non-sectarian and not at all coercive. The village chairman reached out to Jenkins after the latter offered "the standard Catholic grace" before a meal at the house where he and the student stayed.[33] From that prayer and Jenkins's hospitality, the Ugandan recognized Jenkins as a Catholic and invited him to attend Sunday Mass at Our Lady Queen of Apostles Church.[34] Through twinning, the committee learned of Uganda families living in the Milwaukee area. Uganda-born Yvonne N. Ssempijja received the Archdiocese of Milwaukee Vatican II Award in 2010 for her Service to the Missions. St Eugene Parish participates in the annual celebration and fellowship on the feast of the Uganda martyrs.

For the 20th anniversary (2022), the Nkokonjeru parish sent four short videos from their twinning leaders that showed Fr Tamale Lawrence Peter and parishioners working at various dimensions of their relationship with St Eugene over 20 years. These included videos of a church singing and dancing group, a twinning member, the woman in charge of their catechetical programme, and parishioners engaged in farm production. The introduction of electricity and technology in Nkokonjeru – no small task at the start of the relationship – has significantly improved the communication between parishes.

On a practical level, Ugandan parishioners became successful farmers, which, Lawrence wrote, "gives people great food security."[35] Reliability of food sources

---

[31] Jenny Kopetsky, e-mail to author, 26 February 2022.
[32] *Ibid.*
[33] Thomas E. Jenkins, e-mail to author, 24 February 2022.
[34] *Ibid.*
[35] Fr Tamale Lawrence Peter, letter to St Eugene Parish, 2021. St Eugene Parish Twinning files.

for families was especially important, given the earlier traumatic situations in the country. Parishioners grew corn, bananas, coffee plants, and pineapples, among other things; they also raised chickens, ducks, pigs, and cows. Parishioners became known throughout the region for the high quality of their poultry products. The piggery project led to a demonstration farm for the area. The parish used twinning funds for a truck to haul food to the market. Corn was turned into maize through a maize machine driven by a newly installed electrical source. Lawrence noted, "Uganda parishioners now had money to send their children to school and to support their parish."[36]

Over the years, others who knew about St Eugene's twinning relationship contributed their talent or resources for needs in the Uganda parish area. Collaborative groups have included Educate Uganda (Karen Van Dyke), Fair Trade Sales of Uganda women's handicrafts (parishioner Jean Harer), and Catholic Relief Services.

Twenty Years of Twinning

Personal Experiences of Transformation

Fr Knippel was invited to celebrate St Eugene's Sunday liturgies in March 2022 at the 20th anniversary of the twinning relationship. His homily reflected on the day's gospel, Jesus' transfiguration. The story, he said, "reminds me that I never see everything exactly the way it is. There's always something deeper."[37] He recounted a conversation with the first group of St Eugene parishioners to Nkokonjeru in 2002, as they "debriefed their experience at the end of the day." A high school student, there with her parents, remarked to him, "I realize that I've been living in a bubble and that bubble is Fox Point." She saw that parish twinning was not about money but about relationships that "opened a larger world" and "that [have] a transforming effect."[38] In the process of getting to know one's twin, one became "transfigured."[39] Parish twinning was about seeing and working for the common good.

Fr Knippel sent Fr Athy Kaferro a message to remind him that it was 20 years since the start of the two-parish relationship. Kaferro wrote back, saying, "Twenty years of love. Thank you, Lord [...] Please tell the people of St Eugene that since the Twinning we are not the same. With the Holy Spirit we love more globally. We praise God."[40] Many St Eugene parishioners could say the same. At the base of those years was the seed of hospitality and a collaboration in prayer with awareness of different contexts for the meaning of the word "catholic."

Africa is the continent with the highest rate of births of twins, so it seems "natural" that the two parishes are also twinning. Wisconsin is a farming and

---

[36] *Ibid.*
[37] Knippel, notes from Parish Twinning Homily, 12 and 13 March 2022. The Gospel for the day was Jesus' transfiguration (Luke 9:28b–36).
[38] *Ibid.*
[39] *Ibid.*
[40] *Ibid.*

dairy state with cows that provide rich milk for ice cream and frozen custard. Cows raised by Nkokonjeru parishioners are now highly sought there, while corn/maize production has kept them "food secure," as Fr Lawrence remarked, enabling many to assume church leadership. In a more profound way, St Eugene and Our Lady Queen of Apostles parishes seem to have found their twinning relationship on many levels of life and faith. As the US Catholic bishops had envisioned in 1997, "our international responsibilities enrich parish life and deepen genuine Catholic identity. Integrating themes of solidarity into the routines of parish life will make for a richer, more Catholic experience of Church. In giving a little, we receive much more."[41] The 20-year collaboration between Fox Point and Nkokonjeru parishes has borne that out, with a "catholic" emphasis (i.e., according to the whole), in Catholic (denomination) parishes.

St Eugene parishioners look forward to a visit from some Our Lady Queen of Apostles parishioners and pastor in fall 2023. When they come, the recently ordained Fr Tonny Kizza, from Uganda, assigned as the shared associate pastor with St Eugene and St Monica parishes, will be one of the greeters. A new but unexpected form of collaboration emerges! St Eugene Parish has come full circle.

A surprising influence of parish twinning happened recently through a presentation and discussion session sponsored by the St Eugene Parish Committee, Education about Racism. They invited a University of Wisconsin-Milwaukee professor for a dialogue about racism and ways to build healthier relationships between people, no matter their race. About 100 people attended in person, with many others online. In discussion after the talk, an idea formed. Noting the parish's 20-year twinning relationship with Nkokonjeru parishioners, one attendee suggested that a similar twinning relationship might be formed with an African American parish in Milwaukee. The "suggestion was met with a spontaneous round of applause."[42] It will be seen what comes of *this* possible mission collaboration!

---

[41] USCCB, "Called to Global Solidarity."

[42] "St Eugene Parish Community Tackles Race Issue," *Catholic Herald,* 22 January 2022. https://catholicherald.org/local/st-eugene-parish-community-tackles-race-issue/.

COOPERATIVE PROJECTS

Collaboration in Mission:
Theological Education in Mozambique

David W. Restrick

Introduction

A perennial challenge of Protestant churches in southern Africa has been the preparation of national faculty for Bible schools and seminaries. Traditionally, many faculty members were missionaries from the USA or UK. Although missionary faculty make significant contributions, they are not nearly as effective as national faculty. In some cases, potential African faculty members were supported to go to the USA for further studies at the graduate level. This proposition was expensive, and in the case of married students, often required the separation of couples and families for significant periods of time. Additionally, in a significant number of cases, the people going overseas to study opted to remain in their host country rather than return to serve in their home countries.

Although the need for national theological faculty has been the same for Mozambique as its neighbouring countries, the problem was compounded by historical realities. As a Portuguese colony, educational opportunities for Mozambicans were severely limited. After independence in 1975, the government sought to remedy this deficiency by radically improving and expanding the country's educational system. However, within a year of independence, civil war erupted across the country. The primary targets of the rebel fighters were government installations and personnel, including schools and teachers. By the end of the civil war in late 1992, the virtual elimination of educational opportunities outside the principal cities had drastically reduced the number of potential candidates for theological education in general. This lack was especially felt in the search for potential theological faculty. Candidates for theological faculty were limited to persons who had been educated prior to independence.

Although the churches in English-speaking countries had the option of sending leaders to study overseas, this choice was not viable for churches in Portuguese-speaking Mozambique. The two countries where further study was possible were Portugal and Brazil. Portugal was not a desirable option because of the relatively short history of Protestant churches in the country. Brazil had a longer Protestant history, but there were few established options for graduate theological education. The desire for degree level theological education was keenly felt by church leaders in the various Protestant denominations in Mozambique, but satisfying the prerequisites to achieve that goal, particularly the preparation of national faculty, remained elusive. Meeting this need for national faculty would require a new approach: collaboration among churches, and particularly among their theological schools. Such a collaborative approach came to be and functioned for a period of time, in part meeting its goals, but also it laid some foundations for future work to be done.

Historical Background

The Republic of Mozambique has had a history of Protestant missions since the mid-1800s. The first to be established was the Universities Mission to Central Africa (UMCA), an Anglican-oriented mission founded in response to David Livingstone's lectures upon his return to Britain from Africa in 1856. The first expedition of UMCA missionaries reached Mozambique in 1858, but a permanent mission was not established until in 1882. This was located in the far north of the country on Likoma Island in Lake Niassa, not far from the Mozambique shore.[1]

In the same year that the Likoma mission was established, Presbyterian missionaries were entering the southern area of Mozambique. Yosefa Mhalamhala was the first missionary of the Swiss Mission in Mozambique, crossing the border from South Africa from where he had fled during the Nguni invasions.[2] Five years later, the first European missionary of the Swiss Mission, Paul Berthoud, arrived to give administrative assistance.[3] A mission centre and ministerial training school was established at Rikatla, approximately 15 miles outside Lourenço Marques. By the time Mozambique gained independence in 1975, the Presbyterians had become one of the most influential Protestant churches in the country.

The Methodist Episcopal Church in Mozambique marks its beginning in 1890 when Erwin H. Richards, formerly with the American Board of Commissioners for Foreign Missions, joined the Methodists and began working on the coast of Inhambane Province. In 1901, the Methodist mission in Africa was reorganized, and the work in Mozambique became a part of the East Central Africa Mission Conference under Bishop Joseph C. Hartzell.[4] Other Methodist groups also began work in Mozambique at this time. In 1885, both the Free Methodist Church and the Wesleyan Methodist Church from Britain were established as a result of Mozambican mine workers returning from South Africa who sought to continue the Christian experience that they had encountered while working in the mines.[5]

---

[1] Malyn Newitt, *A History of Mozambique* (Bloomington, IN: Indiana University Press, 1993), 435.

[2] Jan van Butselaar, *Africains, Missionaires et Colonialistes: Les Origines de l'Eglise Presbyterienne du Moçambique, 1880-1896* (Leiden: E. J. Brill, 1984), 24.

[3] Adrian Hastings, *The Church in Africa: 1450-1950* (Oxford: Oxford University Press, 1994), 443.

[4] Foreign Missions Board, *Annual Report of the Foreign Missions Board of the Methodist Episcopal Church for the Year, 1929* (New York: Board of Foreign Missions, 1929), 341.

[5] Clara Evans Keys, *We Pioneered in Portuguese East Africa: A Methodist Missionary's Memoirs of Planting Christian Civilization in Mozambique* (New York: Exposition Press, 1959), 31.

The Church of the Nazarene officially began work in Mozambique in 1922 when Charles and Pearl Jenkins assumed responsibility for an earlier independent work begun by Isaac O. Lehman, a missionary resident in Johannesburg. As with the Free Methodists and the Wesleyan Methodists, the nucleus of the Church of the Nazarene was found among miners who had come to faith while working in the mines of South Africa.[6]

Rev. C. Austin Chawner, a missionary working under the auspices of the Canadian Pentecostal Assemblies of Canada began the Mozambique Assembly of God Church in 1937.[7] Chawner was a gifted linguist and evangelist and was responsible for establishing a number of congregations in and around the capital city of Lourenço Marques. He also began a school for the training of pastors.[8]

Protestant work in colonial Mozambique was never easy. As I have written elsewhere, "although Protestants were allowed to enter and work in Mozambique, it was not without restriction or limitation. Prior to 1920, the large majority of missionaries arriving in Mozambique were from non-Portuguese speaking countries. The fear of missionaries 'denationalizing the natives' became a major concern of the government."[9] Because of limitations placed upon all of these Protestant churches by the colonial government, there was a considerable degree of cooperation among the missionaries of these denominations as evidenced by the establishment of the Portuguese East Africa Evangelical Missionary Association. This association provided opportunities for the missionaries of the various denominations to meet for fellowship and mutual support on a regular basis, but its primary role was to serve as a conduit for making appeals to the International Missionary Council on behalf of the churches in Mozambique in an effort to seek relief from the repressive policies of the Portuguese colonial government.[10] With the coming of Mozambican independence in 1975, the work of all Christian denominations in Mozambique was severely curtailed. The Portuguese East Africa Evangelical Missionary Association came under the leadership of Mozambican church leaders and metamorphosed into the Christian Council of Mozambique. Following the example of its predecessor, its primary role was to represent the churches before the government and to speak out against the repressive policies of the now independent Marxist government. Aside from the collaboration through the Christian Council of Mozambique, the various denominations resorted to

---

[6] Russell V. DeLong and Mendell Taylor, *Fifty Years of Nazarene Missions*, vol. 2, History of the Fields (Kansas City, MO: Beacon Hill Press, 1955), 204.

[7] Although the Pentecostal Assemblies of Canada was aligned with the Mozambique Assembly of God Church, historically, they were separate entities.

[8] Graham Charles Woodward, "Rev. Charles Austin Chawner," Geni.com, https://www.geni.com/people/Rev-Charles-Austin-Chawner/6000000017817659834.

[9] David W. Restrick, "The Church of the Nazarene and the Mozambique Revolution: 1975-1982" (ThD diss., Boston University, 2001), 66.

[10] Portuguese East Africa Evangelical Missionary Association, "Minutes of the Annual Meeting," 1 August 1940, International Missionary Council, Conference of British Missionary Societies. Joint IMC/CBMS Missionary Archives, Africa and India, 1910–1945 (Zug, Switzerland: Inter Documentation Co., 1979), micro-fiche.

establishing and maintaining their own programs as best they could, given the repressive government policies designed to curtail the work of the churches.

Prior to independence, the Church of the Nazarene had a functioning Bible school for training pastors. It was located in the rural Manjacaze District of Gaza Province. It had been established in 1955 but was closed and its installations nationalized by the government in 1976. C. Austin Chawner of the Assemblies of God had also established a pastoral training programme for the churches around Lourenço Marques, but its work was limited in scope and duration. As best as can be determined, it was not functioning at the time of independence.

Two Theological Schools Are Born

In 1982, the government restrictions placed upon the churches were markedly relaxed. The Evangelical Assembly of God Church of Mozambique and the Church of the Nazarene took this opportunity to establish schools for the training of ministers. Rev. Dino Amade, pastor of the Portuguese-language Assemblies church in the centre of Maputo (the post-independence name for Lourenço Marques) was the driving force for the establishment of Escola Bíblica da Assembleia de Deus de Moçambique (Bible School of the Assembly of God of Mozambique). In 1981, Rev. William Cornelius, Director of World Missions for the Pentecostal Assemblies of Canada, visited Mozambique. At that time, Amade spoke with Cornelius about his desire to establish a ministerial training school for the church in Mozambique and officially requested assistance from the Pentecostal Assemblies of Canada. The request was positively received, and efforts began to make Amade's dream a reality.[11]

A Canadian missionary couple serving in Brazil, Rev. Bill and Mrs Linda Mercer, were approached about transferring to Mozambique with the task of establishing a Bible school for training pastors. Accepting this assignment, and after making preparations and securing educational resources in Brazil, the Mercers arrived in Maputo in June 1985. Their first task was to establish a governing board for the proposed Bible school, and then to find a suitable location for classes. With these tasks completed and other challenges overcome, the Bible school officially began classes in October 1985 with a total enrolment of 84 students. One of the major challenges was finding qualified instructors. As a result, most of the teaching responsibility was borne by the Mercers, with some help given by two Mozambican pastors. The first class of 61 students completed their course with the school's first graduation programme held on 19 December 1987.[12]

Over the next seven years, the work of Escola Bíblica da Assembleia de Deus de Moçambique was strengthened and expanded with the arrival of other missionary couples who not only provided leadership for the school, but also became teachers in its various programmes. In 1989, Rev. Reinhard and Mrs

---

[11] Bill Mercer and Linda Mercer, "Early History of the Escola Bíblica da Assembleia de Deus de Moçambique," unpublished manuscript, September 2021. Sent to the author by Reinhard Mattheis.

[12] *Ibid.*

Sieglinde Mattheis arrived from Germany to give assistance to the school, particularly in the securing of property in the city of Maputo and the construction of the school's own facilities. The inauguration of the basic installations at that location took place in June 1994. By that time, Mattheis had been selected to serve as director of the school. Under his leadership, the academic programme and faculty were strengthened, primarily with the arrival of new missionary teachers. These additional instructors made it possible to launch a Bachelor of Theology programme, which coincided with the improvement of educational opportunities in the country in general. However, it was clear that the reliance on missionary faculty could not be sustained indefinitely, and their eventual departure would constitute a desperate need for adequately trained Mozambicans to fill their roles as theological faculty for the school's academic programmes.[13] An additional challenge was the fact that the Mozambique government offered no official recognition for any theological academic programme.

While the Assemblies of God school was developing, similar events were taking place within the Church of the Nazarene. With relaxed government restrictions, two Nazarene leaders took steps for training pastors for their denomination. Rev. Simeão Mandlate, at the time pastor of the Maputo Central Church, and Prof. Vicente Mbanze, former instructor at the Instituto Bíblico Nazareno in Gaza, announced the beginning of classes for anyone who had previously studied at the school in Gaza, but whose studies had been interrupted by the closing of the school in 1976. Informal classes at night were begun in local churches, and it soon became evident that a more structured approach was needed. A board was created, consisting of the district superintendents from Maputo and Gaza Provinces as well as missionary Rev. Frank Howie, at that time working among Mozambican miners in South Africa. Assuming the name of the previously closed school, a curriculum was devised using whatever books had been salvaged from the old school's library. Those who served as teachers were the few pastors who had completed the former school's "fourth year class," described as equivalent to the first year of studies for a Bachelor of Theology degree. Because most of the potential students had secular jobs, classes were held in the evenings at various local churches scattered around the city. Basic instructional materials were sent in from South Africa, but there was a marked lack of textbooks or other resources available for use by the students. Initial class sizes were small but increased as instruction was made available to anyone who felt called to ministry.

In 1987, the pastor of the Maputo City Church of the Nazarene, Rev. Jonas Mulate, moved to the northern city of Nampula to begin planting the Church of the Nazarene in that province. A gifted evangelist, Mulate soon had several churches organized and a number of young people expressing a call to ministry. Mulate appealed to the board of the school in Maputo to include these candidates as students. In response to his appeals, and with more people interested in pursuing theological studies, the board in Maputo requested authorization from the denomination's General Board in the United States to transform their ministerial classes into an official theological training school for the church in

---

[13] *Ibid.*

Mozambique. The petition was granted at the board's annual meeting in February 1989, and plans got under way to secure land in Maputo and drawings for the construction of a campus. At the same time, the board recognized the need to strengthen the faculty and curriculum. At the board's request, Frank Howie approached the author, then serving in South Africa, about transferring to Mozambique and becoming academic dean of the newly constituted Seminário Nazareno em Moçambique. These actions coincided with the construction of a new building for the Maputo Central Church. Because of its central location and its more adequate facilities, seminary classes were all transferred to Central Church where Simeão Mandlate served as both pastor of the church and director of the seminary. Shortly after, Mandlate resigned as pastor of the church to devote his full attention to the development of the seminary.

It was not until February 1992 that the author took up his duties as teacher and academic dean at Seminário Nazareno em Moçambique. In the meantime, Mandlate had begun studies at the denomination's theological college in Swaziland to complete his BTh degree. Also, Jonas Mulate, now doing pioneer work in the city of Beira, had sent a large number of students to Maputo to begin their ministerial studies. One of the primary tasks needing to be completed was a thorough revision of the school's curriculum to bring it into line with the denominational standards for ministerial education. The curriculum revision was completed toward the end of 1993. In January 1994, the seminary held its very first graduation as a four-year educational institution granting a diploma in theology to a total of 35 graduates. Shortly after, the new curriculum was implemented with the beginning of the new academic year.

Over the next two years, work progressed on the development of the new campus in the Laulane area of the city. Several groups arrived from the USA to help with construction, and at the end of 1996, the first building was completed and dedicated. In January 1997, the resident students and their families moved from the Central Church grounds to temporary housing on the new campus, and classes began in the new facilities the following month. At the end of the year, the first group of students completing the academic requirements of the new curriculum in its entirety graduated with the diploma in theology. As they did so, voices were being raised from various sources in the Mozambican church about the possibility of establishing a Portuguese-language college-level bachelor's degree programme in Mozambique. However, at that time, the school had no functioning library, and only two faculty members had an academic degree of any kind.

Developments Outside Mozambique

While these developments were taking place in Mozambique, similar events were taking place in the Americas. In 1989, a group of people with a common dream met on the campus of Fuller Theological Seminary in Pasadena, CA. Their dream was to establish a theological school in Brazil that would provide a broad theological education directed toward the necessities of the churches of Brazil. Their goal was to provide a completely biblical and evangelical ministerial preparation that focused on the spirituality of the student along with an emphasis on practical pastoral ministry with a missional perspective.

Leading this meeting was Rev. António Carlos Barro, a Brazilian who was completing his PhD programme in intercultural studies at Fuller. Upon his return to Brazil, he and his brother, Jorge Henrique Barro, also a PhD graduate from Fuller, began to make contacts across Brazil. In addition to seeking financial support, they also developed a faculty and curriculum for their proposed school. By October 1993, a group of Brazilian Christian leaders had joined their efforts and gave their support to the development of a school in the city of Londrina to be named Seminário Teológico Sul Americano (South American Theological Seminary). Four months later, the school launched its first classes with 42 students enrolled. In 1999, the Brazilian Ministry of Education and Culture officially recognized theology as a college-level course for certification and recommended that the name of the school be changed to Faculdade Teológica Sul-Americana (FTSA) to reflect this official recognition.[14]

Twenty years before FTSA was founded, other events were taking place that would have an impact not only in Brazil, but also in Mozambique. In 1974, a group of businessmen from Indianapolis were in South Korea attending the building dedication at the Seoul Theological Seminary. While there, they were informed that many of the students of the seminary did not have the resources to pay for their studies. The group returned home and were determined to raise funds and to establish scholarships for these students. They formed an organization for this purpose, and Overseas Council International was born. Over the next ten years, the scope of the Overseas Council's involvement expanded to include various areas to help seminary leaders improve their institutions, particularly in the strategic development of faculty for the training and development of Christian ministers. The influence of Overseas Council International expanded to include more than 100 evangelical ministerial training institutions in over 70 countries.[15]

Cooperative Efforts in Mozambique

By 2000, there were only a limited number of theological training institutions located in Maputo, Mozambique. Located about 15 miles north of the city centre was the Seminário Unido de Rikatla (United Seminary of Rikatla), supported by the United Methodist Church, the Presbyterian Church of Mozambique and the United Church of Christ (Congregational), also known as "American Board." Closer to the city centre were the Escola Bíblica da Igreja União Batista (Union Baptist Bible School), Seminário Nazareno em Moçambique (Nazarene Seminary in Mozambique), Escola Bíblica Betel (Bethel Bible School) and Escola Bíblica da Assembleia de Deus (Assembly of God Bible School). There was little to no communication and no cooperation at all among these various

---

[14] Faculdade Teologica Sul-America, "Conheça a FTSA: Sobre Nós – Nossa História," Faculdade Teologica Sul-America Website, https://ftsa.edu.br/sobre-nos/.
[15] Overseas Council, "Our Story," United World Mission, https://uwm.org/overseas/learn/story/.

theological schools. Each school functioned in isolation and served the needs of their respective denominations. Contact among the personnel of these schools was largely informal, either through an interdenominational church which held services in English, or through a school for missionary children established by One Mission Society (formerly Overseas Mission Society).

Late in 2005, the author, serving as the interim director of the Nazarene seminary, received an invitation from Rev. João Barbosa, a Brazilian missionary serving with One Challenge mission, to join with several other missionaries involved with theological education to meet with Dr António Carlos Barro, director of FTSA, and with Dr Manfred Kohl, a representative of Overseas Council International. The meeting was held several days later at the Villa Italia on the Maputo seafront and in attendance were Barbosa, Barro, Kohl, Rev. Reinhard Mattheis, director of the degree programme of the Assembly of God Bible School, Rev. Steve Chaloner, mission director for the Pentecostal Assemblies of Canada in Mozambique, and the author, David Restrick. Barbosa chaired the meeting as the person who knew all of the participants. After introducing Barro and Kohl, they presented their personal and institutional backgrounds and their shared vision of cooperating with existing theological schools in Mozambique to establish a masters-level programme in Mozambique to be taught in Portuguese. The purpose of this programme would be to improve the academic quality of seminary faculty and leaders for the churches of Mozambique. Barbosa determined that the two schools most likely to cooperate in such a venture were the Assembly of God Bible School and the Nazarene Seminary in Mozambique.

The basic plan of Barro and Kohl involved investment on the part of FTSA in developing the curriculum and providing faculty who would travel to Mozambique during the course of two years to give intensive classes. Students would then have a third year to do research and write a thesis. The schools in Mozambique would recruit students, provide classroom and library facilities, and arrange accommodation for the visiting professors. The costs would initially be subsidized by Overseas Council, with more of the costs being covered by student fees as the programme became established. Considerable discussion followed their presentation, with questions and answers flowing in both directions. There was a favourable response from all involved in the discussions. In the end, it was decided that the respective school representatives would present the proposal to their constituencies and prepare to meet again in the early part of 2006.

In the interim, the proposal was presented to the leaders of the Assemblies of God Church in Mozambique as well as to the local and regional leaders of the Church of the Nazarene. All of the Assemblies of God leaders were enthusiastic about the venture. The faculty and the Board of Directors of Nazarene Seminary were also in favour of proceeding, but some church leaders both in Mozambique and at the denomination's regional offices in South Africa were less enthusiastic. The decision was taken to proceed, and an ad hoc committee began informal discussions to determine how to establish the programme logistically. It was agreed that the location of classes and professor accommodation would be at the Nazarene Seminary because there were already adequate facilities there. The libraries of both schools would be available for the use of the students, and computer facilities with internet access would also be established at both schools to support the programme.

Another organizational meeting was held on 15 March 2006. According to the minutes of that meeting, those present were Manfred Kohl from Overseas Council International, Bill Houston from Overseas Council: Africa, António Carlos Barro, João Barbosa, Stephen Chaloner, Reinhard Mattheis and David Restrick. By this time, many of the logistical matters had been resolved by the ad hoc committee, and these were presented at this March meeting. Key issues agreed upon included that the programme would be evangelical in theology; a completed bachelor's degree would be a pre-requisite for all applicants; the programme would be open to men and women alike; and students would be required to pay an application fee of 100 US dollars with tuition set at 1000 US dollars. It was agreed that those administering the programme in Mozambique would be Restrick and Mattheis. Restrick, who held a doctoral degree from Boston University, would oversee the academic side of the programme, and Mattheis would be the administrator of the programme. A local working committee consisting of Chaloner, Barbosa, and Restrick was suggested; but when Chaloner announced that he was being transferred to Kenya, Mattheis was substituted in his place. It was also decided that this working committee would seek to enlist church leaders to serve on a proposed Committee of Reference. The proposed members would not only be representatives of the Assemblies of God and the Church of the Nazarene, but members of other denominations were also suggested with the vision of expanding the denominational involvement in the project. Finally, it was decided that by 1 May 2006, the basic working committee would be in place and functioning. In October, an orientation meeting would take place, and the first teaching sessions would be scheduled for December 2006.

Further meetings were held by the local representatives. By the end of April, a constitution had been drawn up stipulating a number of key characteristics for the programme. From the outset, the organizers shared a vision for the programme to eventually become self-sufficient, both financially and academically. With that in mind, they chose to name it Instituto Superior Teológico Evangélico de Moçambique (ISTEM). In the interim, the constitution recognized that the ownership remained with FTSA. The constitution also presented other pertinent information relating to its functioning.[16] With this work completed, and with Manfred Kohl advising, the local committee drafted a proposal to submit to Overseas Council International requesting funding for the project. By autumn 2006, Overseas Council International had pledged funding in the amount of 58,000 US dollars over the course of three years, the amount pledged and paid in 2007 being 16,000 US dollars.

With the receipt of this funding, the organizers could move forward with planning to launch the programme with the first cohort of students. Coordination

---

[16] Reinhard Mattheis, *et al*, "Constitution," Instituto Superior de Teológica Evangélica de Moçambique, unpublished manuscript, ISTEM papers, 30 April 2006. Sent to the author by Reinhard Mattheis.

with FTSA in Brazil resulted in the establishment of a list of classes as well as the professors who would be responsible for each class. In total, students would be required to take ten classes over the course of two years, and then write a thesis with all their work being evaluated by the faculty in Brazil. The classes included: Research Methods in Theology, Biblical Theology of Urban Mission, Biblical Theology of Holistic Mission, Church Planting and Administration, Reconciliation and Pastoral Care, Biblical Leadership and Ethics, The Old Testament in the African Church, Culture and Mission in Theological Perspective, Curriculum Development, and Teaching the Bible in the Contemporary Church. Although the goal of starting classes in December 2006 was not met, it launched in April 2007.

In total, 24 students were enrolled in the first year of ISTEM representing 8 different denominations, 15 of whom were members of the Assembly of God Church of Mozambique. Much work went into planning for this first group of students, and the organizers were pleased when plans came to fruition with a minimum of complications. All ten subjects were taught through 2007 and 2008, and students began work on their theses early in 2009. The first graduation ceremony was held on 1 May 2010 with much celebration by the leaders in Mozambique, by the graduating students, and by those who had conceived of such a programme many years before.

Over the next 12 years, 4 more cohorts progressed through the programme. A total of 71 men and women representing 18 different denominations enrolled. Forty-eight students completed the course and graduated. Unfortunately, with the graduation held in 2019, ISTEM ceased operation.

Several factors led to the end of ISTEM, but the primary factor was financial. While the original director and administrator served the programme as volunteers, everyone knew that eventually workers would need to be paid. Provisional budgetary planning was developed to take this into consideration and to provide a salary for a director and administrator. In the end, although tuition payments from students did cover much of the costs, it was still insufficient to sustain the programme once the funding from Overseas Council International came to an end.

Accelerating this process was the retirement of ISTEM's original leaders in Mozambique. The author, who served as academic director, retired and left Mozambique in early 2013. Reinhard Mattheis retired in 2014, and although he remained in the country for sustained periods over the subsequent three years, efforts to pass responsibility onto Mozambican leadership were not successful. One person did assume responsibility as academic director, and he served with a high level of motivation and expertise. However, the offer of a sponsorship to do further studies in Brazil brought his tenure as director to a close.

A more discouraging reason for the programme's demise was the fact that the Mozambican government never officially recognized the diplomas granted to the students. Official recognition by the government for any academic work was critically important to Mozambicans considering further education. This lack of recognition negatively impacted the attractiveness of the programme, and in the end, contributed to its demise. Prospective students felt that a programme not officially recognized by the government was not worth their financial investment.

Some would say that the whole venture was a failure because it did not endure for more than a few years. However, there were benefits that may not be measurable in terms of numbers. In terms of collaboration among various entities, one would have to conclude that there was a great deal of success. The first obvious result was the collaboration among those who inaugurated the programme. The key players would not normally be expected to be collaborators. The fact that Nazarenes, members of the Assemblies of God, and Presbyterians, with the assistance of Overseas Council International, all came together to develop a programme that would be satisfactory to them all was a significant example of collaboration for the good of the kingdom. One could say that this was due more to the qualities of the persons themselves rather than their denominations, but the effect was to open channels of communication and cooperation among those denominations in Mozambique, and among other theological schools in the area as well.

The cooperation also spawned a sense, not only of collaboration, but also camaraderie and collegiality, among the students. António Chavo, one of the students, reports that the experience "permitted me to better understand how the others thought about a topic, and to better understand some questions that we had criticized without any deeper thought on the matter. They also helped me to better understand the doctrines of my own church."[17] Another student, André Inguane, reports that it was a very positive experience for him to learn of the differences in interpretation and doctrines of other denominations, but especially to establish meaningful relationships with members of other churches.[18] Simão Simbine states, "Initially, it was strange and a bit strained to study with people from other churches, but after a short while, it became quite pleasing. Our differences were used positively as we exchanged experiences and helped each other to learn."[19] This spirit can also be extended to the relationships developed among the Mozambican students and the Brazilian professors who came from FTSA. Although some critics thought that the professors were too liberal, Reinhard Mattheis, programme administrator, believes that it was a benefit to Mozambican church leaders to be exposed to that spectrum of the body of Christ.[20]

Finally, the programme did reach its original goal of providing a more highly trained faculty for the two host theological schools. Graduates serve on the faculty of both schools enriching the quality of instruction. Additionally, it led to the establishment of a pattern and tradition in the various collaborating institutions that anyone who is tasked with the responsibility of teaching others must be trained at, and have successfully attained, a level of education at least one degree higher than that of the students.

---

[17] António Chavo, email to David Restrick, 4 April 2022.
[18] André Inguane, email to David Restrick, 4 April 2022.
[19] Simão Simbine, email to David Restrick, 14 April 2022.
[20] Reinhard Mattheis, email to David Restrick, 15 February 2022.

Conclusions

The development of Instituto Superior de Teologia Evangélica de Moçambique was a successful experiment in substantive collaboration among churches in Mozambique. Looking back at that experience and at the current state of theological education in Mozambique, one cannot help but wonder if that collaborative effort could serve as a model for all theological education within Mozambique. It cannot be denied that adequate financial support is essential for any educational institution to be successful, and this fact is equally and especially true for theological schools. It is a challenge for denominations to support their own ministerial training schools in Mozambique without funding from overseas; and when this funding is progressively being reduced, the challenge becomes even greater. This is especially true in countries like Mozambique where personal disposable income is at a minimum if it exists at all. It is this challenge that makes a collaborative approach to theological education appear more and more attractive.

Historically, the several evangelical denominations which have theological schools in Maputo have been content to maintain their independence for training pastors. However, in the view of the author, the experience of collaboration for graduate level education provides a template for collaboration at the diploma and bachelor levels as well. Of course, financial support would need to be addressed. However, combining faculties and other resources would enhance the educational experience of all the students, and it would still be possible for the denominations to maintain their own distinctives in terms of theology and polity within the curriculum of a combined institution. This system could have ramifications not only in the capital, but could also be applied in other centres of the country, with the overall effect being the strengthening of theological education for all of Mozambique.

The overarching factor in the sustainability of any collaborative approach to theological education in Mozambique is this: it must be seen to be originated by Mozambicans themselves. Although this factor is not overtly stated as a factor in the termination of the ISTEM master's degree programme, nevertheless, one cannot help but conclude that if the originators had been Mozambicans, the final outcome might have been different. Even so, this collaborative approach to theological education did have its successes, and it stands as an example for future possibilities in theological education in Mozambique and elsewhere.

KAIROS – Contributing to Restoring Right Relations with Indigenous Peoples in Canada

Stephen Allen

He has told you, O mortal, what is good;
and what does the Lord require of you
but to do justice, and to love kindness,
and to walk humbly with your God?
Micah 6:8 (NRSV)

In the fall of 1977, Project North, an ecumenical coalition of several Protestant denominations, the Canadian Conference of Catholic Bishops, and several Catholic religious orders organized a tour of Indigenous leaders and elders from the Mackenzie Valley in the Northwest Territories to a number of cities in southern Canada. This tour provided an opportunity for the Indigenous peoples of the Mackenzie Valley to share their concerns and fears with Canadians about the potential impact of the proposed Mackenzie Valley pipeline on the land, the waters, their livelihoods, and their culture. The initiative regarding the Mackenzie Valley pipeline was one component in Project North's programme that reflected a commitment to support Indigenous peoples in northern Canada in their struggles for justice and settlement of their land claims and a commitment to challenge Canadians across the country to become involved in the ethical issues of northern development.

Three years earlier, in March 1974, the Government of Canada established a public inquiry to investigate the social, economic, and environmental impacts of the proposed pipeline. The Government appointed the late Justice Thomas Berger to lead the public inquiry. The Mackenzie Valley pipeline was intended to transport natural gas from the Beaufort Sea, across northern Yukon, and through the Mackenzie Valley delta, to connect with gas pipelines in northern Alberta. In his inquiry, Justice Berger met with representatives from the oil and gas sector, local governments, environmental organizations, and with Indigenous peoples in 30 Dene and Inuvialuit communities in the Yukon and the Mackenzie Valley. Indigenous leaders had begun to inform and consult with Indigenous communities who would be affected by a pipeline.

Justice Berger submitted his report to the late Warren Allmand, the Government of Canada's Minister of Indian and Northern Affairs. Berger's report recommended that the pipeline not be built across northern Yukon due to the Yukon's sensitive ecosystem and that there be a ten-year moratorium of a pipeline down the Mackenzie Valley until land claims with Indigenous peoples had been resolved. Allmand accepted the recommendations of the Berger inquiry and persuaded the federal Cabinet to do so as well.[1] The inquiry's

---

[1] Following his retirement from public life, Warren Allmand became an active volunteer with KAIROS' Indigenous Rights Circle, part of KAIROS' governance structure.

recommendations halted what would have been one of the largest industrial projects in Canadian history. It highlighted the ongoing tension and debate regarding resource extraction projects and their impact on Indigenous peoples and fragile ecosystems in Canada and elsewhere in the world. This issue is still relevant in Canada and in other countries with Indigenous populations.

Project North provided an opportunity for Indigenous peoples to communicate their concerns and fears with Canadians in southern Canada. Created in 1975 by the Anglican Church of Canada, the Canadian Conference of Catholic Bishops and the United Church of Canada, Project North was established as a result of Indigenous leaders challenging the churches to support Indigenous peoples' struggles for justice. Over the next few years, the Lutheran Church in America Canada Section, the Mennonite Central Committee of Canada, The Presbyterian Church in Canada, the Evangelical Lutheran Church in Canada, the Society of Jesus (Jesuits), the Council of Christian Reformed Churches in Canada, the Religious Society of Friends (Quakers), and the Oblate Conference of Canada joined Project North.[2] In 1989, Project North became the Aboriginal Rights Coalition and was one of the ten ecumenical coalitions brought together to form KAIROS in 2001.

This case study explores the ecumenical collaboration and social justice work of KAIROS from its inception in 2001 to 2021. This study will develop the context and identity of KAIROS by exploring its history and creation in its Canadian context and focusing specifically on KAIROS' role as a collaborator and connector in supporting Indigenous peoples' struggles for justice in Canada.[3] Extending from this foundational understanding, the case study will outline one of KAIROS' programmes – the Indigenous Rights Program – and a resource called the KAIROS Blanket Exercise.[4] Through exploring the development and influence of this resource, the study will highlight KAIROS' contribution to non-Indigenous Canadians learning about the history of the relationship between Indigenous peoples and settlers and how events of the past continue to shape relationships today. KAIROS' history and development over the past 21 years offers valuable social, theological, and missiological insight into Christian collaboration in a changing Canadian landscape.

KAIROS: Ecumenical Social Justice in the Canadian Context

As the example of Project North illustrates, KAIROS' roots date back to the ecumenical and social justice movements which emerged in the 1970s and 1980s in Canada. During this period, a number of Protestant denominations, the Canadian Conference of Catholic Bishops, and Roman Catholic religious orders

[2] For background information on Project North, see Peter Hamel, "The Aboriginal Rights Coalition," in Christopher Lind and Joe Mihevc, eds, *Coalitions for Justice: The Story of Canada's Interchurch Coalitions* (Ottawa: Novalis, 1994), 16–36.
[3] Through the Indigenous Rights Program, KAIROS invites non-Indigenous Canadians to critically examine the history of Indigenous and non-Indigenous relations, an important contribution in changing attitudes toward Indigenous peoples.
[4] For information on KAIROS' programmes, see KAIROS Canada, "What We Do," KAIROS, https://www.kairoscanada.org/what-we-do.

came together to establish ecumenical coalitions with mandates to focus on specific regions of the world or specific issues.[5] These coalitions reflected a commitment to the Lund Principle, that churches should "act together in all matters except those in which deep differences of conviction compel them to act separately," and to the gospel call to seek justice in the world.[6]

By the 1990s, however, the context in Canada that engendered the creation of these coalitions was changing. Christopher Lind and Joe Mihevc, editors of *Coalitions for Justice – The Story of Canada's Interchurch Coalitions,* sounded a note of caution in 1994 when they wrote:

> the coalitions were created in a time of optimism as well as hope. In the spirit of ecumenism, church leaders saw that it was possible to do together things that it may have been impossible to do alone. Today, a new spirit is upon us. It is a spirit of pessimism born of scarcity. We fear that this spirit is more protective of the old growth of denominational loyalty and theological retrenchment than of the tender shoots of ecumenical co-operation for justice.[7]

The pessimism and scarcity expressed by Lind and Mihevc signalled a broader change in the church's role in Canadian society. By the late 1990s, the church no longer had the influence and power it once enjoyed. Membership in many Christian denominations was dropping. With fewer members, denominational budgets began to shrink. Staff in some national offices were being laid off. Church programmes were being cut.

In the 1990s, revelations about physical and sexual abuses committed against Indigenous children in residential schools run by the Anglican Church of Canada, a number of Roman Catholic orders and dioceses, The Presbyterian Church in Canada, and the United Church of Canada on behalf of the Government of Canada increasingly came to light. These allegations gave rise to mounting lawsuits by Survivors[8] of the residential schools against the Government, the denominations, and Catholic orders and dioceses. The financial strain on the churches, and by extension on the ten ecumenical coalitions, increased, putting into question their sustainability. A new ecumenical model was required to meet the challenges of the times.

On 1 July 2001, KAIROS: Canadian Ecumenical Justice Initiatives was established and housed in the United Church of Canada. Church representatives took great care to keep their respective denominations and religious communities

---

[5] The ten coalitions were the Aboriginal Rights Coalition; Canada-Asia Working Group; Ecumenical Coalition for Economic Justice; Inter-Church Action for Relief, Development & Justice; Inter-Church Committee on Human Rights in Latin America; Inter-Church Coalition on Africa; Inter-Church Committee for Refugees; PLURA/Presbyterian, Lutheran, United, Roman Catholic, Anglican (PLURA provided grants to anti-poverty groups in Canada); Taskforce on the Churches and Corporate Responsibility; and Ten Days for World Development (an education and advocacy coalition that involved resource people from the Global South visiting congregations in communities across Canada).

[6] The Lund Principle emerged out of the Faith and Order Conference of the World Council of Churches held in Lund, Sweden, in 1952.

[7] Lind and Mihevc, eds., *Coalitions for Justice*, 11.

[8] The word "Survivors" is capitalized based on Indigenous peoples' preference.

informed of the discussions and negotiations that led to KAIROS' creation. The initial membership of KAIROS included the Anglican Church of Canada, the Canadian Catholic Organization for Development & Peace, the Canadian Conference of Catholic Bishops, the Canadian Religious Conference (the 250 men's and women's Catholic orders), the Canadian Yearly Meeting/Religious Society of Friends (Quakers), the Christian Reformed Church in North America (Canadian Corporation), the Evangelical Lutheran Church in Canada, the Mennonite Central Committee of Canada, The Presbyterian Church in Canada, Primate's World Relief and Development Fund (the relief and development agency of the Anglican Church of Canada), and the United Church of Canada.[9]

While recent surveys report that Canadians are divided about the role religion should play in public life, and as public awareness about the harm done in residential schools grows, KAIROS has adapted to a changing social context.[10] Today, KAIROS engages in research, policy development, education, and advocacy, and it offers support to grassroots action. Central themes include ecological justice, gender justice, migrant justice, and Indigenous rights. KAIROS staff support a network of activist volunteers in some 43 local groups across Canada. KAIROS' other programmes deserve equal attention, but this case study focuses on the Indigenous Rights Program.

KAIROS as Collaborator and Connector in Canada: Contributing to Restoring Right Relations with Indigenous Peoples

The Indigenous Rights Program illustrates KAIROS' commitment to collaboration and partnership with Indigenous peoples, communities, and organizations. The effectiveness of one of its resources, the KAIROS Blanket Exercise, has resulted in many invitations from public institutions and non-profit organizations to facilitate the exercise. The Indigenous Rights Program has developed in response to major events addressing the relationship between Indigenous and non-Indigenous peoples in Canada. Two important initiatives include the Royal Commission on Aboriginal Peoples (RCAP) and the Indian Residential Schools Settlement Agreement, which included the Truth and

---

[9] A Memorandum of Agreement, approved by the governing bodies of the denominations and religious orders, spelled out the rights and responsibilities of all signatories. At the time of KAIROS' creation, the United Church of Canada was large enough to meet the Canada Revenue Agency's requirement that no more than 10 percent of a charity's budget could be allocated to advocacy. This is still the case today. The United Church issues charitable tax receipts for donations to KAIROS.

[10] See Angus Reid Institute, "Faith and Religion in Public Life: Canadians deeply divided over the role of faith in the public square," Angus Reid Institute, 16 November 2017, https://angusreid.org/faith-public-square/; Michael Lipka, "5 Facts About Religion in Canada," Pew Research Center, 1 July 2019, https://www.pewresearch.org/fact-tank/2019/07/01/5-facts-about-religion-in-canada; Darrell Bricker and Haley Jones, "Canadians Agree (77%) There Should Be a National Day of Remembrance for Victims of Residential Schools, but Split on Removing Statues (52%)," Ipsos, 9 June 2021, https://www.ipsos.com/en-ca/news-polls/canadians-agree-there-should-be-national-day-of-remembrance-for-victims-of-residential-schools.

Reconciliation Commission of Canada (TRC). Understanding the background of these initiatives shows what has shaped the Indigenous Rights Program and underscores KAIROS' commitment to supporting justice for Indigenous peoples in Canada.

Royal Commission on Aboriginal Peoples/RCAP

The Royal Commission on Aboriginal Peoples was mandated to investigate and propose solutions to the challenges affecting the relationship between Aboriginal peoples (First Nations, Inuit, Métis), the Government of Canada, and Canadian society as a whole. RCAP's final report in 1996 included a recommendation that non-Indigenous Canadians learn about Indigenous people and the relationship between Indigenous people and non-Indigenous people. There were 440 recommendations in this 4,000-page final report which called for fundamental changes in the relationship between Indigenous peoples and Canada. Three recommendations, which were not acted upon until close to a decade later, dealt specifically with Indian Residential Schools. Most of the recommendations have not yet been implemented.

Indian Residential Schools

Between the 1870s and into the 1990s, over 150,000 Indigenous children were forcibly removed and separated from their families and communities and shipped to residential schools, often hundreds of kilometres away from their families. Residential schools were intended to assimilate Indigenous children into the dominant Christian culture.[11] Most schools were closed by the 1970s; the last school was closed in 1996. The physical and sexual abuse suffered by children in the residential schools was systemic. The Rt Hon. Beverley McLachlin, former Chief Justice of the Supreme Court of Canada, described the residential school system as cultural genocide.[12]

In the late 1990s and into the next decade, a growing number of residential school Survivors courageously came forward to speak about the physical and sexual abuse they suffered at these schools. Lawsuits, mounted by Survivors, were filed against the churches and Catholic orders and dioceses that ran the schools. The federal government decided that a comprehensive approach was needed to address the harm done to Indigenous children and communities.

In a process facilitated by a retired Supreme Court of Canada Justice, the Indian Residential Schools Settlement Agreement was reached in November 2005 and implemented on 19th September 2007. The Settlement Agreement included Survivors of residential schools, lawyers representing Survivors, the Assembly of First Nations, Nunavut Tunngavik Inc., Inuvialuit Corporation, Makivik Corporation, the Anglican Church of Canada, the Catholic Entities

---

[11] Aimée Craft, Phil Fontaine, and the Truth and Reconciliation Commission of Canada, *A Knock at the Door: The Essential History of Residential Schools* (Winnipeg: University of Manitoba Press, 2015).
[12] Sean Fine, "Chief Justice says Canada attempted 'cultural genocide' on Aboriginals," *Globe and Mail*, 28 May 2015, https://www.theglobeandmail.com/news/national/chief-justice-says-canada-attempted-cultural-genocide-on-aboriginals/article24688854.

(created to represent the 47 dioceses and religious orders that ran residential schools), The Presbyterian Church in Canada, the United Church of Canada, and the Government of Canada. The Indian Residential Schools Settlement Agreement is the largest class action settlement in Canadian history. In an earlier ruling by the Supreme Court of Canada on 21st October 2005, the churches' liability for abuse suffered by Indigenous children would be capped at 25 percent. The Government of Canada would cover 75 percent.

Indian Residential Schools Settlement Agreement –
Truth and Reconciliation Commission of Canada/TRC

The Indian Residential Schools Settlement Agreement included the creation of the Truth and Reconciliation Commission; a Common Experience Payment to Survivors, that is compensation for each year of attending a residential school; the creation of the Independent Assessment Process run by the Indian Residential Schools Adjudication Secretariat for claims of sexual and/or serious physical abuse; funding support for commemoration activities; measures to support healing such as the Indian Residential Schools Resolution Health Support Program and an endowment to the Aboriginal Healing Foundation.

The Truth and Reconciliation Commission (TRC) held seven national events, which took place between 2010 and 2015. The events gave Survivors an opportunity to share publicly what had happened to them in a residential school. Survivors could also give their testimonies in private. Over 6,000 Survivors gave their testimonies. The TRC's national events included Education Days for children in senior primary grades and secondary school students. KAIROS was invited to several national events as a resource on Education Days and facilitated the Blanket Exercise, an experiential workshop in which participants learn about the impact of colonization on Indigenous peoples in Canada. This exercise includes learning about Indian residential schools. The request for KAIROS to lead Blanket Exercise workshops increased dramatically following the conclusion of the TRC in 2015.

KAIROS contributed to the TRC in other ways. With the approval of the TRC, KAIROS invited Naty Atz Sunuc, a Maya Kaqchikel woman and a KAIROS partner from an Indigenous organization in Guatemala, to participate in a panel at a national event. Naty Atz Sunuc was invited to be an Honorary Witness at a subsequent national event. Honorary Witnesses were inducted at each TRC national event. Toward the end of each national event, Honorary Witnesses would be invited to publicly reflect on what they had heard and learned. They would also be expected to share what they had learned once the TRC event had ended. At the first national event Naty Atz Sunuc attended, she talked about the treatment of Indigenous people in Guatemala. She also learned about the treatment of Indigenous peoples in Canada.

A Programme in Focus: The KAIROS Blanket Exercise

An important resource in the Indigenous Rights Program is the KAIROS Blanket Exercise. It is an experiential workshop that has been effective in educating Canadians about the history of colonization in Canada and its impact on

Indigenous peoples. It was developed following the Royal Commission on Aboriginal Peoples' final report. Staff and volunteers with the Aboriginal Rights Coalition (formerly Project North and later one of the ten founding coalitions of KAIROS), began to develop an exercise to accomplish this goal.[13] That exercise, originally created in 1996, has developed into what is now called the KAIROS Blanket Exercise. Since the conclusion of the TRC, KAIROS has facilitated the Blanket Exercise with a wide range of Canadian organizations.

The KAIROS Blanket Exercise Explained

To begin, blankets are laid on the floor. The blankets touch each other and represent Turtle Island, the name given by some Indigenous peoples to what is now the continent of North America before colonization. There may be up to 30 people on the blankets. For the purpose of the exercise, participants on the blankets represent Indigenous peoples with the exception of one "European" who hands out scrolls and cards to participants. Some participants receive scrolls, others receive cards, and some get both. The scrolls are numbered and are part of the script. When it gets to the appropriate part of the script, the narrator will, for example, ask the person with scroll no. 1 to read it aloud. The scroll may refer to Indigenous people who died of infectious diseases brought by Europeans. The narrator explains that those holding a white card represents Indigenous people who died from infectious diseases. They are asked step off the blankets. A participant holding scroll no. 2 is asked to read it aloud. The scroll may refer to Indigenous children who never returned home from residential school. The narrator explains that those holding a grey card are asked to step off the blankets. Participants who are asked to step off the blankets either sit or stand away from the blankets.

Participants do not stand still but are constantly moving from one blanket to another. During the exercise, the European folds up the blankets. Participants are instructed to stay on the blankets and not step on the floor. Movement is increasingly restricted during the exercise, and participants become more and more isolated from each other. At the end of the one-hour exercise, there are few Indigenous people left on the blankets. Most of the blankets, symbolizing Indigenous territory, have been completely folded or removed. There are few participants left on the blankets. Those that are still on the blankets can no longer get to another blanket.

This powerful exercise sheds uncomfortable light on the colonization of Indigenous peoples. One example of its effectiveness comes from an especially moving occasion when the KAIROS Blanket Exercise was facilitated on the grounds of Parliament Hill in Ottawa in June 2015. Canada's Parliament Buildings and much of the City of Ottawa are on unceded Algonquin territory. No treaty has been signed between the Crown and the Algonquin peoples. The sobering reality of the ongoing effects of colonization and the unrecognized loss of Indigenous land and rights came alive for the several hundred participants who were led in this poignant exercise by Indigenous youth. During the same

---

[13] As described in the previous sections, The Aboriginal Rights Coalition was one of ten ecumenical coalitions brought together to form KAIROS in 2001.

week in Ottawa, the commissioners of the TRC presented their recommendations, referred to as the 94 Calls to Action.[14]

The Evolution of the KAIROS Blanket Exercise

For many years, the KAIROS Blanket Exercise was largely carried out in churches. As noted earlier, this began to change at the national events of the TRC. Following the conclusion of the TRC's mandate in 2015, there was a growing demand for KAIROS to facilitate the exercise. What began as an act of social justice growing out of Canadian ecumenism has become an integral educational tool and contribution to truth telling and reconciliation used in many sectors of Canadian society.

At a KAIROS Steering Committee meeting in June 2019, staff reported that there were 1,200 requests a year to lead the Blanket Exercise.[15] By the end of 2019, the last year when KAIROS could facilitate in-person workshops over a 12-month period, KAIROS led 900 Blanket Exercises. There were 120 institutional partnerships implementing the KAIROS Blanket Exercise.[16] In 2021, in the midst of the COVID-19 pandemic, KAIROS delivered more than 200 virtual exercises to 10,000 participants from coast to coast to coast and overseas. While workshops continue to occur in churches, many of the organizations are not ones that churches generally have contact with. Some of the workshops are provided on a contractual basis. This is the case with federal civil servants and with Royal Canadian Mounted Police (RCMP) recruits.[17] While the RCMP issued a formal apology to Indigenous peoples at a national event of the TRC, racism directed at Indigenous peoples still exists in the RCMP. A point made by the commissioners of the TRC is that reconciliation involves all Canadians and all Canadian institutions.

Below is a partial list of organizations whose members have experienced the KAIROS Blanket Exercise:

- Canada School of Public Service: 627 public servants were trained in 2018–2019.[18]

---

[14] Truth and Reconciliation Commission of Canada, *Calls to Action* (Winnipeg: Truth and Reconciliation Commission of Canada, 2015), https://ehprnh2mwo3.exactdn.com/wp-content/uploads/2021/01/Calls_to_Action_English2.pdf.

[15] KAIROS, Steering Committee meeting, meeting minutes are in possession of the author, 7 June 2019.

[16] KAIROS, Steering Committee meeting, meeting minutes are in possession of the author, 25 February 2020.

[17] The Royal Canadian Mounted Police is Canada's federal police force. It is also the provincial and criminal police establishment in all provinces except Ontario and Quebec and the only police force in the Yukon and Northwest Territories.

[18] In 2017, an agreement was reached with the Canada School of Public Service to offer Blanket Exercise workshops to federal civil servants. In 2018–2019, 30 workshops were given involving 627 participants. The current contract with the Canada School of Public Service ends in 2022. KAIROS is negotiating a new contract that will include training facilitators.

- Canadian Food Inspection Agency: training for staff has taken place in 16 locations across Canada.
- Crown Attorneys: 78 Crown Attorneys have been trained.
- Royal Canadian Mounted Police: KAIROS has led the Blanket Exercise with new recruits at the RCMP's training centre in Regina, Saskatchewan, and is negotiating a new contract with the RCMP.
- Alberta Teachers' Federation.
- Toronto Catholic School Board.
- The Rotary Club of Canada: 750 Rotary Club members across Canada have been trained.
- New Canadians: partnerships have included the Canadian Council for Refugees, the Ontario Council of Agencies Serving Immigrants, and Newcomer Women Organization.
- Migrant workers.
- Churches across Canada: congregations invite KAIROS staff or denominational staff to facilitate the Blanket Exercise.

The KAIROS Blanket Exercise is most effective when delivered by an Indigenous team of two or three facilitators. The initial version of the Blanket Exercise drew on scholarly research provided to the Royal Commission on Aboriginal Peoples. Subsequent editions of the KAIROS Blanket Exercise and new versions are developed in consultation with Indigenous peoples and continue to draw on scholarly research. In the past few years, KAIROS has hired a number of staff, largely Indigenous, to lead the workshops. There are now five editions of the Blanket Exercise. The KAIROS Blanket Exercise is available in English, French, and Spanish, and a youth script has been developed.[19]

The Blanket Exercise is being adapted in a growing number of countries. Naty Atz Sunuc's visit to the TRC's national events led to a Guatemalan youth group visiting Canada in June 2017. Following this visit, a Canadian youth group composed of First Nations, Inuit, Métis, and settler youth visited Guatemala later in August of the same year. The Blanket Exercise is being adapted to the Guatemalan context. It is also being adapted by organizations in Australia, Ecuador, the Philippines, and the United States.

The Blanket Exercise has come a long way since it was first developed following the final report of the Royal Commission on Aboriginal Peoples in 1996. This resource represents an important contribution by KAIROS and its member denominations and religious communities in support of Indigenous rights in Canada and increasingly in support of Indigenous people in other countries. The collaboration with Indigenous peoples that began with the

---

[19] The Blanket Exercise is intended to shed light on a history that is unfamiliar to most Canadians. Whether this includes Indian residential schools or treaties between the Crown and First Nations that in too many instances have not been respected by the Crown, it is a history that is not taught in primary and secondary schools in most provinces, although it is taught in the three territories – the Yukon, the Northwest Territories, and Nunavut.

development of the first edition of the Blanket Exercise continues as new editions are developed.

Conclusions:
Social, Theological, and Missiological Significance Toward Tomorrow

In a post-Christendom Canada, the church no longer has the influence it once had. Sarah Travis observes that the Christian church is now in the process of disestablishment, a process that is painful yet potentially life-giving to the church. Travis acknowledges the fears this process may cause for many, but she also believes that a church that finds itself on the margins is no less equipped to serve.[20] In *Transforming Mission: Paradigm Shifts in Theology of Mission*, David Bosch draws on five models of church, articulated by Dulles and later referred by Burrows.[21] Bosch suggests that the church functions as an institution, a mystical communion, a sacrament, a herald, and a servant. Bosch's models of church find expression in the members of KAIROS. The aspects of KAIROS' programmes presented in the case study most clearly demonstrate how a theology of service is an effective model of church in its context of disestablishment.

Current trends in Canadian society point to a continuing decline in most mainstream Protestant denominations as well as in many Catholic orders. A growing number of Christians in Canada state they are not affiliated to any denomination.[22] A temptation for Christian denominations and organizations, including KAIROS, would be to look to the future with some anxiety or perhaps for some, even despair. Instead, leadership by several Catholic orders have hope, as evidenced in their creation of the Justice Fund in KAIROS. This endowment fund includes gifts and loans from several religious orders as well as churches and individuals. The Justice Fund represents a commitment to KAIROS and to ecumenical justice for the future regardless of the state of the church.

And despite the national decline in many denominations and religious orders, membership in KAIROS has remained stable for the past 20 years. The one exception, which KAIROS' board of directors accepted with regret, was the decision by the Canadian Conference of Catholic Bishops (CCCB) to withdraw from KAIROS in 2016. The CCCB had difficulty with some aspects of KAIROS' structure, namely the fact that KAIROS' letterhead includes the names of all its members. Because the CCCB did not always agree with the content of some of the advocacy letters, it would have preferred having its name removed on letters with which it did not agree with the content. While this difficulty led to the CCCB's withdrawal, Catholic membership in KAIROS thankfully continues with the Canadian Religious Conference and the Canadian Catholic Organization for Development & Peace.

---

[20] Sarah Travis, *Metamorphosis: Preaching after Christendom* (Eugene, OR: Cascade Books, 2019), 14.

[21] David J. Bosch, *Transforming Mission: Paradigm Shifts in Theology of Mission* (Maryknoll, NY: Orbis Books, 2009), 469.

[22] See footnote 10 of this essay.

In the midst of change, KAIROS continues to adapt for the future. Members of KAIROS agreed several years ago to increase the number of positions on the Steering Committee. Two of these new positions provide for an Indigenous presence. In addition, there is a position for an individual involved in migrant rights. These changes to KAIROS' governance structure reflect KAIROS' commitment to Indigenous and migrant rights and leadership.

In the coming years, the church in Canada will look very different than it does today. KAIROS' members will be affected by these changes. Regardless of what these changes bring, KAIROS and its members can build on the ecumenical partnerships which began to develop in the 1970s. KAIROS celebrated its 20th anniversary in 2021. There was much to celebrate and to be thankful for. Nonetheless, the issues KAIROS and its members will face in the future will be challenging and complex. Collaborating with other organizations in Canada and around the world will be necessary and mutually beneficial. The gospel's call to seek justice will be as essential to KAIROS in the coming years as it is today.

Mission is a multifaceted ministry composed of witness, service, justice, healing, reconciliation, liberation, peace, evangelism, fellowship, church planting, contextualization, and much more.[23] Bosch's call for the mission of the church to be constantly renewed and reconceived rings true for KAIROS today and into the future.[24] Historically, as demonstrated throughout this case study, KAIROS' mission has been renewed and reconceived through its commitment to mutual partnership that elevates the voices and lived experiences of its partners. The ecumenical social justice work of KAIROS remains rooted in a missiology of mutuality and advocacy that is "not a passive and semi-reluctant coming together but an active and deliberate living and working together."[25] In the World Council of Churches' *Together towards Life: Mission and Evangelism in Changing Landscapes*, we are reminded that living God's mission "requires a commitment to struggle against and resist the powers that obstruct the fullness of life that God wills for all, and a willingness to work with all people involved in movements and initiatives committed to the cause of justice, dignity and life."[26]

---

[23] Bosch, *Transforming Mission*, 512.
[24] *Ibid.*, 519.
[25] Bosch, *Transforming Mission*, 464. Here, Bosch is referring to ecumenism, and the author extends Bosch's comments to the ecumenical work of KAIROS.
[26] Jooseop Keum, ed., *Together towards Life: Mission and Evangelism in Changing Landscapes* (Geneva: WCC Publications, 2013), 7.

Partnership on the Evangelical Margins: Lausanne's Global Creation Care Network in North America

Tyler Lenocker

One week after Hurricane Sandy swept over Jamaica – and while the storm was still battering America's eastern seaboard – 57 delegates from 28 countries met on the island nation and launched a global network of evangelical creation care leaders. The coalition, eventually named the Lausanne/WEA Creation Care Network (LWCCN), was birthed from the Lausanne movement and its historic 2010 Cape Town congress.[1] LWCCN – a product of intercultural collaboration from the start – has since emerged as the dominant global evangelical network devoted to environmental wellbeing.[2]

This chapter explores LWCCN's development and the challenges and opportunities created by the network's global reach yet enduring North Atlantic organizational centre of gravity. The association and its partners demonstrate how international evangelical bodies founded in the middle of the 20th century have become the most sustainable institutions from which to launch creation care initiatives. Key partners include relief, development, and traditional mission organizations. The environmental impulse among evangelicals has most often expanded the reach of extant organizations rather than birthed new ones, and LWCCN has laboured to join the leaders of such initiatives into networks.

Lausanne's network has not only emerged as the leading global coalition of evangelical creation care leaders but also as the sole regional coalition in North America. The association has filled a void left by marginal and often competitive evangelical organizations in the United States. A time of increasing peril in the natural world has coincided with a time of increasing politicization in American evangelicalism. The Trump era has further narrowed America's signature expression of Protestant Christianity, quieting moderates who would be more open to integrate creation care into their faith and pushing many young supporters of environmental activism out of Christianity altogether. Mediated through the Lausanne network, the still growing global evangelical community provides a stimulating safe haven for Americans seeking to be both godly and

---

[1] The incorporation of the World Evangelical Alliance (WEA) into the Lausanne Creation Care Network in 2016 is described below.

[2] This case study is based partially on eight oral history interviews conducted by the author with evangelical leaders involved in and beyond Lausanne's creation care network. Lowell Bliss, Zoom interview by author, 11 January 2022; David Bookless, Zoom interview by author, 8 March 2022; Ed Brown, Zoom interview by author, 15 December 2021; Jason Fileta, Zoom interview by author, 8 April 2022; Jasmine Kwong, Zoom interview by author, 31 January 2022; Lascelles Newman, Zoom interview by author, 21 January 2022; Mark Polet, Zoom interview by author, 2 February 2022; Lowell Pritchard, Zoom interview by author, 11 January 2022.

green.[3] The network also introduces North Americans to pioneering endeavours in the Global South – often undertaken in partnership with Western expatriates – that integrate spiritual, social, and environmental restoration among the world's most vulnerable people and places.

Lausanne, as a global network, also presents limitations for US-based creation care leaders. LWCCN is more effective at drawing North American creation care advocates into the global evangelical communion than bringing the travails and power of the global church to bear on local environmental action in North America. As products of the 20th century, most global evangelical organizations with North American origins remain rooted in a "from the white suburbs to the world" orientation. Yet, the parachurch is where evangelical ecumenism happens.[4] For evangelicals, Christianity's unitive impulse manifests itself in issue specific networks. The issues themselves, for good or for ill, provide the contours of global Christian belonging. The universality of the ecological threat that respects no borders creates an opportunity. It creates an opportunity to further subvert structures and mentalities dividing the West and the rest. The global threat can drive the global body of Christ into deeper bonds of fellowship marked by shared vulnerability. Whether or not the increasingly nationalist American evangelical church can live into those relationships – and whether Lausanne can facilitate a small piece of that transformation – remains an open question.

A Brief History of Evangelicals and Creation Care

While the current manifestation of evangelicalism in the United States remains one of the great global impediments to humanity's stewardship of God's

---

[3] This study defines "evangelical" as those individuals – and institutions – self-identifying as "evangelical." Self-identification and its relation to institutional identification allows for tensions inherent within term "evangelical" as a national religious identifier and/or global religious identifier. Self-identification also creates space for evangelicals found in mainline Protestant denominations. Mainline evangelicals, along with many non-mainline evangelicals, have promoted creation care initiatives which often go unnoticed given the broader public resistance to environmental efforts among the American evangelical base. A prominent example is the founding of Floresta (now Plant with Purpose) by Tom Woodard out of Mount Soledad Presbyterian Church (USA) in California in 1984. Plant with Purpose integrated economic, environmental, and spiritual restoration from its founding and has become one of the leading evangelical environmental organizations in the world. Like the role of Anglican Communion for evangelical Anglicans described below, US mainline denominations have created institutional and theological space for evangelicals in those denominations committed to creation care. For Plant with Purpose's origins, see Melanie Gish, *God's Wounded World: American Evangelicals and the Challenge of Environmentalism* (Waco, TX: Baylor University Press, 2020), 54–55.

[4] Joel Carpenter also highlights the centrality of the parachurch – rather than denominational structures – in forming fundamentalist associations and identity in the first half of the 20th century. The pattern continued with those later identifying as "evangelicals." Joel Carpenter, *Revive Us Again: The Reawakening of American Fundamentalism* (Oxford: Oxford University Press, 1997), 32.

creation, the early evangelical movement and its forebearers pioneered efforts to protect the natural world. The vigorous reformist impulse of Puritans, non-conformists, and other early expressions of pietist Protestantism extended to human and non-human creation. Driven by Reformed understandings of God's revelation in the natural world and postmillennial eschatologies, Puritans led efforts for the humane treatment of animals and agricultural reforms, including mass tree planting efforts in England.[5] Early participants in the modern Protestant missionary movement likewise demonstrated commitments to reform human relationships to the nonhuman world. Missionary pioneer William Carey founded the Agricultural and Horticultural Society of India in 1820. Members of the evangelical Anglican Clapham Sect – most famous for William Wilberforce's efforts to abolish slavery – helped found the Society for the Prevention of Cruelty to Animals in 1824.[6]

Twentieth century American evangelicals diverged from this legacy. Their embrace of modern business developments, a selective rejection of modern science, and wide adoption of premillennial eschatology created a toxic cocktail of forces that drove most American evangelical heads into the sand as the global ecological crisis unfolded. The movement's leaders welcomed modern technology and the fruits of the fossil fuel industry, especially when they resourced missionary initiatives, gospel crusades, and theological schools.[7] Like most Americans, only with added theological warrant, evangelicals readily embraced a consumptive lifestyle facilitated by the US's expanding commercial empire overseas.

Despite collective resistance to efforts promoting environmental wellbeing, creation care initiatives emerged on the evangelical margins from the beginning of the contemporary environmental movement. Fitting with his broader critique of Western modernity, Francis Schaeffer's *Pollution and the End of Man,* published in 1970, is recognized by many as the earliest evangelical publication to tackle ecological concerns.[8] The first decades of the present environmental movement saw greater openness and debate among evangelicals regarding their engagement in ecological work.[9] Due in part to inheriting fundamentalism's apoliticism, the era predated the politicization of evangelicalism and its later identification with the political, economic, and religious right.

---

[5] Belden C. Lane, *Ravished by Beauty: The Surprising Legacy of Reformed Spirituality* (Oxford: Oxford University Press, 2011), 31–36.
[6] David Bookless, "Jesus is Lord…of All? Evangelicals, Earth Care, and the Scope of the Gospel," in Kapya J. Kaoma, ed., *Creation Care in Christian Mission* (Oxford: Regnum, 2015), 108. For an important historical survey of missions and environmental care, see Dana L. Robert, "Historical Trends in Missions and Earth Care," *International Bulletin of Mission Research* 35, 3 (July 2011): 123–29.
[7] For evangelical entanglement in the fossil fuel industry, see Darren Dochuk, *Anointed with Oil: How Christianity and Crude Made Modern America* (New York: Basic Books, 2019).
[8] Francis A. Schaeffer, *Pollution and the Death of Man: The Christian View of Ecology* (Wheaton, IL: Tyndale House, 1970).
[9] Gish, *God's Wounded World,* 36.

In 1979, Calvin DeWitt pioneered the Au Sable Institute of Environmental Studies, the first US evangelical organization devoted to ecological concerns. Au Sable and its educational emphasis shaped an early generation of evangelical creation care leaders, especially many scientists who went on to establish departments and initiatives devoted to sustainability and ecology at the nation's many private evangelical colleges.[10] Other national evangelical organizations followed, including Plant with Purpose, Christian Nature Federation, Restoring Eden, Blessed Earth, and the Evangelical Environmental Network (EEN). Founded in 1993, EEN began not as a grassroots evangelical effort but rather as an interreligious initiative that sought to develop an evangelical arm to carry out environmental advocacy. The EEN's early dependence on secular funding sources demonstrated its lack of connection to its evangelical base and the general challenge of all US evangelical environmental organizations to secure funding from its constituency. Also, for most of its history, the EEN was not a network but an advocacy group, another organization that other fledgling evangelical environmental groups had to compete against for scarce resources – both financial and human.[11] The perpetual absence of US evangelical coalescence in the promotion of creation care opened organizational space for a global association to provide leadership where national initiatives faltered.[12]

Creation Care and the Lausanne Movement

The Lausanne/WEA Creation Care Network emerged in the early 21st century as North America's predominant evangelical environmental association. Its formation demonstrates how organizations coming from 20th century evangelical missionary initiatives – in tandem with evangelical relief organizations founded mid-century – created the most enduring networks in which to embed national evangelical creation care efforts. Other evangelical missionaries promoted aspects of creation care prior to LWCCN. In 1975, W. Dayton Roberts, a missionary with Latin America Mission, wrote *Running Out: A Compelling Look at the Current State of Planet Earth*.[13] In a 1994 book, Roberts called for a "Fraternity of Missionary Earthkeepers."[14] Missionary and mission professor

---

[10] Early books by DeWitt included Calvin DeWitt, *Earth-Wise: A Biblical Response to Environmental Issues* (Grand Rapids, MI: CRC Publications, 1994); Calvin DeWitt, *Caring for Creation: A Responsible Stewardship of God's Handiwork* (Grand Rapids, MI: Baker Books, 1998).

[11] Bliss, interview by author; Brown, interview by author.

[12] Despite the inability to sustain a national network, evangelicals active in environmental work have come together at numerous occasions to issue national statements on evangelical commitment to creation care. These include statements by the National Association of Evangelicals in the early 1970s; "An Evangelical Declaration on the Care of Creation" issued in 1994; and the "Evangelical Climate Initiative" from 2006. For accounts of these statements see Gish, *God's Wounded World*, 36, 71–77.

[13] W. Dayton Roberts, *Running Out: A Compelling Look at the Current State of Planet Earth* (Ventura, CA: Regal Books Division, G/L Publications, 1975).

[14] W. Dayton Roberts, *Patching God's Garment: Environment and Mission in the 21st Century* (Monrovia, CA: MARC, 1994).

William Dyrness wrote on creation care beginning in the 1980s.[15] Lausanne's own embrace of creation care as a part of mission has its roots in the first Lausanne congress in 1974. Latin American evangelicals like C. René Padilla, with the support of British theologian John Stott, ensured that social action be included in the *Lausanne Covenant* as a component of mission. The expansion of mission beyond verbal proclamation of the gospel in Padilla's *misión integral* paradigm created space for the incorporation of other missiological priorities in the future.[16]

Lausanne leaders' openness to the incorporation of creation care as an aspect of mission also emerged from international Christian bodies beyond the evangelical community. The impact of Anglicanism – mediated through John Stott – on global and American creation care advocates looms large to this day. Stott began preaching on environmental stewardship in the 1970s and became one of the first council members for the Christian conservation organization A Rocha, founded in 1983.[17] A Rocha was started in Portugal by Anglican church-planter, and friend of Stott's, Peter Harris. Stott's advocacy for A Rocha helped it become the preeminent evangelically rooted conservation organization in the world.[18] Stott's integration of creation care did not, however, occur in a vacuum. Beginning in the late-1960s, the Church of England began promoting forums and publications devoted to the environment.[19] In 1990, the Anglican communion added promotion of the "integrity of creation" to its "Marks of Mission."[20] David Bookless and Lascelles (Las) Newman, both Anglican leaders in Lausanne, credit the "Five Marks of Mission" in shaping their views on environmental stewardship. The Anglican Communion shapes evangelical discourse, and the reverse, with evangelical Anglicans bridging the two global networks.

John Stott also illustrates the role of conciliar Protestant bodies in resourcing evangelical engagement in creation care. Despite common narratives of evangelicals abandoning World Council of Churches (WCC) circles wholescale after the 1968 Uppsala assembly, many, like Stott, maintained connections with the WCC. The missiological work of J. Andrew Kirk evidences the influence of conciliar conversations on global evangelical networks. Kirk was a regular

---

[15] William Dyrness, "The Stewardship of the Earth," in Wesley Granberg-Michaelson, ed., *Tending the Garden: Essays on the Gospel and the Earth* (Grand Rapids, MI: Eerdmans, 1987).

[16] The holism found within what was eventually termed integral mission/*misión integral* is found throughout C. René Padilla, *Mission Between the Times: Essays on the Kingdom* (Grand Rapids, MI: Eerdmans, 1985).

[17] R.J. Barry and Laura S. Meitzner Yoder, eds., *John Stott on Creation Care* (London: Inter-Varsity Press, 2021), 13.

[18] The US-based Plant with Purpose (PWP) is also a leading global evangelical environmental organization.

[19] G.W. Dimbleby, *Man in His Living Environment: An Ethical Assessment* (London: Church Information Office for the Church Assembly Board for Social Responsibility, 1970).

[20] Anglican Communion, "History of the Five Marks of Mission," Anglican Communion Office, Last accessed 2022, https://www.anglicancommunion.org/mission/marks-of-mission/history.aspx.

participant in both WCC and Lausanne circles and his 1999 missiological text *What is Mission?* devoted a chapter to environmental care and promoted the WCC emphasis on protecting the "Integrity of Creation."[21] While "Creation Care" has become the dominant moniker among evangelicals, "Integrity of Creation" was introduced into WCC discussion by theologian Jürgen Moltmann at the 1983 Vancouver Assembly.[22] The phrase was adopted later by the Anglican Communion, influencing the many Anglicans who have shaped the Lausanne Movement. The evangelical movement remains porous, shaped by global Christian conversations that predated or paralleled Lausanne's own prioritization of creation care as a core component of mission. Thus, when 4000 evangelicals from 198 countries gathered at Lausanne's 2010 Cape Town Congress, many were already engaged in an international Christian dialogue on the church's role in stewarding the environment.

The 2010 Cape Town Congress devoted a "multiplex" breakout session to the topic of creation care. The session created a space where evangelical environmental pioneers working regionally prior to the gathering formed a global network. The session was organized by Ken Gnanakan (1940–2021) from India and Lascelles Newman from Jamaica. David (Dave) Bookless from England and Edward (Ed) Brown from the US joined Gnanakan and Newman after Cape Town to launch Lausanne's creation care efforts. The group reflected the British imperial legacy – and the dominance of the English language – that still shapes the contours of global evangelical networks to this day. Gnanakan held a PhD from the University of London, had worked as a professional musician and travelling evangelist, and then as a theological educator and administrator. His ACTS Ministries school promoted environmental work from its founding in 1979, and Gnanakan wrote *God's World: A Theology of the Environment* in 1999.[23] Lascelles Newman was also a theological education administrator, an Anglican lay minister in his native Jamaica, and a long-time participant in the Lausanne Movement. He worked for decades with the International Fellowship of Evangelical Students (IFES), through which he met Ed Brown. The two had already promoted creation care gatherings through IFES.[24] The global IFES network originated in late-19th century England and then expanded as InterVarsity Christian Fellowship in the United States in the mid-

---

[21] J. Andrew Kirk, *What Is Mission? Theological Explorations* (Minneapolis, MN: Fortress Press, 2000), 167. See also Allen Yeh, *Polycentric Missiology: Twenty-First-Century Mission from Everyone to Everywhere* (Downers Grove, IL: InterVarsity Press, 2016) for a contemporary example of an evangelical intentionally crosspollinating conciliar and evangelical missionary networks.
[22] "Integrity of creation" was then added by the WCC to earlier emphases on peace and justice, to create the council's "Justice, Peace, and the Integrity of Creation" initiative. R.J. Barry, "Creation Care: A Brief Overview of Christian Involvement," in Colin Bell and Robert S. White, eds., *Creation Care and the Gospel: Reconsidering the Mission of the Church* (Peabody, MA: Hendrickson, 2016), 112.
[23] Ken Gnanakan, *God's World: A Theology of the Environment* (London: SPCK, 1999).
[24] Newman, interview by author.

20ᵗʰ century. The network served as an early site for international evangelical initiatives in creation care.[25]

Dave Bookless, also an Anglican, grew up in India as the son of Church Missionary Society (CMS) missionaries and was also part of IFES networks from his university days. In 2001, Bookless helped found A Rocha-UK and then served as Director of Theology for A Rocha International. Ed Brown also grew up as a child of missionaries. His parents served as Baptists in Pakistan. Brown worked with InterVarsity Christian Fellowship at the University of Wisconsin-Madison and then as chief operating officer for the Au Sable Institute. In 2005, he helped found Care of Creation, an organization which promoted environmental missions in Kenya. Beyond their robust international connections, the stories of Brown and Bookless demonstrate the enduring importance of missionary children – and the generational power of their parents' pioneering cross-cultural commitments – in promoting entrepreneurial and sometimes unpopular initiatives on the margins of their religious communities. Maverick missionary kids – Brown and Bookless – and Global South evangelicals – Newman and Gnanakan – drove the early formation of Lausanne's international creation care network.[26]

The Cape Town Congress also gave the network, and the global evangelical family, theological license to place creation care at the heart of their missionary calling. "The Cape Town Commitment" (CTC) was unequivocal in its integration of creation care in mission, including the topic in both its "confession" and "call to action" sections.[27] Like the Lausanne Covenant, the CTC was crafted by an evangelical Anglican, Christopher Wright. Wright, an Old Testament scholar and protégé of John Stott, brought prior commitments to environmental care to his work on the CTC. The finalized CTC called for "urgent and prophetic ecological responsibility" by "living out the biblical truth that the gospel is God's good news [...] for individual persons, *and* for society, *and* for creation. All three are broken and suffering because of sin; all three are included in the redeeming love and mission of God; all three must be part of the comprehensive mission of God's people."[28]

The Jamaica Consultation

As Lausanne expanded the theological scope of mission, so the organization expanded the variety of sub-networks within the movement. The Cape Town gathering catalyzed a global evangelical network committed to promoting creation care through churches and parachurch organizations around the world. Through conversations between Ed Brown, Lascelles Newman, Lausanne

---

[25] Brown, interview by author.
[26] Dana Robert highlights the importance of missionary children in pioneering ecological initiatives in Dana L. Robert, *Christian Mission: How Christianity Became a World Religion* (Malden, MA: Wiley Blackwell, 2009), 111.
[27] *Cape Town Commitment* I.7.A; II.6 in J.E.M. Cameron, ed., *The Lausanne Legacy: Landmarks in Global Mission* (Peabody, MA: Hendrickson, 2016).
[28] Italics in original. *Cape Town Commitment* I.7.A.

International Director Lindsay Brown, and Chairman Douglas Birdsall, creation care was chosen as the first follow up consultation after Cape Town.[29] Newman, in conversation with Brown, put the Caribbean forward, specifically his native Jamaica, to host the creation care consultation. The choice of Jamaica was both pragmatic and symbolic. Brown and Newman had already partnered to host an IFES creation care gathering with North American student leaders in Jamaica in 2008. Also, for Newman, the Caribbean stood on the frontlines of a warming and volatile climate. Appearing providential, Hurricane Sandy swept through the Caribbean and up the eastern American seaboard only one week before the event. The impact of Sandy almost derailed the consultation, reminding participants of the urgency of their task.

The Jamaica gathering drew 57 participants from 28 countries, but the gathering pulled heavily from Anglophone nations, most notably from the Anglophone North Atlantic. The participants included a strong contingent of Christian scientists, theologians, and Bible scholars, but practitioners dominated. The consultation discovered that at least four global mission organizations already had a staff member devoted to creation care: Wycliffe/SIL (Summer Institute of Linguistics), TEAM (The Evangelical Alliance Mission), OMF (Overseas Missionary Fellowship), and Christar.[30] The most heavily represented organization at the event was A Rocha, along with multiple attendees from World Vision and Tearfund. Tearfund (the Evangelical Alliance Relief Fund) grew out of the UK-based Evangelical Alliance and the fund they created in 1959 to provide assistance to Cold War-era refugees.[31] Tearfund has become a global evangelical leader in creation care initiatives, often embedding environmental projects in their relief and development work as well as working to mobilize churches around the world to better care for God's creation. UK-led organizations like Tearfund and A Rocha have often stepped in to fill the institutional vacuum created by grassroots American evangelical resistance to the environmental movement.

Tearfund has also set up a branch in the United States and now employs Jason Fileta, one of the most pioneering evangelical creation care activists in the country. Fileta, son of Egyptian immigrants, mobilizes young evangelicals for environmental advocacy at the grassroots through cultural mediums. He does this through Christian artists, musicians, and worship gatherings and partners with the 24/7 Prayer movement through their digital prayer app to call for prayer for those in the global church suffering from climate change.[32] Fileta's work demonstrates how our current ecological crisis has evolved the strategies and priorities of evangelical relief and development. The evolution has entailed not simply an expansion of mission priorities but also a growing focus on community-based solutions that wed spiritual and environmental renewal at the

---

[29] Brown, interview by author.
[30] Ed Brown, "Report on the Lausanne Consultation on Creation Care and the Gospel," 5 February 2013, Ed Brown Personal Papers. Document emailed to author.
[31] Brian Stanley, *The Global Diffusion of Evangelicalism: The Age of Billy Graham and John Stott* (Downers Grove, IL: IVP Academic, 2013), 63.
[32] Fileta, interview by author.

local level. Examples include Tearfund's promotion of its "Umoja" church mobilization curriculum in environmental initiatives as well as Plant With Purpose's growing prioritization of spiritual and ecological restoration in damaged watershed zones.[33] Such localized integral mission activities offer perhaps the most promising models from LWCCN partners for evangelical creation care endeavours.

In addition to creating a global network of evangelical environmental leaders, the 2012 Jamaica gathering produced a written statement, "The Jamaica Call to Action," and led to a book, *Creation Care and the Gospel: Reconsidering the Mission of the Church*.[34] The "Jamaica Call to Action" was oriented, as its title suggested, to action rather than theological reflection. Such actions called for included "environmental missions among unreached people groups," "radical action to confront climate change," and promoting "an economy that works in harmony with God's creation."[35] The document set apart its closing, and longest, section for a call to prayer – prayer that is "intentional and fervent, soberly aware that this [creation care] is a spiritual struggle."[36] The emphasis on prayer – a conspicuous characteristic of many evangelical creation care gatherings – formed a core part of not just the "Call to Action" but also the programme of the Jamaica gathering itself. Indian leader Ken Gnanakan was most responsible for shaping the activities in Jamaica, including its time devoted to collective prayer. Gnanakan also provided the structure for *Creation Care and the Gospel* and its section divisions of "God's Word," "God's World," and "God's Work."[37]

The most enduring product of the Jamaica gathering was a commitment to plan regional gatherings to bring together local creation care leaders to share resources and catalyze actions. The gatherings took place for Southeast Asia in the Philippines in 2014; East and Central Africa in Kenya in 2015; North America in the US in 2015; Latin America and the Caribbean in Peru in 2015; West Africa in Ghana in 2015; South Asia in Nepal in 2016; East Asia in Pakistan in 2017; Europe in France in 2017; Southern Africa in South Africa in 2018; and Oceania in Australia in 2018. After a pause due to the COVID-19 pandemic, the conferences resumed in 2022, with Eastern Europe gathering in Croatia and the Middle East/North Africa gathering in Jordan.

The Lausanne Creation Care Network in North America

After Jamaica, Ed Brown was formally appointed Lausanne's Creation Care Catalyst to help organize the subsequent regional consultations. The 2015 North American gathering was held at Gordon College, a private evangelical liberal arts school in the Boston suburbs. The gathering helped bring cohesion to the

---

[33] Pritchard, interview by author; Francis Njoroge, Tulo Raistrick, Bill Crooks, and Jackie Mouradian, *Umoja: Transforming Communities* (Teddington, UK: Tearfund, 2009).

[34] Bell and White, *Creation Care and the Gospel*.

[35] "Jamaica Call to Action," in Bell and White, *Creation Care and the Gospel*.

[36] *Ibid.*

[37] Bell and White, *Creation Care and the Gospel*, v–vii.

still marginal and fragmented evangelical creation care movement in the US.[38] Also, with the Lausanne emphasis on regions rather than countries, the "North American" gathering included Canadian evangelicals from the beginning. Canadian evangelicals had long been more amenable to the integration of the creation care into their churches and ministries and continue to wield disproportionate influence in LWCCN. Katherine Hayhoe, the Canadian-born Chief Scientist for The Nature Conservancy and professor at Texas Tech University, participates in Lausanne events, including Jamaica 2012. Jasmine Kwong, a Toronto native of Chinese descent based in the Philippines, works as the Creation Care Advocate for the mission organization OMF. Kwong's journey to eco-mission began through secular community development work on food security and then an internship with International Justice Mission in the Philippines.[39] Through OMF, she partners with the non-profit Reefs for Life, a group that organizes Filipino fishermen to help restore coral reefs in their local communities. Kwong will soon transition into the Creation Care Catalyst role with LWCCN.[40]

Given its short lifespan, the current global Lausanne creation care network and its influence over North American evangelicals remains tenuous. The 2015 gathering produced Lausanne's relationship with the World Evangelical Alliance (WEA) through New Zealand-born, US-based Christopher Elisara, director of the WEA's Creation Care Task Force. The Lausanne-WEA bond has expanded the network's reach but has also created confusion among LWCCN participants regarding who leads specific initiatives. The 2015 meeting produced a design team – a mix of college professors and non-profit administrators – to build and promote a new North American network of evangelicals devoted to the environment.[41] The organization never materialized. The COVID-19 pandemic holds partial blame, as does the perennial challenge of launching an initiative with little funding and no full-time staff. Also, while professors and non-profit and mission organization leaders dominated the regional gathering, few clergy or denominational leaders attended the event. LWCCN's formal gatherings, especially in North America, operate more as professional societies for creation care specialists rather than drawing a diverse set of actors representing the broader North American evangelical community.

After the 2015 Boston meeting, LWCCN hosted digital global gatherings: "Creation Care at the Crossroads" in 2020 and "Creation at the Crossroads 2.0" in 2021. The 2020 event gathered over 70 participants from 25 countries. North American participants unfamiliar with Lausanne gatherings were introduced to

---

[38] Bliss, interview by author.

[39] Kwong, interview by author.

[40] Kwong also participated in a pilot project of the Oikos Network, launched in the fall of 2022. The Oikos Network is a joint initiative of the LWCCN, A Rocha, Tearfund, the Anglican Alliance, and Renew Our World. Oikos groups bring together small cohorts of Christian leaders involved in creation care "to be a space to build friendships and connections with like-minded individuals from across the globe through online peer-support groups and events." "Oikos Network," World Evangelical Alliance Sustainability Center, Last accessed 2022, https://wea-sc.org/en/oikos-network.

[41] Bliss, interview by author.

the diversity of the global evangelical community. Speakers included Filipino Rei Lemuel Crizaldo, Tearfund's theological education coordinator in Southeast Asia; Latin American Ruth Padilla DeBorst, theological education leader with Resonate Global Mission; and Filipino Efraim Tendero, General Secretary of the WEA. The programme was sponsored by the University of Wisconsin-Madison's Loka Initiative through a friendship developed by Ed Brown, who lives in Madison, with Loka's Buddhist director, Dekila Chungyalpa. Brown convinced the university's organizers that evangelicals were best engaged as a distinct global community rather than being mashed together with interfaith efforts. Through the partnership, three science professors from the university also spoke at the gathering. Lack of funding from the evangelical grassroots helped push Lausanne into partnership with a secular public university. The second gathering in 2021 opened with prayer by Ed Brown and then mindfulness breathing exercises led by Dekila Chungyalpa. The interreligious and secular partnerships promoted by evangelical efforts to build global creation care networks signified the pioneering nature of their eco-mission efforts as well as their continual disconnect from the American evangelical grassroots and their money.

The Peril and Promise of Business

Evangelical non-profit dependence on private US-based funding from wealthy conservative donors has limited sustained global efforts to promote creation care. Despite the demographic diversification of global Christianity, the bulk of institutional and financial resources still lie in the West. Private donors and family foundations can promote a type of fiscal colonization through causes donors choose or choose not to underwrite. While funders pour millions into American organizations reaching unreached people groups abroad, groups promoting evangelical engagement in environmental wellbeing struggle to garner grants in the tens of thousands of US dollars at best.[42] When donor-funded missionaries begin to shift their work to environmental causes, funders quietly pull their money away.[43] Wealthy evangelical donors are more willing to open their pocketbooks for organizations working against poverty, like World Vision or World Relief. However, explicit talk of promoting environmental work not only fails to elicit donor enthusiasm, but also imperils future funding for non-environmental work.[44]

While evangelical ties to business have often limited the work of creation care activists, an alternative network of evangelical business entrepreneurs with connections to the mission movement may offer the most creative and effective pathways and partnerships for environmental work. Another product of Cape Town 2010 was BAM Global, launched by Lausanne in 2011 to act as a network for leaders and practitioners of "Business as Mission." The BAM movement

---

[42] Brown, interview by author.
[43] Bliss, interview by author.
[44] Jason Fileta, interview by author. Ed Brown commented that World Vision engages in many more creation care endeavours overseas than it reports to its US-based donors. Brown, interview by author.

began when traditional missionaries used "shell businesses" to gain visas to restricted countries, but the movement slowly developed into a global network of legitimate Christian business people seeking to promote holistic transformation through their for-profit endeavours.[45] The BAM Global network encourages its members to promote four "bottom-lines": "People (social), Planet (environmental), Purpose (discipleship), and Profit (sustainable)."[46] In 2019, Canadian Mark Polet, who participates in LWCCN, started as BAM Global's Ambassador for Creation Care. Polet, a biologist by training, had founded and then sold a waste management company in Canada. His family simultaneously began participating in short-term mission trips through their church, where Polet witnessed the potential for transformational business endeavours overseas.

Polet has networked a younger, emerging contingent of creation care-oriented BAM entrepreneurs. The leaders include Christopher Chukwunta, the Canadian-based and Nigerian-born Vice President of International Renewable Energy Systems, a company promoting solar and wind technologies. American Mike Mannina, also a participant in BAM Global, leads the non-profit Thrive Worx and first launched the for-profit Thrive Farmers that promotes sustainable cultivation of coffee and tea. Colby May, another evangelical entrepreneur, worked in the field of energy efficiency in Texas prior to attending Gordon-Conwell Theological Seminary for an MA in Ethics. To pay for graduate school, with his wife Amanda May, the Mays launched Energy for Purpose (EFP), a company promoting energy efficiency in churches and Christian colleges and seminaries. After seminary, the Mays started the non-profit Energy for Mission (EFM), using 40 percent of their for-profit revenue to fund and administer holistic mission projects around the world. Many of the projects integrate creative energy projects like solar to promote spiritual, social, and environmental wellbeing in DR Congo, Myanmar, India, and the urban US.[47] Beyond businesses with explicit commitments to creation care, a younger generation of evangelical business leaders lacks many of their elders' phobias of the environmental movement. The younger business leaders will be tomorrow's donors, and global networks like Lausanne do well to connect them to pioneering works that wed mission and creation care.

Conclusion: A Return to People (then Places)

In a recent conversation between the author and a Puerto Rican Pentecostal minister from inner city Boston, the minister described the disconnect between his own community and its needs and the evangelical creation care conversation and its priorities. He critiqued the educated middle-class elitism of the broader environmental movement that still characterizes most North American evangelical participants in the LWCCN. The pastor argued that an emphasis on caring for *the generations* (of people) and promoting *community health* would

---

[45] C. Neal Johnson, *Business as Mission: A Comprehensive Guide to Theory and Practice* (Downers Grove, IL: InterVarsity Press, 2009), 31–38.
[46] Mark Polet, interview by author.
[47] The author, Tyler Lenocker, served as the Executive Director of Energy for Mission.

most animate his own congregation to engage in holistic care for their urban environment. His congregation was a community of humans fighting to survive in a dehumanizing city.[48]

In debates between a biocentric and anthropocentric approach to environmental work, evangelical theologians involved in Lausanne increasingly argue that a theocentric perspective should guide Christian environmentalism.[49] Theocentrism, it is argued, guards against the total devaluation of human uniqueness in biocentrism and the exploitation of the natural world caused by the anthropocentrism that dominated Western modernity. The theocentric shift seems the appropriate horizon of all Christian work and worship in the world. However, the evangelical movement is likely on its surest footing in the present moment as it centres its environmental energies and priorities on people. As this study has demonstrated, the institutions that often best sustain evangelical environmental work began not as conservation organizations but as relief and development organizations. Furthermore, the younger generation of creation care leaders like Jasmine Kwong and Jason Fileta, both from immigrant families, began their vocational lives working for social justice, not saving endangered species. This people-centred ethic is communicated by the title of evangelical scientist Katherine Hayhoe's recent book: *Saving Us*.[50] Evangelicalism is its best as a popular movement of transformed lives transforming lives. Lausanne's creation care leaders should harness evangelical populism, not avoid it.

Thus, while evangelical authors of the Cape Town Commitment have expanded holistic mission to include the nonhuman world, the origins of *misión integral* best anchor the evangelical creation care community. These origins were human suffering caused by humans. If any group in the United States best represents the Christian face of suffering caused by a volatile climate, it is poor, Latin American, and Pentecostal. These communities and their experiences are conspicuously absent from Lausanne's North American network. Yet with Lausanne's robust experience in intercultural partnership abroad, the network stands poised to promote similar partnerships in North America. LWCCN and its participants already find themselves on the margins of the declining white suburban evangelical base in its money. This marginality provides an opportunity for a novel evangelical network to emerge which more fully embodies the collective wisdom and suffering of the global Christian community that already exists both within North America and around the world.

---

[48] Anonymous, interview by author, 1 April 2021, Boston, MA.
[49] Bookless, interview by author.
[50] Katharine Hayhoe, *Saving Us: A Climate Scientist's Case for Hope and Healing in a Divided World* (New York: One Signal Publishers, 2021).

DECOLONIZING FRONTIERS

A Prophetic Vision of Just Intercultural Community: The Canadian School of Missions and The Forum for Intercultural Leadership and Learning

Jonathan Schmidt

Originally established as the Canadian School of Missions, the Forum for Intercultural Leadership and Learning (FILL) celebrated 100 years in 2021. It continues to be a unique resource to both global and Canadian Christianities.[1] FILL's current work draws from these 100 years of experience with Canadian and global ecumenism, a time for developing understandings of and responses to changing contexts, crafting intentional pedagogy as a praxis of justice, creating and supporting community, learning and incorporating changes from the margins and the marginalized, and building relationship across cultural difference. In 2015, Pope Francis declared, "We are not living an era of change, but a change of era."[2] Living faithfully in this change of era requires creative space to imagine new ways of being, and FILL offers a promising example. Born of the Canadian churches' mission history and global and local colonial relationships, FILL's contemporary expression offers the church relevant tools for discerning its faithful witness.

This case study explores FILL's vision of Just Intercultural Community as the radical process needed for Canadian churches striving to be faithful in the emerging era in their ministries, relationships, and structures. Drawing from the research and findings from the author's Doctor of Ministry thesis, this study demonstrates how the history, context, and programmes of FILL have come to create profound experiences of interculturality. These experiences provide hope that Canadian churches might become communities in which all might be fully

---

[1] The singular "Christianity" is the more commonly accepted term encompassing the many expressions and experiences of Christianity both globally and in Canada. FILL in its work intentionally uses "Christianities" as an act of decolonizing. Most participants in FILL programmes are shaped by Western European Christianity and have difficulty comprehending other expressions of Christianity, let alone their full validity. "Christianities" creates a cognitive dissonance. Just as the Canadian ethnobiologist Wade Davis declares in the 2009 Canadian Broadcasting Corporation Massey lectures, "other cultures are not failed attempts at being us; they are unique manifestations of the human spirit." In its Engage Difference! programmes, FILL maintains that "other Christianities are not failed attempts at our Christianity; they are unique manifestations of the Spirit."

[2] Joshua J. McElwee, "Catholicism can and must change, Francis forcefully tells Italian church gathering," National Catholic Reporter, 10 November 2015, https://www.ncronline.org/news/vatican/catholicism-can-and-must-change-francis-forcefully-tells-italian-church-gathering.

themselves as created by God.[3] Informed by FILL programme alumni, facilitators, and stakeholders, this study suggests that the core outcome is experiences of Just Intercultural Community that result from people negotiating their way of being together to bring about that vision of belonging rather than any specific tools or "head knowledge" for facilitating Intercultural Community. FILL's role in leading this intercultural movement spurs optimism that the Canadian church might, in the words of one research participant, "grow the circles of voices and champions, 'a pantheon of wrestlers' that can help us slowly push this thing up the hill and actually decolonize the Gospel, the Church, the society."[4]

The first section of this study offers a brief history of the Canadian School of Missions and its evolution into the Forum for Intercultural Leadership and Learning. The history provides the foundation for understanding FILL's vision of interculturality. The next section provides definitions, discoveries and challenges of Just Intercultural Community and explains how FILL adapted along its journey in mission. Finally, the case study concludes with key findings, commentary, and remarks on FILL's call to the Canadian church to embrace interculturality.

FILL's History: The Foundation Leading to a Radical Vision

In 1917, following the Edinburgh World Missionary Conference of 1910, representatives from several Protestant mission boards and theological colleges at the University of Toronto desired a Canadian expression of the ecumenical and missiological energy of the time. They began a conversation that resulted in the founding of the Canadian School of Missions.[5] The opening worship for the newly founded school was held at Knox College, Toronto, in 1921. The Canadian School of Missions would uphold ecumenism as one of its primary characteristics through its history. The dedication of the school's first building included prayers "that the confines of knowledge may be ever enlarged and all

---

[3] For a more complete assessment of the prophetic vision, history, and work of FILL, see Jonathan Schmidt, "Living into the Emerging Ecumenical Paradigm: A Process of Conscientization and Discernment Toward Just Intercultural Community for Christianity in the Canadian Context" (DMin thesis, University of Toronto, 2021), https://tspace.library.utoronto.ca/handle/1807/107419.

[4] FILL stakeholder representative during focus group interviews conducted over Zoom as part of the author's Doctor of Ministry Research. Documented in "Living into the Emerging Ecumenical Paradigm: A Process of Conscientization and Discernment Toward Just Intercultural Community for Christianity in the Canadian Context" (DMin thesis, University of Toronto, 2021), 176, https://tspace.library.utoronto.ca/handle/1807/107419.

[5] The history of FILL is documented at "The History of the Forum for Intercultural Leadership and Learning," based on an address given by Teresa Burnett at the 75th Anniversary Celebration of the Canadian School of Missions/Canadian Churches' Forum for Global Ministries, https://www.interculturalleadership.ca/our-history/.

good learning flourish and abound."[6] This commitment to learning continues to be a core mandate of the organization.

As a religious and cultural product of Canadian Christianity, the School of Missions endeavoured to train Christian missionaries to go out into the world in the 1930s. It founded the Toronto School of Linguistics and provided courses in mission for the Student Volunteer Movement and for medical and education colleges. Lectures attracted prominent international scholars and were featured in Toronto newspapers. The school also functioned as a learning and social centre for returned missionaries. This emphasis on fostering intentional community runs through the school's history and is evident in FILL's focus on learning in community and on building networks of intercultural ministry practitioners across Canada.

The 1960s would see one of the organization's many moments of discernment and response to a changing context. Global ecumenism was changing, and a special conference was held in 1962 out of which The Canadian School of Missions and Ecumenical Institute began operations described as "an arms-length agency under the aegis of The Canadian Council of Churches (CCC)."[7] While there was agreement to create this new organization, enough difference prevented a full merger. This difference was politely explained as, "the School [of Missions] attended to mission in unity and the [Canadian] Council [of Churches] to unity in mission."[8] These similar but different approaches remain a source of creative tension in FILL's relationship within the CCC today.

The institute's courses in ecumenics attracted both Protestant and, in a significant development in Canadian ecumenism in the wake of the Second Vatican Council, Catholic students. Shaped by engaging the global church, the school increasingly focused on issues of justice in both global engagement and in encounters between cultures. This shift in focus would lay important groundwork for the focus on justice in relationships of today's programme offerings. One notable contribution was a programme of women's Bible studies in an era when women remained marginalized in society and the church. The creation of space for marginalized groups grounds the agency's current work, which recognizes the gifts that come from integrating marginalized voices.

During this time of independence movements and global resistance to colonial rule, Canadians were rejecting many institutions, including the national, centralized churches that made up the CCC. Canada's major Protestant churches

---

[6] The Canadian School of Missions, *Service of Dedication of The Canadian School of Missions. 97 St George Street, Toronto, Canada. Monday Afternoon, January Sixth Nineteen Hundred and Thirty at Three O'Clock*, located at the archives of The Canadian Council of Churches, Toronto, Ontario.

[7] The Canadian Council of Churches By-Laws 2020, Section X, "Agencies under the Aegis of the Council," the archives of The Canadian Council of Churches.

[8] The Canadian School of Missions, *The Order for Service for the Inauguration of the Canadian School of Missions and Ecumenical Institute and the Installation as Director of the Reverend Canon H.L. Puxley, M.A., D.D., D.C.L., eight o'clock in the evening on Friday, the eighteenth of October Nineteen hundred and sixty-three in Knox College Chapel, Toronto*, the archives of the Canadian Council of Churches.

were no longer seen as providing a moral vision for Canadian society.[9] In 1965, the school reorganized again and renamed itself the Ecumenical Institute of Canada. Confusion with the Ecumenical Institute of Chicago prompted a name change to the Ecumenical Forum of Canada.

In 1973, the Ecumenical Forum participated in the "An Affection for Diversity" report initiated by several of the Canadian churches to gauge the churches' needs and willingness to work ecumenically. Decades later, the organization continues to aspire to the report's recommendation that the Ecumenical Forum "help end ethnocentric pride and narcissism, racial bigotry, and mono-cultural blindness."[10] The report also recommended that the Institute become a centre for inter-faith encounter, study, and reflection, again grounding the broad visions of ecumenism and community that shape today's programmes and activities.

Programme emphasis began to shift from academic courses on mission to cross-cultural education for member denomination mission personnel in the 1980s. The organization changed its name to the Canadian Churches Forum for Global Ministries (CCFGM). The 1970s to 1990s also charted the emergence of the Canadian justice coalitions which came together to form "KAIROS: Canadian Ecumenical Justice Initiatives" in 2001.[11] The life of CCFGM was intertwined with these coalitions, which were shaped by issues of global justice encountered in the mission field and often staffed by former mission personnel who had come through CCFGM's programmes.

There was a proposed moratorium on sending missionaries and money from the North, and an alternative proposal came about for more justice in mission relations in the early 1970s.[12] In Canada, there were calls for a shift from the model that saw "missionaries go from the West to the rest, from what had been seen as superior to the inferior, from the religious to the pagan" and for no longer seeing the purpose of mission as conversion, development, or civilizing.[13] Within the global ecumenical movement, "mission as conversion" shifted to "mission as witness." A key moment in this shift was the 1989 World Mission Conference in San Antonio, Texas. This meeting led to a consensus statement on the relation between Christianity and other religions, saying, "we cannot put any limit to

[9] Daniel C. Goodwin, "The Canadian Council of Churches: Its founding vision and early years, 1944–1964," *Journal of Ecumenical Studies* 41: 2 (Spring 2004), 147–73.
[10] Janet Somerville and Charles Hendry, *An Affection for Diversity: A Report of a Consultation on Education Ecumenically for the Canadian Council of Churches* (Toronto: The Canadian Council of Churches, 1973), 53.
[11] The stories of these coalitions are well-documented in Christopher Lind and Joe Mihevic, eds., *Coalitions for Justice: The Story of Canada's Interchurch Coalitions* (Ottawa: Novalis, St Paul University, 1994).
[12] See World Council of Churches, "History", Commission on World Mission and Evangelism History, Last Accessed 2022, https://archived.oikoumene.org/en/what-we-do/cwme/history/.
[13] Loraine MacKenzie Shepherd, "From Colonization to Right Relations: The Evolution of United Church of Canada Missions within Aboriginal Communities," *International Review of Mission* 103: 1 (April 2014), 153–71.

God's saving power."[14] Overseas partners, and, increasingly, Canadians born in other cultures and contexts, were seen as having equally valid experiences of God and faith. Recognizing the need to resource these diverse voices was one of the seeds that continues to grow in the current work of the FILL.

At the end of the 20th century, Canadian churches entered a process of apology and reconciliation with Indigenous peoples in Canada as the abuses and damage to culture done by the church-run Indian Residential school system were being revealed more widely.[15] FILL's valuing of diverse voices and recognition of the cultural damage of the residential schools is part of the intentional attention to pedagogy of the current FILL intercultural programmes. FILL strives to recognize the potential for damage, and the potential resources, of learning across cultural, power, privilege, and other differences.

Through much of the 20th century, overseas mission and theological and cross-cultural preparation of missionaries were the Canadian denominations' way of recognizing that there was an "other" in the world. In the early 21st century, Canadian cities became increasingly diverse. CCFGM, located in Toronto, was in a city where the majority of its residents were visible minorities and almost

---

[14] World Council of Churches, "History".

[15] This decades-long process continues to shape the Canadian churches. The 2015 "Truth and Reconciliation Commission of Canada: Calls to Action," Truth and Reconciliation Commission of Canada, https://web.archive.org/web/20200506065356/http://trc.ca/assets/pdf/Calls_to_Action_E nglish2.pdf, directed ongoing reconciliation for the churches, including a covenant process for Canadian denominations that were not directly involved in the running of the Indian Residential Schools. Within denominations, there are processes of reconciliation with their Indigenous members and relationship. The parties to the Residential Schools (institutions that were involved in the running of the schools) issued individual apologies. The Anglican Church of Canada, through the Primate, Archbishop Michael Peers, made apologies to the National Native Convocation Minaki, Ontario, on 6 August 1993 ("A message from the Primate, Archbishop Michael Peers, to the National Native Convocation Minaki, Ontario, Friday, August 6, 1993," https://www.anglican.ca/tr/apology/english/). The Presbyterian Church in Canada apologized through adoption of a confession at its General Assembly on 9 June 1994 ("The Confession of the Presbyterian Church in Canada as adopted by the General Assembly, June 9th, 1994," http://presbyterian.ca/downloads/35607/). In 1986, the Moderator of the United Church of Canada, the Right Rev. Bob Smith, issued an apology ("1986 Apology to Indigenous Peoples" and "The 1988 Response", https://united-church.ca/sites/default/files/apologies-response-crest.pdf). The Missionary Oblates of Mary Immaculate issued an apology in 1991 through the Oblate Conference of Canada ("An Apology to the First Nations of Canada by the Oblate Conference of Canada," https://www.cccb.ca/wp-content/uploads/2017/10/oblate_apology_english.pdf). The Royal Canadian Mounted Police issued an apology for their involvement in 2004 ("Indian Residential School apologies," https://www.rcmp-grc.gc.ca/indigenous-autochtone/apo-reg-eng.htm). Through Prime Minister Stephen Harper, the Government of Canada apologized in Parliament in 2011 ("Statement of apology to former students of Indian Residential Schools," https://www.rcaanc-cirnac.gc.ca/eng/1100100015644/1571589171655).

half were immigrants to Canada.[16] The context had changed and the organization reimagined its mandate again. Consultations identified need to support Canadian denominations responding to diversity in Canada. In 2012, an ecumenical group of programme designers and facilitators created a new programme, "Engage Difference! Deepening Understanding for Intercultural Ministry." This 3-day residential programme has been offered in and shaped by contexts across Canada, now with over 200 alumni who form the core of a Canadian intercultural ministry network. The primary focus of the agency became intercultural ministry and the prophetic challenge to engage the other in more just ways within Canada.

In 2017, CCFGM became the Forum for Intercultural Leadership and Learning (FILL), a reference group of the CCC.[17] The Canadian Ecumenical Anti-Racism Network (CEARN), previously connected to the Council's Commission on Justice and Peace, became a subgroup of FILL. This network was a Canadian response to the 2001 United Nations World Conference Against Racism, held in Durban, South Africa.[18] A 2018 consultation identified the need for ongoing training for intercultural ministry and racial justice and highlighted the unique pedagogy and program delivery developing within the work of FILL.[19] The consultation also named the need for well-done theologies of intercultural ministry and racial justice. In response to these needs, two other subgroups of FILL emerged. A "Training for Transformation" group provides space for development of programme and pedagogy as well as mentoring of design and facilitation skills. A "Research and Theology" group invites, fosters, and amplifies the many people working toward theologies of interculturality, connecting faith-based intercultural ministry to the learning of other disciplines. It also initiates and brings together research on intercultural ministry in the churches.

---

[16] City of Toronto, *T.O. Health Check: An Overview of Toronto's Population Health Status*, "Chapter 1: Population Demographics," 2019, https://www.toronto.ca/wp-content/uploads/2019/11/99b4-TOHealthCheck_2019Chapter1.pdf.

[17] Terms of Reference: Forum for Intercultural Leadership and Learning (F.I.L.L.) A Reference Group of the Canadian Council of Churches. Adopted by the Governing Board of the Canadian Council of Churches 24 May 2017. https://www.interculturalleadership.ca/wp-content/uploads/2022/06/Terms-of-Reference-Forum-for-Intercultural-Leadership-and-Learning-Reference-Group-Canadian-Council-of-Churches.pdf.

[18] Learn more about CEARN at The Canadian Council of Churches, "Anti-Racism Network: The Canadian Ecumenical Anti-Racism Network (CEARN)," Council of Churches, https://www.councilofchurches.ca/social-justice/ undoing-racism/anti-racism-network/.

[19] The Canadian Council of Churches, "Summary Report CCC FILL-CEARN Consultation Spring 2018," https://www.interculturalleadership.ca/wp-content/uploads/2022/11/Summary-report-CCC-FILL-CEARN-Consultation-sping-2018.pdf.

Definitions, Challenges and Discoveries

As the history and evolution of FILL's mission and programme demonstrates, commitment to Just Intercultural Community has emerged as a central mandate. Just Intercultural ministry seeks to interrupt the kind of harm reflected in the churches' involvement in the tragedy of the Canadian Indian Residential Schools, its participation in colonial projects, the "othering" that makes possible war, genocide and societal inequality, and participation in environmental damage and climate change. Just Intercultural Community may be essential for the survival of the church in Canada as it can draw on the wisdom and gifts of global theologies and ways of being church. Finally, providing space for the voices of many cultures allows for a fuller experience and expression of our faith as "no human culture has a final definitive grasp of the gospel."[20]

Living into its new mandate, resourcing intercultural ministry, and responding to the prophetic challenge of engaging diversity in more just ways within Canada has been a journey of learning that has shaped FILL in unexpected ways. The Engage Difference! programme, alumni gatherings, and FILL sponsored conversations and research on diversity have been a "laboratory" in which a community wrestles with, discovers, and learns interculturality. Evolving visions of interculturality and Just Intercultural Community emerged that are not yet widely held by the Canadian church. Rather, these visions are an invitation and prophetic challenge to the Canadian church. Extending this invitation and challenge requires clear definitions and descriptions of interculturality, naming and countering the barriers to interculturality in Canadian cultures and contexts, and providing tools, methodologies, and pedagogies that create space for the unlearning and learning for communities to move toward.

Defining Interculturality

Many organizations and communities are negotiating an increasingly diverse Canada and responding to diversity globally. The language around these initiatives needs to be interrogated to challenge unbalanced power relationships and marginalization of communities. FILL's prophetic challenge and vision of interculturality describes these relationships and requires definitions of terms like "multicultural," "cross-cultural," and "intercultural."

"Multicultural" is simply a descriptive term. There are many cultures. This term does not include how and if those cultures interact. "Cross-cultural" is the term historically used in describing overseas mission personnel relationships. It states that two or more cultures are interacting and does not describe relationships across culture that include issues of power and privilege (in which a dominant culture is able to set the norms and rules of interaction).

"Intercultural" is something to which communities aspire. In cross-cultural settings, typically others must relate to a dominant culture. In contrast, intercultural communities allow each person and culture to stand in full dignity of difference, fully aware of themselves and able to engage from a position of equal power and influence. Intercultural is what Eduardo Galeano described as

---

[20] George R. Hunsberger, "Contrast and Companionship: The Way of the Church with the World," *Cultural Encounters* 7: 2 (2010), 7–16.

"fighting for a world that must be the house of everyone."[21] Intercultural Community acknowledges, celebrates, and gives voice to the differences and diversity within the community as gifts.

One of the issues in defining intercultural is that it has become a common term, used in several disciplines to describe very different understandings of interaction or relationships across cultures without an emphasis on justice.[22] To distinguish from these uses, FILL utilizes the term "Just Intercultural" to describe just relationship between people and with all of creation. The expression also invites a reclamation of the term "interculturality." In Just Intercultural spaces, relationships are shaped by justice and an awareness of power and privilege that cause harm or prevent individuals, communities, or cultures from being fully themselves. There is awareness of self and one's impact on others. Just Intercultural would extend this awareness beyond the Christian churches. It aspires to these kinds of relationships between all of humanity and with all of creation or, to use an Indigenous understanding, "all my relations."

Extending from this holistic Indigenous understanding, FILL has drawn inspiration from several sources in the development of the vision of interculturality. Scriptural images such as shalom or "Peace be with you" (Lk. 24:36, Jn. 20:19) provide notions of wholeness or completeness, prosperity and security, right relationships between people in community, right relationship and covenant with God, and even a harmonious relationship with nature.[23] In the baptism of Jesus, John the Baptist recognizes the visitor as being a gift (Mt. 3:13–14). In the story of Zacchaeus (Lk. 19:1–10), Jesus encourages Zacchaeus to be fully himself by encouraging an invitation from Zacchaeus: "Zacchaeus, hurry and come down; for I must stay at your house today" (Lk. 19:5–6). Martin Luther King Jr. described "Beloved Community," a vision of inclusiveness, both economic and social, in which all persons are valued and able to live fully as themselves.[24] The African Nguni Bantu term, "Ubuntu," describes interconnection as the "very essence of being human" in which "my humanity is caught up, is inextricably bound up, in yours."[25] Letty M. Russell's *Just Hospitality* envisions church as "a community of Christ where everyone is welcome and Christ's presence among us calls us to be open to each other" and

[21] Eduardo Galeano, "Vivir sin Miedo" ("Living Without Fear"), audio recording, YouTube Channel: Mario Benedetti, Uploaded: 5 May 2019, https://youtu.be/X7lC4Bxojb8.
[22] Hennig Wrogemann, trans. Karl E. Böhmer, *Intercultural Theology*, vol. 1, *Intercultural Hermeneutics* (Downers Grove, IL: IVP Academic, 2016), 22.
[23] Scripture quotations are taken from the New Revised Standard Version Updated Edition (NRSVUE). National Council of Churches of Christ in the United States of America, 2021.
[24] Martin Luther King Jr, "Facing the Challenge of a New Age" [1957] in James M. Washington, ed., *A Testament of Hope: The Essential Writings and Speeches of Martin Luther King, Jr.* (New York: Harper Collins, 1986), 135–44.
[25] Desmond Tutu, *No Future without Forgiveness* (New York: Doubleday Random House, 1999), 29.

a place that "[gives] priority to the perspective of the outsider."[26] Drawing on her own experience as someone outside the dominant culture who yet participates and interacts with it, Stephanie Spellers offers *Radical Welcome* as "the spiritual practice of embracing and being changed by the gifts, presence, voices, and power of The Other."[27]

The Research and Theology group of FILL has recognized the need to reclaim the term intercultural as a community project shaped by local contexts. Toward this project, the group created "Interculturality Framework and Guiding Principles: An Invitation to Conversation and Dialogue."[28] Included as an appendix to this chapter, this living document and invitation to conversation and dialogue invites the reader of this case study into the project of describing interculturality.

Canadian Barriers to Interculturality

Interculturality requires a process of naming barriers that prevent all from being fully human. In Canada and around the world, the trauma of, and Christian complicity in, the White[29] European colonial project must be acknowledged. Edward Said argued that "the major component in European culture is precisely what made it hegemonic both in and outside of Europe: the idea of European identity as a superior one in comparison with all non-European peoples and cultures."[30]

Several Canadian "myths" maintain this identity and are barriers to interculturality. At the beginning of the 20th century, Canada saw itself as the ideal British colony, fully embracing the USA vision of Christianity and layering onto it the grandeur and accomplishments of British Empire and civilization.[31] Daniel Coleman describes the myth of Canada as the ideal civilized British colony and argues that "English Canadian Whiteness has been modelled upon a specific form of British civility, a form of Britishness that is a uniquely settler-colonial project."[32] Paulette Regan argues that the myth that Canada is a peace-

---

[26] Letty M. Russell, *Just Hospitality: God's Welcome in a World of Difference*, eds. J. Shannon Clarkson and Kate M. Ott (Louisville, KY: Westminster John Knox Press, 2009), 45.

[27] Stephanie Spellers, *Radical Welcome: Embracing God, the Other, and the Spirit of Transformation* (New York: Church Publishing, 2006), 6.

[28] Forum for Intercultural Leadership and Learning Research and Theology Group. "Interculturality Framework and Guiding Principles: An Invitation to Conversation and Dialogue." Updated versions in French and English can be found at: https://www.interculturalleadership.ca/theology-and-research/.

[29] In the work and circles of FILL, the capitalization of "White" is the accepted norm.

[30] Edward W. Said, *Orientalism* (New York: Vintage Books, 1978), 7.

[31] Robert A. Wright, *A World Mission: Canadian Protestantism and the quest for a new international order, 1918-1939* (Montreal, Quebec: McGill-Queen's University Press, 1991), 3–37.

[32] Daniel Coleman, *White Civility: The Literary Project of English Canada* (Toronto: University of Toronto Press, 2006), 211.

making nation is a barrier to reconciliation.[33] Canada's Truth and Reconciliation process is an opportunity to examine the Canadian myths about ourselves as benevolent peacemakers who brought British law, justice, and the Christian message of the peaceable kingdom. The Indian Residential Schools, supported by a theology and evangelism shaped by a desire to civilize the other, point to a need to look critically at the theology of the dominant Canadian Christianity. Baldwin, Cameron, and Kobayash connect Canadian racism and notions of Whiteness to Canadian myths about their relationship to the land, framed as "The Great White North," as central themes in our identity that shape our relationships with others and stand in the way of reconciliation.[34] Himani Bannerji and others identify the official Canadian policy of multiculturalism as maintaining Canada's dominant culture and preventing critique of inequalities, power, and privilege, while maintaining unjust relationships.[35]

Intercultural Pedagogies

Beyond naming barriers or deconstructing the dominant culture, the church requires processes through which communities can discover and co-create visions of interculturality in their contexts. This process requires local theologies, local praxes, and local *poiesis*, or the "poetic dimension as the church contributes to social transformation."[36] Within the Canadian context, Indigenous ways of knowing and decision-making provide examples of alternative ways of learning as possible. Discerning visions of Intercultural Community requires *creative imagination.*[37] Rather than a formula for interculturality, FILL invites the church into "the art of intercultural ministry" as a process of discovering tools for ministry in the emerging ecumenical paradigm in their contexts.[38] FILL has developed a pedagogy toward change of heart and right relationship that provides spaces in which all gathered can be fully themselves as they shape communal visions, theologies, and praxes of interculturality.

---

[33] Paulette Regan, *Unsettling the Settler Within: Indian Residential Schools, Truth Telling, and Reconciliation in Canada* (Vancouver, British Columbia: UBC Press, 2010).
[34] Andrew Baldwin, Laura Cameron, and Audrey Kobayashi, *Rethinking the Great White North: Race, Nature, and the Historical Geographies of Whiteness in Canada* (Vancouver, British Columbia: University of British Columbia Press, 2011).
[35] Himani Bannerji, *The Dark Side of the Nation: Essays on Multiculturalism, Nationalism and Gender* (Toronto: Canadian Scholars Press, 2000), 110.
[36] Charles J. Fensham, "The Transformative Vision: Public Witness and the Poiesis of Christian Social Transformation," *Missiology: An International Review* 44: 2 (2016), 155–66.
[37] Marilyn J. Legge, "In the Company of God and One Another: Feminist Theo-Ethics, Heterogeneous Publics and Intercultural Churches," in Anita Monro and Stephen Burns, eds., *Public Theology and the Challenge of Feminism* (New York: Routledge, 2015), 46–62.
[38] Forum for Intercultural Leadership and Learning, Engage Difference! Deepening Understanding for Intercultural Ministry program description. https://www.interculturalleadership.ca/duim/.

In Conclusion: Key Findings and Commentary

The original research and doctoral thesis of FILL's impact, conducted by this chapter's author in 2020, has informed the content for this case study.[39] FILL programme alumni, facilitators, and stakeholders described FILL's programmes as profound experiences of interculturality providing hope for Canadian churches to become inclusive communities of belonging for all. The original research revealed how participants in FILL's programmes experienced optimism for the future of the church in Canada, brought changes of heart, and facilitated glimpses of Just Intercultural Community through in-person gatherings and new relationships.

The research used an Appreciative Inquiry methodology through which the interview participants and the FILL Reference Group presented several invitations to the Canadian church.[40] These invitations, born out of the insights of the unique Canadian context and experience, are gifts to the wider global church in its faithful responses to the change of era.

- An invitation to recognize, name, and faithfully respond to a new era; an invitation to communities of faith to describe their contexts, discern local theologies, and develop and discover the tools, pedagogies, and praxes, or ways of being faithful, in those contexts.
- An invitation to see that Canada's Indigenous communities, migrant communities, and other diverse communities are gifts and sources of theologies and praxes that will help church communities respond to their contexts, survive, and remain faithful.
- An invitation to reclaim the terms "intercultural" and "interculturality" and to create well-articulated theology(s) and language(s) of Just Intercultural Community.
- An invitation to recognize the multiplicity of intersecting axes of power, privilege, marginalization, and resistance. The diversity and the plurality of cultures, theologies, and praxes found in and outside the church draw it to understand the nature of these relationships and to discern God's visions for right relationship with each other and with all of creation.
- An invitation to discover and develop pedagogies for the new era and practice the "art of intercultural ministry." There are multiple ways of knowing and learning.
- An invitation to church communities to examine whether they will be, in their national and local expressions, a homogenous church, a diverse church, an inclusive church, or a community where all present experience belonging.
- An invitation to church communities to embrace a vision of interculturality and to a process of becoming Just Intercultural Communities.

---

[39] Schmidt, "Living into the Emerging Ecumenical Paradigm."
[40] For a description of Appreciate Inquiry, see David L. Cooper, Diana Whitney, and Jacqueline M. Stavros, *Appreciative Inquiry Handbook for Leaders of Change*, 2nd ed. (Brunswick, OH: Crown Custom Publishing Inc., 2008).

FILL is a source of hope and encouragement as communities strive for a more just world. Participants named "possibility" as an important theme in their experience of FILL. Just Intercultural Canadian churches and interculturality are possible. Participants come away with a clearer sense of God's vision of a more just world and how they have been and will be active agents in living into this vision.

Rinaldo Walcott argues that Canadian society is in the throes of what Ruth Wilson Gilmore calls "organized abandonment."[41] Deindustrialization and the emergence of a neoliberal economy in which the welfare state has been significantly undermined means that Canadians have all become responsible only for our individual selves. Interculturality is an alternate radical vision that will be resisted by structures of power. Interculturality is a call for revolution, a retaking of the commons, and a reclaiming of the common good. It is a revolution in the way Canadians think. Canadians need to again be confident that our society, our institutions, our communities, and our neighbours will care for us and act in our best interests.

The prophetic challenge of FILL is that Canadian churches might become communities in which all persons might be fully themselves as created by God and extend an invitation to that hopeful vision for a society. FILL challenges expressions of church in Canada to live Jesus' promise of shalom, or "Peace be with you." As the church responds faithfully in a change of era, hope is in the promises of the One who declares, "See, I am making all things new" (Rev. 21:5).

Appendix

Interculturality Framework and Guiding Principles:
An Invitation to Conversation and Dialogue

The Forum for Intercultural Leadership and Learning (FILL)
A Reference Group of The Canadian Council of Churches (April 2021)

The FILL Theology and Research Working Group

This group offers this living document as a framework and guiding principles as it attempts to be open to and live out interculturality in our various church communities. This group recognizes that interculturality is a complex and painstaking process of mutual learning and of undoing inherited structures that privilege a small segment of society over others. As a living document, this will change over time as we become more sensitive to hearing God's calling to become a prophetic community. This group offers this document as an invitation to conversation and dialogue.

---

[41] Rinaldo Walcott, *On Property: Policing, Prisons, and the Call for Abolition* (Windsor, Ontario: Biblioasis, 2021), 38.

The FILL Theology and Research Working Group has adopted a framework and guiding principles:

1. The celebration and welcoming of the diverse voices of faith communities to be part of the conversation, with the recognition that each of us speak from **different ethnocultural vantage points**;

> Diverse here denotes inclusion of all varying expressions of the human experience, including but not limited to: ethno-racial, cultural, religious traditions, age, gender, sexual orientation and identity, class, ableness, citizenship, education, geographic location…

2. And to acknowledge that each of us encounters each other with our own unique experiences, ways of knowing, and **diverse spiritual and theological traditions**.

3. We intend to **interrogate the available language** and to **develop and create new language** to speak about intercultural exchanges.

> Intercultural exchanges are the multilevel dynamics by which members of different ethnocultural communities interact with each other and draw from their own sources of knowledge and wisdom to make sense of life, interact with each other, the environment, and make sense of the divine. Cultural traditions are not understood here as finished products and uniform. They are conceived as porous and dynamic and in a constant process of fluctuation or change.

As part of our objective, we are committed to reflect on the meaning of **interculturality**. We do this by:

    a. naming and challenging the **duality between theory and practice in Western Euro-centric contexts**, and **validating and affirming the holistic nature of life**;

> Holistic nature of life: Being in touch with all our relationships, with each other, with our own bodies, with all of nature. All of it is not reducible to concepts or categories but is encompassed in everyday life. This is the Indigenous concept of "All my relations".

> Duality: In Western Euro-Centric contexts the tendency is to separate all experiences of life into disconnected pieces without necessarily bringing all the pieces together at the end, for example: we think; we feel; we do; we intuit, are all separate. Another example is we separate the private and the public. Life is reduced to all of its parts, but the linkages are not made explicit.

b. reclaiming and learning from the lived-experiences of ethnocultural communities on the ground as sources of theological material;

Intercultural engagement imposes an ethical imperative so that no one group can claim to have any kind of privileges over other communities. It entails an action of mutual welcoming of all parties recognizing that all stand on equal ground.

c. **challenging Western Eurocentric and Euro-Canadian-centred forms of knowledge and ways of encountering the Divine** which discount other forms of learning, along with other forms of knowledge, of doing theology, and other forms of living life;

In light with the holistic nature of life, intercultural engagement requires that dominant communities abandon denial, distraction, or deflection of historical grievances. Instead, engage in an intentional unlearning of the colonising mentality and learning decolonising ways of right relationships.

d. **celebrating and valuing of Indigenous cultural traditions** and knowledges, as well as the **celebrating and valuing of the many other ethnocultural, epistemological and faith traditions** that call Canada home.

Interculturality requires that cultural diversity becomes a characteristic of the social context. It also requires that different communities become mutually receptive of each other, and the different ways they view life, understand God, and interact with each other in ways that are dignifying, just, and life-giving.

For permission to reproduce please contact:

The Theology and Research Working Group of The Forum for Intercultural Leadership and Learning. www.InterculturalLeadership.ca

Edited April 29, 2021

Forum for Intercultural Leadership and Learning | Forum pour le leadership et l'apprentissage interculturels

"Engaging Our Diversity: Interculturality and Consecrated Life": A Program of the Center for the Study of Consecrated Life (CSCL) at Catholic Theological Union at Chicago

Roger Schroeder, SVD

Multicultural Reality of the Life and Ministry of Catholic Religious Congregations

The Catholic Church and communities of Consecrated Life (religious congregations) in North America are blessed by the giftedness, commitment, and vitality of those coming from the Majority World. At the same time, embracing these gifts requires some degree of openness for adaptation on various levels in ministry and religious communities. Such multicultural situations require a minimum of basic toleration and peaceful co-existence, hopefully followed by an openness for adaptation and an interest in truly appreciating and understanding another social-cultural group. However, Christians and members of religious communities are expected to strive even further.

Jesus preached and witnessed to the inclusiveness of the reign of God through the parable of the Good Samaritan (a "half-Jew"), his interactions with the Samaritan woman at the well and the Syro-Phoenician woman,[1] and his table fellowship with those considered marginalized in society. The early church – tracing its action through the Acts of the Apostles – took the major step of accepting Gentiles as fellow Christian women and men.[2] Paul's image of the "Body of Christ" (1 Cor. 12:12–27), which points to the diversity and unity of gifts of the early Christian communities, clearly offers the Catholic Church and religious congregations a vision and challenge for living as multicultural communities witnessing to the reign of God with a spirit of mutual understanding, respect, and exchange. This further stage is referred to today as "interculturality," which is understood here as the "mutual exchange between cultures that can lead to transformation and enrichment of all involved."[3] It is important to note that "culture" is understood, in its post-modern sense, to

---

[1] See Adriana Carla Milmanda, SSpS, "The Intercultural Journey of Jesus," in Maria Cimperman, RSCJ, and Roger Schroeder, SVD, eds., *Engaging Our Diversity: Interculturality and Consecrated Life Today* (Maryknoll, NY: Orbis Books, 2020), 65–76.

[2] See Stephen Bevans and Roger Schroeder, *Constants in Context: A Theology of Mission for Today* (Maryknoll, NY: Orbis Books, 2004), 10–31.

[3] Lazar Stanislaus, SVD, and Martin Ueffing, SVD, eds., *Intercultural Living* (Sankt Augustin, Germany: Steyler Missionswissenschaftliches Institut; New Delhi: ISPCK, 2015), xxiv.

include the following: ethnicity, race, and nationality; social change; social location (i.e., female/male, rich/poor, social status, location within power dynamics, different generations); and particular individual and communal circumstances.

Interculturality is a key element of mission for witnessing to the reign of God in our world today. It requires a spirit of listening, vulnerability, and discernment in order to promote mutual enrichment and challenge for the sake of God's mission. Theologically, this process includes a recognition by all of both the signs (enrichment) and counter-signs (challenge) of God's reign in everyone's "culture" or context. The agricultural parables of Jesus refer to "good seed" and "weeds," respectively, that exist in everyone's (individual and communal) "garden."[4] This lifelong process can be understood within the dynamic framework of the theology, practice, and spirituality of "prophetic dialogue."[5] Based on these strong theological, biblical, and missiological foundations, we propose that interculturality is an engaging paradigm of mission.[6]

Furthermore, the pursuit of interculturality needs to be an integrative process that engages the mind, heart, and hands – knowledge, motivation, conversion, and action – on both the personal and communal/systemic levels. Strategies and knowledge need to be accompanied by a deep spirituality and ongoing conversion from all forms of prejudice.[7]

Catholic religious congregations in North America realize that they often do not achieve the ideals of true interculturality in their religious community life and their ministry contexts, due to misunderstanding, miscommunication, and prejudice. How welcome do those of underrepresented groups feel in religious life? How do prejudices impact the decisions made by leaders, finance personnel, formation directors, and liturgy planners? How do the members of religious congregations contribute to exclusiveness and racism within their ministry? In response, many religious congregations recognize the urgent need to develop more clearly and deeply the intercultural "body of Christ." A failure to do so could lead to strained and broken relationships and a counter-witness to the reign of God both within the religious community and their ministry. On the positive side, the development of a fuller expression of interculturality can provide an

---

[4] See Roger Schroeder, "Entering Someone Else's Garden: Intercultural Mission/Ministry," in Stephen Bevans and Roger Schroeder, eds., *Prophetic Dialogue: Reflections on Christian Mission Today* (Maryknoll, NY: Orbis Books, 2011), 72–87.
[5] See Roger Schroeder, "Prophetic Dialogue and Interculturality," in Cathy Ross and Stephen B. Bevans, eds., *Mission on the Road to Emmaus: Constants, Context, and Prophetic Dialogue* (London: SCM Press, 2015), 215–26.
[6] See Roger Schroeder, "Interculturality as a Paradigm of Mission," in Lazar Stanislaus, SVD, and Martin Ueffing, eds., *Intercultural Living: Explorations in Missiology* (Maryknoll, NY: Orbis Books, 2018), 172–85.
[7] For example, see Roger Schroeder, "Enriched by the Spirituality of the 'Other,'" in Lazar Stanislaus, SVD, and Christian Tauchner, SVD, eds., *Becoming Intercultural: Perspectives on Mission* (Sankt Augustin, Germany: Steyler Missionswissenschaftliches Institut; New Delhi: ISPCK, 2021), 75–89; María Salomé Labra Madariaga, SSpS, "Intercultural Spirituality in Relationships: Challenges and Prospective Actions," in *Becoming Intercultural: Perspectives on Mission*, 90–106.

even stronger prophetic vision for the church and the broader society of the United States. Moreover, the interaction and engagement of different cultures can be an opportunity for mutual transformation and enrichment – an "already and not yet" experience and experience of the reign of God. These opportunities and challenges of boundary crossing in the process of striving for true interculturality apply both to *life* within the multicultural Christian community or religious community (*ad intra*) and to *ministry* among the great diversity of God's people (*ad extra*).

Rationale and Structure of the Project

In order to address the above challenges and opportunities, the Center for the Study of Consecrated Life (CSCL) at Catholic Theological Union (CTU) in Chicago sponsored a three-year (2017–2020) project, called "Engaging Our Diversity: Interculturality and Consecrated Life." Financial support was provided by the Conrad N. Hilton Foundation, and the Catholic Sisters Initiative gave other valuable assistance. The overall supervision of this project was under Maria Cimperman, RSCJ, the Director of CSCL, and Roger Schroeder, SVD, the faculty advisor. Maria Nguyen, OSB, and Joanne Jaruko Doi, MM, also joined the organization team.

Twenty US-based women's and men's religious congregations participated in this multi-year project with a core team (of three to five persons) from each community, who would serve as the catalyst and resource to guide their community of consecrated persons through this intercultural process.[8] Each team intentionally included representation of the diversity of cultures, generations, and community roles (including leadership). Interestingly, about half of the team members identified as belonging to an underrepresented group in their congregation (in terms of ethnicity, race, generation, nationality, or other categories).

Growing in intercultural living and ministry requires 1) providing the necessary knowledge and developing certain skills and behaviours, 2) nurturing the necessary motivation, spirituality, and ongoing process of "conversion" from all forms of ethnocentrism (by all parties), and 3) developing action steps and possible changes. These changes can include shifts in formation programmes, leadership styles, decision-making processes, and practices in ministry. A thumbnail description of these three elements would be "head," "heart," and

---

[8] The criteria for acceptance into the programme was that a congregation had a significant number of members (more than 20) in the United States and that they already had some ethnic/racial diversity within their congregation. One group was not accepted due to the second criterion, since they were only exploring the possibility and had no living experience of it. Each community had a commitment to external ministry, although it took many different forms. No cloistered religious congregation applied, although interculturality is also a challenge and opportunity for them. Schroeder on other occasions has conducted in-person intercultural workshops with the cloistered local women's communities of the Trappistines (Cistercian) and the Perpetual Adoration Sisters of the Holy Spirit (SSpSAP), who share the same founder with the SVD and SSpS.

"hands." The CSCL-CTU project provided the necessary framework of accompaniment, support, and sharing of insights and best practices through this process of discernment and transformation within each religious congregation and among the participating congregations.

Each core team did background reading, developed case studies, used sociological tools and questionnaires, developed action plans, and posted progress reports on a common platform called Desire to Learn (D2L). They also participated in three conferences. The first two in-person weekend conferences in November 2017 and 2018 (before COVID-19) included presentations, small-group discussions, participant exercises, intercultural prayer/liturgies and core work sessions. The third 24-hour conference, which switched to a Zoom format due to COVID-19 and was held in May 2020, served as a wrap-up to the multi-year project.

The seven plenary speakers in the November 2017 conference were born in seven different countries – Argentina, Australia, England, South Korea, Mexico, USA, and Vietnam. They covered some foundational topics like intercultural living and ministry for religious congregations, cultural frameworks for understanding differences, intercultural spirituality, the intercultural journey of Jesus, and intercultural sensitivity and competence. In response to feedback from the participants, the November 2018 conference addressed further underlying issues and more particular aspects of interculturality, such as reconciliation, cultural models of conflict resolution, practical suggestions for intercultural living, personality and culture, interculturality and leadership, and race and gender dynamics. Based on earlier feedback, a set of workshops, a panel, and a special professional story-telling session on race were new additional features in this second conference. The addition of race was due to a number of strong voices during the first conference and the new Black Lives Matter movement within the North American context of the CTU programme. The presenters represented not only different nations of birth (including Lebanon, Nigeria, Philippines, Poland, and Tanzania), as in the first conference, but now also the cultural-racial diversity among US citizens. The shortened third Zoom conference included plenary addresses on the two dimensions of interculturality, that is, religious life (*ad intra*) and ministry (*ad extra*), respectively, and various break-out small group discussions around particular sub-themes. The latter provided a platform through which religious congregations could share their learnings and future plans regarding interculturality.

Specific Goals of the Project

The particular goals of the project, based on the rationale and description above, were grouped under three levels.

First of all, the core team of each religious community, individually and as a team, would demonstrate the ability to 1) expand their sensitivity for and knowledge of the cultural diversity in their congregation and ministry; 2) acknowledge and identify the internal dynamics (positive and/or negative from different perspectives) within their religious community around the issue of cultural diversity; 3) engage in a respectful conversation about cultural differences with others; and 4) demonstrate a willingness to change and adapt through the process of cultural engagement.

Secondly, the core team would demonstrate the ability to a) work with their congregational leadership to develop and facilitate action plans for developing a stronger sense of interculturality within their congregation; b) develop, if necessary, a network with others within and/or outside their congregation for following through with their action steps; c) assess and make adjustments to their plan over time; and d) share the actions and results of their work with the central planning group of the CSCL according to the designated timetable and format.

Thirdly, the religious communities participating in the CSCL project would strengthen their understanding and practice of interculturality according to their action plans within their community (*ad intra*) and in ministry (*ad extra*). Later, the goal of networking with other religious congregations and organizations present in North America was added to this goal.

Results and Evaluation of the Project

External consultants Charles DeNault and Dominic Perri of "Essential Conversations" reviewed and analyzed the individual conference evaluations and the results of the 2017 and 2019 Survey Monkey questionnaires (which included many identical questions for the sake of comparing and analyzing results). They concluded that 1) the 2017 and 2018 conferences hosted at CTU provided an environment conducive to learning; 2) the conferences provided both the knowledge and the inspiration for the core teams to develop and implement plans for their communities; and 3) the participants, core teams, and the larger communities were using ethnic stereotypes less frequently, discussing interculturality more frequently, sharing meals with those of other cultures more frequently, and having more positive experiences in conversations about ethnic and cultural differences with those from other backgrounds.[9]

DeNault and Perri then prepared a final evaluation of the "Engaging Our Diversity: Interculturality and Consecrated Life"[10] programme based on the 2019 questionnaire and final reports submitted by the core teams from all 20 religious communities in February and March 2020. The latter included at most three major activities, three major obstacles, and three best practices from their participation in the CSCL interculturality programme. A summary of their findings in these three areas follows.

Major Intercultural Activities

First of all, the 20 participating communities reported having 52 major activities, examples of which are listed below. There was an average of 165 people involved in each activity, which means that approximately 9,000 people were directly involved in at least one activity. Applying a modest network multiplier

[9] Charles DeNault and Dominic Perri, Executive Summary of Final Report, "Engaging Our Diversity Report on Participating Communities' Interculturality Plans" (Chicago, IL: Essential Conversations LLC: 21 April 2020), 4.
[10] *Ibid.*

(0.5), DeNault and Perri believe that number rises to over 17,000 people in total.[11] Beyond the issue of quantity, the consultants found that very significant qualitative changes occurred in terms of growth in interculturality in the following areas.[12]

- All of the religious communities reported an increase in formal and/or informal discussions with respect to interculturality.
- Thirteen of the twenty communities (65 percent) reported improvements in the area of leadership and interculturality.
- Half of the communities reported improvements in terms of formation and interculturality.
- Nearly half (45 percent) reported the activities have resulted in changes to community policies.
- Half reported an increase in sharing meals with people from culturally diverse groups.
- Forty percent reported improvement in the area of ministry and interculturality.
- Over one third (35 percent) say they have greater attendance and participation of culturally diverse groups due to their activities both within their communities and ministry.

The many intercultural activities are represented by the following examples (including the name of the religious congregation).[13]

- Provided a study guide for a chapter on intercultural living in *Our Own Words: Religious Life in a Changing World* and a case study of a woman in formation in the Philippines, which was included on the congregation's web page (Adrian Dominican Sisters, MI).
- Made presentations on intercultural living and led discussion activities four times with the religious community, which included the leadership, formation directors, and the entire community (Benedictine Sisters of Mount St. Scholastica, KS).
- Engaged the topic of interculturality through presentations, intentional conversations, and movie discussions with leadership and communities in the United States and Mexico (Dominican Sisters of Mission San Jose, CA).
- Held a two-day workshop for lay men and women who govern and administer the educational institutions sponsored by the congregation, and a 2.5-hour in-service for congregation employees or "directors" of a congregation office or department (e.g., communications, philanthropy, COO, CFO, liturgy) (Dominican Sisters of Sinsinawa, WI).

---

[11] *Ibid.*, 6.
[12] *Ibid.*, 8–9.
[13] Charles DeNault and Dominic Perri, compilers, "Activities, Obstacles and Best Practices: An Addendum to the Summary of Final Reports" (Chicago, IL: Essential Conversations LLC: April 2020), 1–6.

- Sponsored congregational assemblies in Brazil, Jamaica, and the United States, developed the theme of interculturality within the Franciscan spirituality, and continued the congregation's activities regarding anti-racism (Franciscan Sisters of Allegany, NY).

- Held weekly classes on intercultural diversity for novices and formators in Chicago, provided international General Chapter preparations for younger congregation members who met in Seoul, and prepared a paper on intercultural competency for the General Chapter in New York state (Maryknoll Fathers and Brothers, NY).

- Conducted monthly discussions on white privilege and intercultural living for a year at the central house (New York state) and two (three-day) phases of a programme for local congregational communities around the world (Maryknoll Sisters, NY).

- Gathered historical information to construct and understand the process of interculturality in their community, with the successes and challenges, as background for sponsoring appropriate discussions and activities at all levels, including the General Chapter (Cenacle) (Missionary Servants of the Most Holy Trinity, MD).

- Developed a congregational plan for initial formation, including intercultural goals for each stage of formation; prepared materials for the leadership of all provinces/regions; the International Leadership Team (ILT) facilitated reflections with local groups of sisters in every province/region (in India, Peru, USA, etc.) over a two-year period (School Sisters of St. Francis, WI).

- Prepared a presentation at an international general assembly of their religious community in Bangalore, India, and every three months (beginning December 2019) sent out educational materials and processes to be used within the local communities and by associates (Sisters of Charity of Nazareth, KY).

- Prepared a programme in English and Korean with a lecture and discussion, translated and administered the Intercultural Competency Scale tool in Korea and the USA, and facilitated reflection and small group discussions (Sisters of Charity of Seton Hall, NJ).

- Prepared presentations on micro-aggression for the Associates of the Sisters of Mercy and the Institute Leadership Team of the Sisters of Mercy to raise awareness in a non-threatening way of people's racist and prejudiced attitudes (Sisters of Mercy of the Americas).

- Prepared a day and a half interculturality experience and programme at the annual summer congregational meeting in 2018 and 2019, which included reading materials, videos, talks, panel sharing, prayer, and reconciliation rituals (Sisters of Providence, St. Mary of the Woods, IN).

- Prepared delegates for the international General Chapter held in Shillong, India, on the theme of interculturality; presented a programme on intercultural living for a total of 31 novices over a period of three years, and prepared and used eight videos of Sisters telling personal stories of their positive and negative experiences of multi-cultural encounters (Sisters of the Holy Cross).

- Facilitated a process for 16 local communities to have at least two sessions, which included input, discussion, and a penance service, and used resources from the US Catholic Conference of Bishops (USCCB) on Racism (The Salesians of Don Bosco).
- Held formal meetings with an external consultant to strengthen teamwork among those with cultural differences, organized three half-day gatherings for sisters, sponsored intentional monthly spirituality days for congregational leaders and formation groups, and developed a three-day formation programme for the USA sisters on interculturality (Verbum Dei Missionary Fraternity).

Obstacles

The second set of materials consists of the 38 obstacles that the core teams faced when they were creating and implementing their interculturality plans. Consultants DeNault and Perri organized them into five categories, presented here in descending order of frequency.[14]

- Lack of time (42 percent): This most common obstacle most likely reflects the increasing demands on time and the many complex issues religious institutes must engage. One respondent describes this obstacle as follows: "Limitations of team's time, distance from each other, responsibilities of ministry, and [limited] energy."
- Attitude (18 percent): The second most common obstacle was convincing other community members that addressing interculturality is necessary.
- Technical obstacles (16 percent): This included problems with translations, a variety of technical issues, and the inability to know how many people had watched a posted video.
- Educating a diverse audience (13 percent): Some teams ran into difficulty with their diverse audiences – one response noted the difficulty in creating materials that "a wide variety of people could understand and engage with. The very young in formation to our Seniors, [and] those that English is not their first language." Although respondents considered these as obstacles, the consultants noted that these points "might be thought of as part of the process of instituting the changes demanded as a community becomes more interculturally aware."[15]
- Community politics (11 percent): Some core teams failed to gain the support they needed from leadership to implement part of their plans.

In analyzing the obstacles, DeNault and Perri noted the following:

---

[14] DeNault and Perri, Executive Summary of Final Report, "Engaging Our Diversity Report on Participating Communities' Interculturality Plans," 11–12. For the detailed data, see DeNault and Perri, compilers, "Activities, Obstacles and Best Practices: An Addendum," 7–12.
[15] DeNault and Perri, Executive Summary of Final Report, 11.

One third of the impediments caused a significant delay and one third caused a minor delay. Nearly one third (30%) of the obstacles forced the core team to make changes to their plan, with minor changes outweighing major changes by a two to one ratio. The core teams indicate that challenges persist for over 80% of obstacles. However, most teams indicate that they were moving forward despite having been slowed or having to adjust their plans. And two teams have resolved their time and attitude issues.[16]

Best Practices

The third set of responses from the core teams falls under the category of best practices. They shared over 30 best practices which they uncovered while developing and implementing their plans. Consultants DeNault and Perri proposed three categories: programmatic elements that work well, how to work well together, and personal commitment.[17]

Programmatic elements that work well

These best practices centre on deliberate and concerted efforts to engage multiple cultures in the community through shared stories, traditions, food, dance, and music. Some communities were highly intentional about processes that mixed people of different cultures and created immersive experiences. Another insight is that intercultural programmes are more successful when they are integrated with other community activities, rather than being offered as standalone interculturality programmes. Here is a shortened list of the best practices:

- Celebrate each culture's traditions and holidays. Enrich oneself by trying new foods, dance, and music.
- Sharing stories can be very powerful, whether at workshops or on video.
- Increase diversity and invite guests from different cultures to join.
- Assign diversity by pairing old with young and mixing races.
- Survey to assess progress.
- Create a map to show where everyone comes from.
- Consider immersive exchanges, because spending time together is important.[18]
- Integrated programmes are better received than independent intercultural programmes. Collaborate with other committees.
- When you find a practice that makes sense and works, move quickly to incorporate it into congregational policy.

---

[16] *Ibid.*, 12.

[17] DeNault and Perri, Executive Summary of Final Report, 13–14. For the detailed data, see DeNault and Perri, compilers, "Activities, Obstacles and Best Practices: An Addendum," 13–16.

[18] During the early times of COVID-19, these exchanges became more difficult. However, during the later period of COVID-19, people found that Zoom and other forms of social media provided a venue for engaging encounters among diverse peoples who were distant geographically and spatially (within communities themselves).

How to work well together

The success of intercultural initiatives is connected to best practices in collaboration, smart meeting design, effective teaming, and effective use of organizational structures. Best practices include the following:

- Tap into the strengths of the core team. Have the creative people create, and have the administrative people do administration, etc;
- Work within the congregation's organizational structures;
- Consider using a contemplative approach to decision making;
- Prepare your group, large and small. For team meetings or large assemblies, send out materials, points of discussion, and agendas in advance. This preparation yields better interaction because people can prepare; it also helps the non-native-English speakers follow and participate;
- Translate materials (when necessary for better communication).

Personal Commitment

Achieving good results with intercultural initiatives also depends on strong interpersonal best practices, such as active, deep listening, self-awareness, and engaging in experiential as well as academic learning. These findings suggest that successful intercultural leaders are those who are willing to invest personally in this work. The core teams shared the following personal commitment best practices:

- Know ourselves and our culture and share this knowledge with others;
- Ask clarifying questions;
- Take feedback and be flexible;
- Practice behaving more naturally when among diverse groups of people;
- Realize that becoming more intercultural requires more experiential learning than academic learning;
- Listen and listen again as you learn more about other cultures;
- Realize that this process takes time and patience. Give the time to absorb words and concepts; clarify understanding. Personal conversion is a process of deepening one's faith that diversity is valued by God.

Missiological Reflections on the Case Study

This particular case study represents the efforts, on the one hand, of 20 Catholic women's and men's religious congregations to address the need for stronger explicit interculturality within the particular contexts of both their communities and their very diverse ministries.[19] Drawing upon the feedback from conference evaluations, the Survey Monkey questionnaires, and especially the final reports by the core teams, the consultants DeNault and Perri provided an excellent description and analysis of activities, obstacles, and best practices. It appears that the majority of the teams were able to begin to address the goals of the overall

---

[19] See footnote 8 above.

project, which of course will require many more years to address fully. Some built upon already-existing programmes, while others were just beginning to acknowledge and address the need for interculturality. It seems that most of the religious congregations are continuing to follow-up on their commitment to interculturality after the end of the CTU-CSCL project.[20] The later addition to the third goal of the project – networking with other religious congregations and organizations – did not receive much attention. However, two of the women's Franciscan congregations explicitly collaborated around Franciscan spirituality and interculturality. These congregations learned from each other during the small group table discussions, plenum sessions, and coffee breaks during the three conferences.

During this project, the core teams facilitated a process for the better understanding, enrichment, and collaboration among the community members with diverse backgrounds within their community life and among the diverse peoples with whom they were ministering. Remembering what was described at the beginning of this chapter, this diversity includes "ethnicity, race, and nationality; social change; social location (i.e., female/male, rich/poor, social status, location within power dynamics, different generations); and particular individual and communal circumstances."

The methodology of this project was based on the theological and pedagogical principle that change and transformation takes place from within a community, rather than being determined or imposed by "outsiders." The members of the individual core teams were primarily "insiders" within their congregational and community life – to act as catalysts and facilitators. In terms of ministry, the congregational members are to engage the local communities in which they minister primarily as appropriate "outsiders" and partners in the process of developing and deepening interculturality in those ministerial contexts. In other words, the agency of the insiders is to be acknowledged and affirmed in all situations.[21]

The needs for tolerance, as a minimum, and interculturality, as an ideal, are urgent for our human family, Christian communities, and religious congregations within the United States and around the world. The desire to address this situation is strong on the international scene. Some of this desire was evident among the international religious congregations who participated in the CTU-CSCL programme. Furthermore, building upon the pedagogy and goals of this Chicago programme, the author chaired the organizing team for a two-week interculturality programme in Rome held from 21 January to 1 February 2019 for 180 religious women (four core team members from 45 international congregations). This programme was sponsored by the International Union of Superiors General (UISG), translated simultaneously into four languages (English, Spanish, French, and Italian), and streamed into two halls. Roger

---

[20] Roger Schroeder has been involved in follow-up programmes with several of religious congregations who participated in the CTU-CSCL programme.
[21] On the spirituality of "insiders" and "outsiders" in such a complex dynamic, see Stephen Bevans, "Letting Go and Speaking Out: Prophetic Dialogue and the Spirituality of Inculturation," in *Prophetic Dialogue*, 88–100.

Schroeder, SVD, also co-chaired with Adriana Milmanda, SSpS,[22] the organization team for a three-week international programme (English and Spanish) on "Spirituality and Interculturality" for 25 SVD, SSpS, and Lay Partners in Steyl, the Netherlands, from 26 January to 14 February 2020. These two programmes were held prior to the outbreak of COVID-19. During the pandemic, international programmes on interculturality continue to be sponsored for Catholic religious congregations by UISG and others virtually using Zoom and other online formats.

The plenary and workshop presentations from the 2017 and 2018 CTU-CSCL conferences were published as Engaging Our Diversity: Interculturality and Consecrated Life Today in 2020 and as Comprometernos con la diversidad: Interculturalidad y vida consagrada hoy in 2022.[23] Such publications provide valuable resources for promoting interculturality in the church and mission within and beyond North America.[24]

During the CSCL-CTU project, it became clear that anti-racism was the prominent issue on interculturality in the context of religious life, the church, and society in the United States. During COVID-19, racism and all forms of prejudice became even more urgent challenges. Racism began to be addressed more explicitly and centrally during the second CSCL conference in November 2018, in response to feedback from the participants. As a next step, CTU applied for and was granted funding again through the Hilton Foundation to develop and execute a three-year project (2022–2025) to prepare religious women as more effective agents of reconciliation and transformative action toward a more racially just Catholic Church and world. This programme will also fall within the auspices of the Center for the Study of Consecrated Life (CSCL) and collaborate with the National Black Sisters' Conference. It will follow a similar methodology of working with core teams of each of the participating religious congregations.

The image of the banquet, which appears throughout the Hebrew and Christian scriptures, represents the call of God for people of all nations and backgrounds to gather as sisters and brothers around one table. Jesus reinforced

---

[22] The Society of the Divine Word (SVD) and the Holy Spirit Missionary Sisters (SSpS) share the same founder, Arnold Janssen, and they also share missionary vision and work.

[23] Cimperman and Schroeder, eds., *Engaging Our Diversity* (Maryknoll, NY: Orbis Books, 2020); trans. Niels Berthel Johansen, *Comprometernos con la diversidad: Interculturalidad y vida consagrada hoy* (Estella, Spain: Editorial Verbo Divino, 2022).

[24] Other recent publications on interculturality include the following: Anthony Gittins, *Living Mission Interculturally: Faith, Culture, and the Renewal of Praxis* (Collegeville, MN: Liturgical Press, 2015); Lazar Stanislaus, SVD, and Martin Ueffing, SVD, eds., vol. I: *Intercultural Living*, vol. II: *Intercultural Mission* (Sankt Augustin, Germany: Steyler Missionswissenschaftliches Institut, and New Dehli: ISPCK, 2015); Lazar Stanislaus and Martin Ueffing, eds., trans. Niels Berthel Johansen, *Interculturalidad: En la Vida y en la Misión* (Estella, Spain: Editorial Verbo Divino, 2017); Lazar Stanislaus and Martin Ueffing, eds., *Intercultural Living: Explorations in Missiology* (Maryknoll, NY: Orbis Books, 2018); Lazar Stanislaus, SVD, and Christian Tauchner, SVD, eds., *Becoming Intercultural: Perspectives on Mission* (Sankt Augustin, Germany: Steyler Missionswissenschaftliches Institut; New Dehli: ISPCK, 2021).

the inclusivity of this call through his ministry of table fellowship to the marginalized "other." The call to interculturality and anti-racism is central to the mission of the reign of God today. The CSCL-CTU three-year project of "Engaging Our Diversity: Interculturality and Consecrated Life" was an attempt to address this pressing mission issue both within the church and religious life and in our ministries and society. It also highlighted the importance of collaboration among religious congregations.

Ministry at the Margins: Outreach to the LGBTQ+ Roman Catholic Community in San Francisco

Amanda D. Quantz

Introduction

In a neighbourhood buzzing with a cast of characters as varied as dog walkers, tourists, software developers, sex workers, undocumented restaurant employees, billionaire entrepreneurs, retirees, and scores of people who are unhoused, the GPS coordinate 37.7625° N, 122.4348° W is the queerest intersection on the globe.

On 20 June 2021, during San Francisco's Pride Week, the inaugural "Faithful & Fabulous Interfaith Drag Street Eucharist" was celebrated in the Castro District. Shortly before the annual Pride festivities, I had heard about the celebration from a colleague whose seminary formation has included several street ministry programmes. This unique eucharistic celebration was designed by the San Francisco Night Ministry, an organization which has been serving the city since 1964:

> The heart of our work occurs at night. We offer spiritual and emotional care and referral services on the streets, in the middle of the night, every night of the year [...] We provide companionship to those who are lonely and isolated. We attend to mental and physical needs. We provide harm reduction for those at risk to themselves and others. We encounter many of the most vulnerable, who fall between the cracks of the city's social services.[1]

Those who serve the church through the San Francisco Night Ministry are intrepid pastoral sensei.

One of several Christian celebrants at the drag liturgy, my colleague, along with numerous congregants, dressed for the occasion. There were colourful wigs, glitter eyeshadow, platform boots, sequined miniskirts, feather boas, and rainbow accessories. The event was advertised on Facebook as an occasion "to honour our queer ancestors, our cloud of witnesses." Celebrants included "Rev. Seminarian Bené Diction, ELCA, Rev. Blessya Hartz, UCC, and Bonnie Violet, a queer chaplain and host of the online series 'Drag & Spirituality.'" The advertisement noted that "in drag or out of drag, all are invited to walk the Runway of the Spirit to the beats of DJ Jihan. Join us for Pride & claim public space for queer faith."[2]

---

[1] San Francisco Night Ministry, "What We Do", SF Night Ministry, https://sfnightministry.org/programs.

[2] Faithful&Fabulous Drag Street Liturgy, Facebook post, 11 June 2021, Event page: 21 June 2021, https://www.facebook.com/events/jane-warner-plaza-castro-sf/faithfulfabulous-drag-street-eucharist/637966964270602; San Francisco Night

A church without walls, the pulsating intersection at 17th and Castro, provided an improvised aisle carpeted with two hot pink runways made of satin fabric duct-taped to the asphalt. The traffic-stopping event was to include another concelebrant, a retired Roman Catholic missionary priest whose ministry to the LGBTQ+ community is fully supported by his religious order. Unfortunately, he was unable to attend the celebration in person due to a last-minute scheduling conflict. Rather than absent himself entirely, the priest made a bold decision to send the pre-consecrated host to the liturgy. He instructed the presiders to state clearly that anyone at this interfaith gathering who wished to be fed by the body and blood of Christ was welcome to receive the eucharist. He also wrote a letter to the Roman Catholics in attendance. His message offered a wholehearted affirmation that LGBTQ+ people are not only loved by God but are also a blessing to the Catholic Church – a Church that has been the cause of moral injury for so many.

The drag eucharist impelled me to reach out to numerous lay and ordained Roman Catholic ministers who serve in the Bay Area. Interviews conducted in 2021–2022 contributed to several missiological insights that resulted in this case study. Its main focus is the Catholic Church's successes, failures, and missed opportunities in ministering to LGBTQ+ Roman Catholics in the Bay Area. A spotlight on key positions, documents, and organizations that present obstacles to effective ministry serve as counterpoints to these innovative approaches to Roman Catholic missionary activity for 21st century North America. This study highlights several points of light that confront institutional recalcitrance. In providing a snapshot of what the Catholic Church is and is not doing, as well as what it could do to minister more effectively to this disenfranchised group, the case study offers a challenge and an opportunity to Roman Catholic missioners who wish to reach people who have been ignored or forgotten by the church. In other words, if the Roman Catholic Church can see LGBTQ+ San Francisco as a vibrant, hope-filled mission field, they should feel prepared to engage in similar ministries anywhere in North America. The narrative below indicates a starting point for disentangling issues of faith, free will, and self-sabotage as the church struggles (or fails to struggle) to live the mission of Jesus.

An ancient parable interpreted by several religious traditions describes two realms: The Land of Incessant Suffering and the Land of Utmost Bliss. A visitor to the Land of Incessant Suffering sees a wonderful array of foods laid out for a banquet, yet everyone is gaunt, angry, and exhausted. In a Buddhist account, the people are surrounded by tempting delicacies, but the only utensils available are three-foot-long chopsticks. The residents' efforts to eat result in eternal frustration.

While touring the Land of Utmost Bliss, the visitor also comes across a banquet. Once again, the only utensils are three-foot-long chopsticks. This time, the visitor is fascinated to see that each cheerful resident feeds the person across the table. The difference between misery and bliss has nothing to do with the tools provided. Rather, exasperation or joy results from people's responses to the

---

Ministry, "Faithful Fabulous," SF Night Ministry, https://sfnightministry.org/faithful-fabulous/.

sustenance provided by the generous host. Those in the Land of Utmost Bliss make a commitment to sustain each person's life, without exception.

In a Christian worldview, these settings parallel Heaven and Hell, both of which the church believes are final destinations. Roman Catholics believe that people eventually reach one or the other state at the journey's end. Hell is final, not because God is merciless, but because our merciful God provides everything that we need in order to practice mercy in the wayfaring state, where life is shaped by interpersonal relationships and ethical decisions. One person's life might involve late conversion, while another's life is marked by a slow-burning love for God. Occasionally, there are prodigious child-saints. The church maintains that our quality of life – of the world and its politics, of family life, of adversarial relationships, of friendships, of careers, and of personal encounters with God and self – whether long or short, determines our final state of bliss or alienation from God. The church, too, is subject to its own teaching.

Church Teaching on Homosexuality

According to the *Catechism of the Catholic Church*, "the number of men and women who have deep-seated homosexual tendencies is not negligible [...] Every sign of unjust discrimination in their regard should be avoided."[3] However, often the Catholic Church's actions are shaped by the document's claim that both "homosexual acts" and a "homosexual inclination" are "intrinsically/objectively disordered."[4] What the Catechism says and how it reads are different. It reads: "They must be accepted with respect, compassion, and sensitivity," but it means that the Church should receive and treat LGBTQ+ people in accordance with these values. However, as Father James Martin indicates, it is not possible to practice authentic sensitivity towards people we do not know.[5] Unfortunately, because it includes statements made by heterosexuals that a huge swath of humanity is "intrinsically/objectively disordered," the Catechism does not help Catholics recognize that assessing one another's wisdom, self-understanding, and holiness is a very speculative activity. Because the phrase "genuine affective and sexual complementarity"[6] refers to genital complementarity, the Catechism does not impel the church "to accept" LGBTQ+ Christians in a way that reflects the embodiment of divine light within them.

---

[3] *Catechism of the Catholic Church*, second edition (Washington, D.C.: United States Catholic Conference, 2011), part 3, "Life in Christ," section 2358, 566.
[4] *Catechism*, section 2357: "Basing itself on Sacred Scripture, which presents homosexual acts as acts of grave depravity, tradition has always declared that 'homosexual acts are intrinsically disordered,'" https://www.usccb.org/sites/default/files/flipbooks/catechism/568/. For an analysis of homosexuality and other "abominations" listed in Leviticus 18 and 19, see my recent book, *Radical Hospitality for a Prophetic Church* (Lanham, MD: Lexington Books/Fortress Academic, 2020), 17–18.
[5] James Martin, *Building A Bridge: How the Catholic Church and the LGBTQ Community Can Enter into a Relationship of Respect, Compassion, and Sensitivity* (New York: HarperCollins, 2017), 41.
[6] *Catechism*, section 2357.

While the church works to confront what it sees as "unjust discrimination," cited in section 2358, it defends a number of discriminatory practices through its interpretation of scripture. In *Mere Christianity*, C. S. Lewis offered a masterful bit of wisdom about hermeneutical humility needed for the difficult task of saying anything meaningful about another person's experience:

> What can you ever really know of other people's souls – of their temptations, their opportunities, their struggles? One soul in the whole creation you do know: and it is the only one whose fate is placed in your hands. If there is a God, you are, in a sense, alone with Him. You cannot put Him off with speculations about your next door neighbours or memories of what you have read in books. What will all that chatter and hearsay count (will you even be able to remember it?) when the anaesthetic fog which we call "nature" or "the real world" fades away and the Presence in which you have always stood becomes palpable, immediate, and unavoidable?[7]

Lewis' prophetic words should remind the church that no individual or institution owns the rights to divine light. God is refracted through each human prism, as a single colour or as the full spectrum of the rainbow, in whatever way God chooses.

The teachings found in the Catechism of the Catholic Church present a predicament for the institution given its stated commitment to a consistent ethic of life. Why, when Jesus' mandate is to be generous with everyone who is spiritually and physically hungry, do some withhold nourishment from hungry guests seated across the table? Jesus welcomed everyone to the banquet, yet there are servant leaders who bar the door to some of his followers.[8] The Catechism's exclusion of words such as gay, lesbian, gender, intersex, or trans is unfortunate. Furthermore, there is no evidence in a recently discovered 2018 draft of the USCCB pastoral letter on LGBTQ+ ministry that anyone who identifies with that community was among the lay staff members who assisted the bishops.[9]

As recently as 2019, Father Bob Bussen, a priest in Park City, Utah, who was outed after celebrating mass for an LGBTQ+ community, said that most gay priests are not safe. Regarding their position, he said, "It is not a closet. It is a cage." Their livelihood is at stake, especially because in the United States, health insurance is tied to employment. Unwarranted scrutiny of gay priests even

---

[7] C.S. Lewis, *Mere Christianity* (New York: HarperCollins, 2000), 216–17.

[8] As Martin says, "Jesus recognizes all people, even those who seem invisible in the community. In fact, he reaches out specifically to those on the margins." *Building a Bridge*, 20–21.

[9] "In the Image of God: A Compendium for Bishops in View of Particular Challenges of Our Time," *The Pillar* (online news source), https://www.pillarcatholic.com/draft-usccb-lgbt-doc-calls-for-clarity/. A 2021 article from *The Pillar*, titled "Vatican and USCCB Leave Transgender Policy Texts Unpublished," indicates that some laypeople were consulted for the draft document: "A task force of USCCB staffers and bishops worked in 2016 to develop a text, former USCCB staffers told The Pillar, with most staff drawn from the Office of Laity, Marriage, Family Life, and Youth, and the Office of Doctrine." "Vatican and USCCB leave transgender policy texts unpublished," *The Pillar*, 17 December 2021, https://www.pillarcatholic.com/p/vatican-and-usccb-leave-transgender.

affects those who are faithful to their vow of celibacy.[10] The tepid form of "acceptance" referenced in the Catechism undermines the institution's own stated commitment to advocating for those who are marginalized. However, as we will see below, the news from the nation's chanceries and parishes is not entirely bleak.

The Buddhist scholar Thich Nhat Hanh explained beautifully the differences between *noumena* and *phenomena*: things as we presume they are versus things as we experience them. Drawing on the example of the relationship between water and waves, he notes the problem of conflating waves with water, of failing to take note of their uniqueness: "Of course there is a relationship between water and wave, but this relationship is very different from the relationship between waves and waves [...] When we say this wave is made of all the other waves, we are dealing with the phenomenal world [...] But it's very different when we say that this wave is made of water."[11]

Hermeneutical humility requires that we do not impose limitations on *noumena* by dismissing or misunderstanding divine-human *phenomena*. Theological reflection that respects cultural diversity must practice generosity. The only way for Catholic leaders to appreciate the lived realities of LGBTQ+ Catholics is through toil. Whether they welcome the analogy or not, bishops are aware that Pope Francis sees an effective minister as a shepherd who smells like the sheep. If the disconnect, which Pope Francis dreads, is true of what he calls "sad priests," how much more urgent is his appeal to the bishops?[12]

Without exception, each minister interviewed for this case study identified one fundamental step that Roman Catholic leaders must take in order to serve LGBTQ+ members more effectively and pastorally. They believe that the *magisterium*, a focal point among the interviewees, should be open to the change of heart that flows from genuine love and understanding. This change, several suggested, should begin with bishops' decisions to seek out and develop relationships with LGBTQ+ members of their own families. Bishop Gumbleton, now-retired auxiliary bishop of Detroit, publicly shared his struggle to understand and eventually embrace his brother Dan, who is gay.[13] Twenty-five years ago, he also encouraged those who work for the church, including gay bishops and priests, to come out. One can only imagine the blessing this would be for priests like Father Bussen.[14]

---

[10] Elizabeth Dias, "It Is Not a Closet. It Is a Cage: Gay Catholic Priests Speak Out," *New York Times*, 17 February 2017, https://www.nytimes.com/2019/02/17/us/it-is-not-a-closet-it-is-a-cage-gay-catholic-priests-speak-out.html.

[11] Thich Nhat Hanh, *Going Home: Jesus and Buddha as Brothers* (New York: Riverhead Books, 1999), 4–7.

[12] "Chrism Mass Homily of Pope Francis," 28 March 2013, https://www.vatican.va/content/francesco/en/homilies/2013/documents/papa-francesco_20130328_messa-crismale.html.

[13] PBS Frontline interview with Bishop Thomas Gumbleton [2005], https://www.pbs.org/wgbh/pages/frontline/shows/pope/sex/gumbleton.html.

[14] Francis DeBernardo, *Book of Memory and Thanksgiving: Celebrating the 25th Anniversary of the Foundation of New Ways Ministry in 1977*, 5, https://www.newwaysministry.org/wp-content/uploads/2021/03/Book_of_Memory.pdf.

Advocates and Adversaries

The LGBTQ+ community has an ally in Father James Martin. In *Building a Bridge*, he notes that "many Church leaders do not know, on a personal level, LGBT people who are public about their sexuality. That lack of familiarity and friendship means it is more difficult to be sensitive. How can you be sensitive to people's situations if you don't know them? So, one invitation is for the hierarchy to come to know LGBT Catholics as friends."[15] Martin offers some questions that Catholic leaders might ask LGBTQ+ individuals: "What was it like growing up as a gay boy, a lesbian girl, or a transgender person? What is your life like now? How have you suffered as a result of your orientation? Where do you experience joy in your life? What is your experience of God? What is your experience of the Church? What do you hope for, long for, pray for?"[16]

It seems fair to say that Pope Francis sees himself as an LGBTQ+ ally. For example, unlike the Catechism, he has publicly used the word "gay." This move is a small step towards healing the moral injury experienced by many current and former Catholics.[17] In the 2020 documentary *Francesco*, Pope Francis said, "What we have to create is a civil union law. That way they are legally covered [...] Homosexuals have a right to be a part of the family [...] they're children of God and have a right to a family. Nobody should be thrown out, or be made miserable because of it."[18]

Juan Carlos Cruz, a victim of clerical sexual abuse in Chile, reported that Pope Francis told him "God made you gay, and God loves you like you are." He also told Andrea Rubera that he and his husband Dario De Gregorio should freely raise their three children as Catholics.[19] Still, Pope Francis opposes the idea of celebrating same-sex sacramental marriages. For faithful LGBTQ+ Catholics who are asking the church they love to bless their civil unions to those they love, this refusal is a cause of great suffering. Made in the image and likeness of God, each person who seeks God is continually moving towards abundant life. Human experience is comprised of bio-psycho-social-spiritual factors, and each Christian of any gender or sexual identity comes to know Jesus in and through continual integration and reintegration of our unique constitutions. So, what does the Catholic Church's refusal to bless civil unions say to the children of Andrea Rubera and Dario De Gregorio? There seems to be two possibilities: either that Christian marriage is inessential for any Catholic or that two people of the same sex are incapable of forming a sacred bond with one another, despite their fidelity to their spouse and God. If it intends to suggest the latter, a more incisive theology of marriage is needed than the church currently offers.

---

[15] Martin, *Building a Bridge*, 40.

[16] *Ibid.*, 33.

[17] As early as July 2013, Pope Francis said during a press conference on his return from Rio de Janeiro to Rome, "If someone is gay, and he searches for the Lord and has goodwill, who am I to judge?" Rachel Donadio, "On Gay Priests, Pope Francis Asks, 'Who Am I to Judge?,'" 29 July 2013, https://www.nytimes.com/2013/07/30/world/europe/pope-francis-gay-priests.html.

[18] *Francesco*, directed by Evgeny Afineevsky (Tolmor Production, 2020), Discovery+.

[19] *Ibid.*

LGBTQ+ Parish Ministries

In 1969, Father Patrick X. Nidorf, OSA, began DignityUSA in southern California to meet the needs of LGBTQ+ Catholics. On 1 October 1986, in a letter signed by Joseph Cardinal Ratzinger, then-prefect of the Congregation for the Doctrine of the Faith, the Vatican stated that groups that disagree with Catholic teaching cannot meet on church property, which resulted in the eviction of most Dignity groups from parishes.[20] In the wake of that decision, priests were gradually informed by dioceses that they were no longer to preside at the eucharist for DignityUSA gatherings. While DignityUSA continues to live its mission, meetings usually occur in Protestant churches. Thirty-five years after the Vatican ban was issued, a common theme I found among San Francisco parish ministers is that Catholic leaders have to walk a fine line with regard to LGBTQ+ ministry. For example, a pastor at one parish tries to accommodate the community, but he also requires that he be consulted before they choose retreat leaders. Another approach is for these groups to keep a low profile. Other priests and lay ministers will take calculated risks, asking as needed for forgiveness rather than permission.

With one exception, the LGBTQ+ ministers interviewed for this case study participated under the condition of anonymity. A young laywoman, whom I will call Annie, coordinates an LGBTQ+ parish group with a listserv of more than 60 people. The group has regular social gatherings after the morning mass, evening prayer meetings, and community-building opportunities with facilitators. Annie's group has the full support of the pastoral staff, including a priest who worked with an LGBTQ+ prison population. She described her pastoral goal as helping integrate the community as one body of Christ with many parts. Her pastor has invited former inmates to join their church community, including trans women. Following Annie's suggestion, parishioners also began introducing themselves with their pronouns of choice. Under the leadership of the previous pastor, the community hosted a series about healing homophobia. He also issued an apology on behalf of the Catholic Church.

At mass during Pride week in 2021, a San Francisco-based guest celebrant at Annie's parish wore a chasuble adorned with rainbow stripes. Rather than preach at the time of the homily, he noted that Annie would offer a reflection after communion. She later told me that it bothers her that women's voices are only permitted at the end of mass. An even-tempered optimist, Annie's reflection highlighted the goodness of diversity and noted that the rainbow Pride flag,

---

[20] "Special attention should be given to the practice of scheduling religious services and to the use of Church buildings by these groups, including the facilities of Catholic schools and colleges." "Letter to the Bishops of the Catholic Church on the Pastoral Care of Homosexual Persons," 1 October 1986, https://www.vatican.va/roman_curia/congregations/cfaith/documents/rc_con_cfaith_doc _19861001_homosexual-persons_en.html. With regard to the ban on priests presiding at Eucharist for DignityUSA groups, see Hank Stuever, "Spurned by the Archbishop of L.A., Members of Dignity, an Organization of Gay Catholics, Maintain Their Allegiance to the Church but…: They Pray Alone," *Los Angeles Times*, 29 August 1990, https://www.latimes.com/archives/la-xpm-1990-08-29-vw-231-story.html.

created by Gilbert Baker in 1978, has a powerful symbolic function. "The rainbow is so perfect," she said, "because it really fits our diversity in terms of race, gender, ages, plus it is natural; it's in nature, it's from the sky. We are each unique, diverse, and natural."[21] The emphasis on the word "natural" challenges section 2357 of the Catechism, where homosexuality is referred to as "intrinsically disordered." A born activist, Annie concluded her reflection by inviting parishioners to learn about sexual identities that they do not understand.

When asked to describe what she believes LGBTQ+ Catholics need, Annie emphasized respect, saying that "they want to be seen, valued, and accepted, which some do."[22] She finds that the LGBTQ+ voices at her parish are welcomed by the pastor, but she is also aware that the parishioners who feel the most comfortable are older, white, gay men. Annie, therefore, tries to lift up the different experiences of women, people of colour, immigrants, families, and those with multiple intersecting identities. She is optimistic about helping create this experience for other LGBTQ+ parishioners and would-be members. With regard to the role of the archdiocese, Annie noted that "essentially, they ignore the LGBTQ+ community unless they perceive that queer expression has gone too far or become too public." Around the globe, Roman Catholic communities have received angry calls from their dioceses for using the rainbow flag as the altar cloth during Pride week. Their complaint is that the gesture goes too far and signals idolatry.[23]

A doctoral student in theology, Jonathan is a gay San Francisco Catholic high school educator who has found refuge in the young adult group at another parish with a sizeable LGBTQ+ population. He is using the synodal process to encourage bishops to cultivate a *habitus* of listening, with the goal of reconciling the LGBTQ+ community to the wider Catholic Church.[24] Working at local and global levels of Catholic governance, Jonathan recently issued a challenge to his Young Adults' Council to be more inclusive. At his Catholic high school, LGBTQ+ groups have to function strategically. For example, the faculty work within a "don't say gay" culture. They are not authorized to encourage students to ask questions about LGBTQ+ issues, but they do so unofficially because the kids bring their questions when they are in a safe space. These limitations are present even at a school with a large student-led organization in which more than 75 percent of its members identify as queer.[25]

Mark Guevarra requested that I use his name in this case study. The father of a young daughter and a long-time partner of an ordained Presbyterian minister, Mark is a former Catholic lay minister whose work as an openly gay man cost him his job.[26] Before he began doctoral studies at the Graduate Theological

[21] Annie, reflection offered during a Pride mass, 2021.

[22] Annie, Zoom interview with the author, 30 December 2021.

[23] My request to interview Archbishop Cordileone for this case study went unanswered.

[24] The Roman Catholic "Synod 2021–2023: For a Synodal Church" was implemented by Pope Francis in 2021 and will conclude in 2023.

[25] Jonathan, interview with the author, 25 March 2022.

[26] Francis DeBernardo, "Fired for Not Answering Question About His Relationship Status," 12 February 2018, https://www.newwaysministry.org/2018/02/12/fired-not-answering-question-relationship-status.

Union in Berkeley, Mark worked in three parishes in Alberta, Canada. In 2018, he was fired from St Albert Catholic Parish in part because he did not ask permission to form an LGBTQ+ prayer group at church. A core group of conservative Catholics complained; an investigation was conducted; and evidence was produced from social media about his relationship status. He was also asked directly whether he was gay and in a relationship. When the process became heated, Mark requested a meeting with the archbishop, who refused. When he was fired, Mark received hundreds of emails from around the world in support of his work, including from a well-known US Catholic priest and from New Ways Ministry. He believes that governance structures need to be reassessed rather than continue in a constant dance. Narratives, he said, need to be challenged.[27]

When asked about transformative experiences he has witnessed within his LGBTQ+ ministry, Mark reflected on his own life, which I would describe as courageous and authentic. Noting that this response sometimes pains him, he explained that closeted priests and seminarians find him a threat. But, "being an Easter people causes us to go back to the cross. Peer support sometimes leads to dating, crying together [...] we place our lived experiences in dialogue with the Church. Being Catholic doesn't mean we turn our brains off and replace them with a catechism."[28] Mark wants the Catholic Church "to authentically listen with our minds and hearts and effectively and lovingly respond." He believes that the response has been painfully inadequate. Silence from ecclesiastical authorities makes LGBTQ+ people feel invisible. They ask: Did anyone hear me? How would I know? Is a non-violent response the best we can hope for?

Like Jonathan, Mark's doctoral work focuses on synodality, an ecclesiological commitment to mutual listening on the part of laity and church leaders. He understands that the laity's unique wisdom makes them partners with the bishops in living the mission of the Catholic Church. Synodality is a continuation of insights explored in *Lumen gentium*, the Dogmatic Constitution on the Church produced by the Second Vatican Council (1962–1965). Synodality is a true process of walking together. In 2020, a grant was funded by the Louisville Institute: "New Agenda for Catholic Theology and Ministry: Perspectives from Queer Theologians of Color." A group of scholars and activists gathered at Loyola University, Chicago, from 20–22 October 2021. Recognizing that issues of race, class, and gender are interlocked, these queer Catholic theologians called for deep listening not only by church leaders, but by the whole Catholic Church.[29]

At World Youth Day in Panama in 2019, Mark spoke with a number of LGBTQ+ groups. He is currently advocating for restorative justice on the part of the Catholic Church to address the hurts and harms suffered by the LGBTQ+ community. As a point of light, Mark offered a recent example of a local ordinary

---

[27] Mark Guevarra, Zoom interview with the author, 20 April 2022.
[28] *Ibid.*
[29] Global Network of Rainbow Catholics, "Perspectives from Queer Catholic Theologians of Color," 28 October 2021, https://rainbowcatholics.org/queer-catholic-theologians-of-color.

who allowed a parish to choose what they saw as best for its community. The parish, which is in an archdiocese that he described as very conservative, is striving to become welcoming to LGBTQ+ people. Mark surmises that he was permitted to offer a retreat because his CV demonstrated that he was eminently qualified. Mark also recently received an affirming email from the Vatican in response to his offer to assist with the synodal process.

Brian, a middle-aged man in a same-sex marriage, has provided spiritual direction for dozens of young adult gay men in the last seven years. He described the approach at his parish as "don't ask, don't tell," meaning "discretion that errs on the side of being closeted." When asked to reflect on the spiritual needs of the LGBTQ+ people he serves, he emphasized the issue of language: "How do you talk about (and thereby think about) gay Catholic sexual integration in a Church whose celebrity influencers speak a weird pop-Freudian version of Theology of the Body? How do you talk about gay couples or the goals of dating and friendship formation? How do families of choice fit into the visible parish?" One of the challenges facing a church that often approaches LGBTQ+ sexuality as a simple matter of choosing celibacy is that "the young single folks have found solid spiritual counsel beyond 'just say no.'"[30] The church is called to meet all people where they are, not where they hope or imagine people to be.

A self-described theological traditionalist, Brian views the Catholic Church's teaching around homosexuality as "a beautiful prescription for gay flourishing that is misrepresented by the ineffective and unrealistic talking points of bishops and straight Catholic influencers." He facilitates theological reflection with his spiritual directees using sources as varied as the Catechism, Thomas Aquinas, and Pope Benedict XVI. When Brian read Aquinas' texts on friendship with a couple in a "monogamish" agreement, they arrived at the realization that recreational sex was not contributing anything to holiness or happiness. A visionary lay minister, Brian said, "I struggle to understand why this needs to be [seen as] boundary crossing. In other words, where are all the openly gay and Catholic leaders? Who are those natural bridges with one foot in LGBT and the other foot in the Church?"[31]

"Neither hot nor cold"

In Revelation 3:16, Jesus condemns the town of Laodicea by alluding to the danger presented by tepid water, saying, "So, because you are lukewarm – neither hot nor cold – I am about to spit you out of my mouth." Water that was neither hot nor cold presented the danger of spreading disease. There are some officially-sanctioned Roman Catholic outreach ministries for LGBTQ+ believers who are struggling to reconcile their sexual identity with Christian faith; however, these organizations fall short and are dangerous. Essentially, they fail to address some basic truths. First, LGBTQ+ people share in the full range of human experiences. Second, they are capable of cultivating sacred, intimate, sexually responsible, and resourcefully procreative relationships. Third,

---

[30] Brian, email communication with author, 31 January 2022.
[31] *Ibid.*

conversion therapy has not only failed miserably in its crusade to change people's sexual orientation, it has also done enormous emotional and psychological damage.[32] Fourth, any theological anthropology that fails to support the full dignity of LGBTQ+ people is offensive to God. Fifth, the church views the call to celibacy as a rare gift. Those who support the ministries discussed below surely realize that celibacy is untenable for most heterosexuals. However, they proceed as if all LGBTQ+ Catholics can and should live celibately. At best, this stance involves magical thinking. At worst, it is fuelled by contempt. All of these disordered positions impede effective ministry.

As the first of five goals listed on its website, *Courage International* is for those who seek "to live chaste lives in accordance with the Roman Catholic Church's teaching on homosexuality (Chastity)."[33] Brian described *Courage International* as having three requisite "A's": "You must view your sexuality (thoughts, words, deeds) as an Addiction. You must Alienate yourself from gay culture and community. You must remain Anonymous."[34] Given its name, it is ironic that *Courage International* promotes anonymity. This practice perpetuates a climate of shame, making it not only an ineffective apostolate, but also a harmful one.

In 2017, Anna Carter and Shannon Ochoa co-founded *Eden Invitation*, an organization that has ties to the *New Evangelization*. It describes itself as a movement for young adult Christians "experiencing same-sex desires and gender discordance." It promotes "original personhood beyond the LGBT+ paradigm," but it does not publicize a substantive theology to support it.[35] While *Eden Invitation*'s approach to homosexuality is problematic, I am optimistic about Carter's growth trajectory from a comment she made during an interview with Claire Swinarski on the *Catholic Feminist* podcast: "Your life is not a problem to be solved; your life is a mystery to be unveiled." Perhaps *Eden Invitation* will evolve as an organization that supports the full, embodied, divinely-loved personhood of LGBTQ+ individuals. Currently, however, with ecclesiastical support, it perpetuates the disheartening view that healthy sexual intimacy is only possible for people who identify as heterosexual.[36]

There can be no integrated-yet-intrinsically-disordered experience of God. The ministries highlighted in this case study place a fine point on a theological question that the Roman Catholic Church must clarify for contemporary

---

[32] An illuminating contemporary film about the damaging effects of conversion therapy is *Pray Away*, a Netflix documentary directed by Kristine Stolakis, 2021.
[33] Archdiocese of Milwaukee, "Courage/EnCourage home page", https://www.archmil.org/Nazareth-Project/CourageEnCourage.htm.
[34] Examples of the propaganda promoted by *Courage International* are Daniel Mattson's book *Why I Don't Call Myself Gay: How I Reclaimed My Sexual Reality and Found Peace* (San Francisco: Ignatius Press, 2017) and "Desire of the Everlasting Hills," directed by Erik Van Noorden, 2015. The film features Mattson as well as two other "same-sex attracted" individuals.
[35] Eden Invitation, see "Community" and "Original Personhood Beyond the LGBT Paradigm" tabs, https://www.edeninvitation.com.
[36] "Living and Thriving on the Sexuality Spectrum," *The Catholic Feminist* podcast, produced by Claire Swinarski, https://thecatholicfeminist.com/shownotes/anna.

believers – that either it does or does not believe that God is perfectly creative, loving, good, wise, and that God fully embraces God's own creation. For the Catholic Church to be credible in proclaiming these divine attributes, it cannot maintain that part of God's perfect creation is inherently disordered. If it is not disordered, then it is ordered. The challenge, then, is for individuals to wrestle with the difficulty of being creatures rather than the Creator and to wrestle with the fact that we do not have the right to reject what is beautifully made, however different or unfamiliar. The church must engage in the ongoing task of understanding, rather than condemning, others and affirming the full dignity of each person.

Conclusion

There is a systemic problem with the application of Church doctrine to an entire group of God's children who have long been ignored. In *Building a Bridge*, Father James Martin, a passionate LGBTQ+ ally, inadvertently reveals the pervasiveness of an anti-LGBTQ+ bias even among well-meaning Catholic scholars. He uses the story of Zacchaeus (Lk. 19:1–10), a despised tax collector, to note that Christians should stand with and befriend LGBTQ+ people, just as Jesus refused to condemn sinners. In an otherwise innovative, discerning book, Martin points to the community's judgment of Zacchaeus, the "chief sinner"[37] whose profession implicated him in an unjust taxation system. However, tax collecting is an occupation rather than an identity, in contrast to sexual orientation, which cannot be separated from the person. In this oversight, Martin fails to challenge the outdated, dehumanizing view that LGBTQ+ Catholics, who embrace the whole of who they were made to be, are sinning by doing so. The Catholic Church should clearly make this distinction in its preaching and teaching.

Church leaders can learn from the work of these lay ministers about sharing more fully Christ's love for all. There are powerful reminders that the Holy Spirit cannot be circumscribed, such as the Faithful & Fabulous Interfaith Drag Street Eucharist in San Francisco. Spirit-filled mavericks, such as the missionary priest who sent the pre-consecrated host to the motley assembly in the Castro, model for the church how to live more fully the mission of Jesus. Such missioners realize that God is still speaking a love language. Prophetic ministers such as the women and men featured in this case study demonstrate for the church that radical inclusivity is at the heart of the Gospel – that it is an enlivening, self-diffusive fruit of discipleship and is our entire reason for being church.

When Copernicus (1473–1573) promoted his theory of heliocentrism, some Catholic leaders, even perhaps including Pope Clement VII, suspended judgment about the evidence, seeing it as plausible rather than threatening. Scepticism among lay scholars led Copernicus to proceed cautiously. It sometimes seems that a truly synodal approach to Church governance would be a type of Copernican Revolution. In this case, too, the laity, who are accustomed to hierarchy, might actually delay progress. Finding a path forward will require

---

[37] Martin, *Building a Bridge*, 45.

reticent Catholic leaders to hold lightly to their own positions and to adopt a spirit of openness. Calling for a long view of history, Bishop Gumbleton reflected on the developmental nature of doctrine: "it's wrong for the Church, officially in any way, to try to stop the development of thought, the development of ideas, the evolution of understanding about various issues. Because, at some point we discover the ones that were silenced were actually saying the truth."[38]

It is impossible to overextend love in the name of Jesus. It would also be a mistake to consider radical love to be an Olympic-level achievement accessible only to contemplatives, mystics, and saintly activists. Rather, it is a basic premise of Christian faith. Perhaps the process by which the Catholic Church gradually accepted that the earth is not the centre of the universe can help us move more gracefully through the 21st century. Leaders can cultivate their own curiosity about the lived experiences of LGBTQ+ lay Catholics, who themselves can initiate dialogue rather than wait for an invitation. Together, the faithful can practice reflective listening, re-evaluate views that we have perhaps formed uncritically, and embrace those who, despite being marginalized or even rejected, choose to remain in the church.

---

[38] PBS Frontline interview with Bishop Thomas Gumbleton.

Notes on Contributors

Stephen Allen served as Associate Secretary for Justice Ministries with The Presbyterian Church in Canada for 20 years. His responsibilities included serving on KAIROS' board of directors, preparing statements on a variety of social issues for the church's General Assembly, and overseeing a Healing and Reconciliation Program. This programme was established by the General Assembly in 2006 to assist The Presbyterian Church in Canada in restoring right relations with Indigenous people.

Dustin D. Benac is Visiting Assistant Professor of Practical Theology and Co-Founding Director of the Program for the Future Church at George W. Truett Theological Seminary at Baylor University (Waco, TX, USA). He is the author of *Adaptive Church: Collaboration and Community in a Changing World* (Baylor University Press, 2022), co-editor, with Erin Weber-Johnson, of *Crisis and Care: Meditations on Faith and Philanthropy* (Cascade, 2021), and Associate Editor of *Practical Theology*.

Carlos F. Cardoza-Orlandi is Frederick E. Roach Professor of World Christianity at Baylor University (Waco, TX, USA). He is the author of *Mission: An Essential Guide* (Abingdon, 2002), also available in Spanish, Portuguese, and Korean, and he is co-author, with Justo L. González, of *To All Nations, From All Nations: A History of the Christian Missionary Movement* (Abingdon, 2013), also available in Spanish and Portuguese.

Britta Meiers Carlson is a PhD candidate at the Boston University School of Theology (Boston, MA, USA). She is a practical theologian who studies intercultural relationships between historically white Christian churches and Latin American immigrant communities to better understand how ecclesiology is evolving in the United States. Supporting areas of interest include postcolonial and liberation theologies, race studies, and church history. Britta is an ordained pastor in the Evangelical Lutheran Church in America.

Morgan Crago is a PhD candidate in the history of Christianity at the Boston University School of Theology (Boston, MA, USA). She studies modern Christianity in transnational perspective, focusing on the Americas. Her areas of particular interest include Protestant denominational missions to Latin America, ecumenical movements in 20th century Brazil, and the emergence of Latin American Protestant theologies and practices of social engagement.

Glory E. Dharmaraj is President of the World Association for Christian Communication (North America) and the former Director of Mission Theology for United Methodist Women. She is the co-author of *Many Faces, One Church: A Manual for Cross-Racial and Cross-Cultural Ministry* (Abingdon, 2006) and *A Theology of Mutuality of Mission: A Paradigm for Mission in the Twenty-first*

Century (United Methodist Women, 2014). She recently published an article on mission and intersectional sisterhood in *Methodist History* (2021).

Angelyn Dries, OSF, is Professor Emerita, Department of Theological Studies, Saint Louis University (St Louis, MO, USA). She is the author of *The Missionary Movement in American Catholic History* (Orbis, 1998) and *Be Centered in Christ and Not in Self: The Missionary Society of Saint Columban: The North American Story, 1918–2018* (Edwards Brothers Malloy, 2017). She has also served as President of the American Society of Missiology and the American Catholic Historical Association.

William P. Gregory is Associate Professor of Religious Studies at Clarke University (Dubuque, IA, USA). He is the author of "Pope Francis's Effort to Revitalize Catholic Mission" in the *International Bulletin of Mission Research* (2019) and the editor of *Go Forth: Toward a Community of Missionary Disciples* (Orbis, 2019), a collection of Pope Francis's teachings on mission. He has served as President of the Association of Professors of Mission.

Christopher B. James is Associate Professor of Evangelism and Missional Christianity at University of Dubuque Theological Seminary (Dubuque, IA, USA). He is the author of *Church Planting in Post-Christian Soil: Theology and Practice* (Oxford, 2018).

Allison Kach-Yawnghwe is a PhD candidate at the Boston University School of Theology (Boston, MA, USA). For 15 years, she has served as a mission worker and trainer in Central America, Eastern Europe, and North America, predominantly with Youth With a Mission (YWAM). Her dissertation research on the early history of YWAM focuses on the intersections between modern global mission movements, pentecostal history, youth movements, and women's history. Allison is ordained with the Ministers Network in Canada.

James R. Krabill is a Core Adjunct Professor at Anabaptist Mennonite Biblical Seminary (Elkhart, IN, USA) and Dallas International University. He served with the Mennonite Board of Missions and Mennonite Mission Network for 42 years, first as a mission worker in Europe and Africa, then as director for West Africa, vice president of mission advocacy and communication, and senior executive for global ministries. In retirement from mission administration, he devotes time to writing and teaching.

Tyler Lenocker is Visiting Researcher at the Center for Global Christianity and Mission at the Boston University School of Theology (Boston, MA, USA), the VP of Global Research at Haggai International, and Adjunct Professor at Gordon-Conwell Theological Seminary (Hamilton, MA, USA). His scholarship focuses on the impact of urbanization and migration on World Christianity in the 20th century.

Christopher P. Ney is a PhD candidate in Practical Theology at the Boston University School of Theology (Boston, MA, USA). Ordained in the Christian Church (Disciples of Christ), his interest in church and society has developed through engagement with social movements and religious communities in the US and Latin America. His doctoral dissertation focuses on a mission partnership between the United Church of Christ and The Pentecostal Church of Chile.

Amanda D. Quantz is Professor of Theology at the University of Saint Mary (Leavenworth, KS, USA). She is the author of *Radical Hospitality for a Prophetic Church* (Fortress Academic, 2020). She has written articles and chapters on several topics, including spiritual care, Franciscan religious history, and World Christianity. A former hospital chaplain and prison minister, she provides spiritual care for people who are unhoused. Her primary pastoral work is with members of the LGBTQ+ community.

David W. Restrick is the former director of the Instituto Superior Teológico Evangélico de Moçambique (Maputo, Mozambique) and former Academic Dean and Professor at the Seminário Nazareno em Moçambique (Maputo, Mozambique). His doctoral dissertation was on the experience of the Church of the Nazarene in the early years of Mozambican independence in the late 1970s and early 1980s.

Dana L. Robert is William Fairfield Warren Distinguished Professor at Boston University and Director of the Center for Global Christianity and Mission at the Boston University School of Theology (Boston, MA, USA). She is author of *Faithful Friendships: Embracing Diversity in Christian Community* (Eerdmans, 2019), *Christian Mission: How Christianity Became a World Religion* (Wiley-Blackwell, 2009), and *American Women in Mission: A Social History of Their Thought and Practice* (Mercer University Press, 1997).

Jonathan Schmidt is the Associate Secretary: Intercultural Leadership; Justice and Peace for The Canadian Council of Churches (CCC). He staffs the CCC's Commission on Justice and Peace, The Forum for Intercultural Leadership and Learning (FILL), and other justice and intercultural work of the Council.

Roger Schroeder, SVD, is Louis J. Luzbetak, SVD, Professor of Mission and Culture and Professor of Intercultural Studies and Ministry at Catholic Theological Union (Chicago, IL, USA). He is the co-author, with Stephen Bevans, of *Constants in Context: A Theology of Mission for Today* (Orbis, 2004), also available in Indonesian, Spanish, Italian, Chinese, Vietnamese, and Korean. Most recently, he published *Christian Tradition in Global Perspective* (Orbis, 2021).